SAGE was founded in 1965 by Sara Miller McCune to support the dissemination of usable knowledge by publishing innovative and high-quality research and teaching content. Today, we publish over 900 journals, including those of more than 400 learned societies, more than 800 new books per year, and a growing range of library products including archives, data, case studies, reports, and video. SAGE remains majority-owned by our founder, and after Sara's lifetime will become owned by a charitable trust that secures our continued independence.

Los Angeles | London | New Delhi | Singapore | Washington DC | Melbourne

MANY VOICES, MANY WORLDS

MANY VOICES, MANY WORLDS

Critical Perspectives on Community Media in India

EDITED BY

FAIZ ULLAH

ANJALI MONTEIRO

K. P. JAYASANKAR

Los Angeles | London | New Delhi
Singapore | Washington DC | Melbourne

First published in 2021 by

SAGE Publications India Pvt Ltd
B1/I-1 Mohan Cooperative Industrial Area
Mathura Road, New Delhi 110 044, India
www.sagepub.in

SAGE Publications Inc
2455 Teller Road
Thousand Oaks, California 91320, USA

SAGE Publications Ltd
1 Oliver's Yard, 55 City Road
London EC1Y 1SP, United Kingdom

SAGE Publications Asia-Pacific Pte Ltd
18 Cross Street #10-10/11/12
China Square Central
Singapore 048423

Published by Vivek Mehra for SAGE Publications India Pvt Ltd. Typeset in 10.5/13 pt Bembo by AG Infographics, Delhi.

Library of Congress Control Number: 2021940889

ISBN: 978-93-91138-46-2 (HB)

SAGE Team: Rajesh Dey, Shipra Pant and Anupama Krishnan
Cover Image: *The Half of It* (2020, Acrylic on Khadi, 30.5 x 33 in), painting by Nityan Unnikrishnan

To students, workers and Dalit and minority communities who use community media to build solidarities and give voice to their concerns, thus working towards a just and equitable society for all of us.

Thank you for choosing a SAGE product!
If you have any comment, observation or feedback,
I would like to personally hear from you.

Please write to me at **contactceo@sagepub.in**

Vivek Mehra, Managing Director and CEO, SAGE India.

Bulk Sales

SAGE India offers special discounts
for purchase of books in bulk.
We also make available special imprints
and excerpts from our books on demand.

For orders and enquiries, write to us at

Marketing Department
SAGE Publications India Pvt Ltd
B1/I-1, Mohan Cooperative Industrial Area
Mathura Road, Post Bag 7
New Delhi 110044, India

E-mail us at **marketing@sagepub.in**

Subscribe to our mailing list
Write to **marketing@sagepub.in**

This book is also available as an e-book.

Contents

Section I: Waves of Freedom: Community Radio and Its Discontents

Section II: In Their Own Moving Image: Community Video Practices

Section III: Durable Margins: Asserting Citizenship

Section IV. Trajectories of Change: Spaces of Hope

Foreword

As a practitioner of community media for over 25 years, I am confronted with two questions as I read this thought-provoking volume: first, is what I am practising backed by much intellectual 'baggage'; and second, is community media a product of this enormously complicated thought process, or has the practice of community media given birth to this complex thinking?

In any case, the thoughts and arguments presented in this volume provide a body of existing theoretical thought to those who are quietly working with local communities on their own media, whether in Uttarakhand in the snowy Himalayas or in Pastapur in the dusty Deccan. The practitioners will continue to actively exercise their communication efforts without even knowing the theoretical perspectives underlying what they are doing.

But for the outsiders, the academics, policymakers and students of development studies, this book is a great source of diverse thoughts and critiques of community media. The concepts such as 'citizenship of the image' provide an exciting context to the discourses that emerge across this volume. However, whether all of them have catered to make the marginalized communities participate and own this process is not so clear. Nor is the discussion on communication rights. How should communication rights be defined in order to achieve the goal of 'empowering' communities to ask, nay demand, that those on the console pass on the control? This raises the question of who empowers whom. My own experience as a person who set up India's first community radio, as well as an authentic rural women–owned and rural women–managed community media, tells me that in this process, my colleagues and I have been 10 times more empowered than the communities we work with. In fact, my entire thinking and action have been re-fashioned and reconstructed by the community vision. Therefore, I do believe that a blind 'empowering' thought should not override the community media efforts. In the community media space, everyone empowers everyone; the outsider stands to gain much more than the locals.

The understanding that community media are more correctly 'people's media' is a post-participation phenomenon. Participation theories stopped at making people participate vigorously in the development effort. There were some vibrant discussions around the issue of 'who holds the stick'. But people's media made a quantum jump and, without trapping itself in theoretical discussions of who holds the stick, simply handed over the stick, the mic and the camera to the communities. This made the outsider just what he was—an outsider, a bystander, an academic, at best. As people carried out their own media and defined their own rules and limits, many theories evolved around this process; this volume is an excellent illustration of those multiple perspectives that form the tapestry of theories around community media.

It is not all about theorizing though. There are many descriptions of actual initiatives, their success and failures. One rather sad story is from Bundelkhand region of Uttar Pradesh narrated by Dash. He describes how Dalits and adivasis, who form the majority of the Bundelkhandi population, have failed to get a truly representational space in the community radios of the region. This is, according to Dash, due to the re-feudalization by non-governmental organizations (NGOs), who behave like middle-class bourgeois at the expense of the interests of marginalized communities. This question throws up the challenge faced by the marginalized communities as to how they should negotiate a space for themselves even in the community media that is intent on excluding them. In fact, the larger political atmosphere also contributes heavily to this phenomenon. The marginalized communities that could create a democratic upsurge when the Bahujan Samaj Party (BSP) was in power had to take a back seat when the right-wing Bharatiya Janata Party (BJP) came to power in the state. All this happened under the very eyes of civil society organizations, who seem to remain unaffected by the changes in political regimes. This is an interesting observation and invites critical scrutiny.

While the marginalized sections of the society are the focus in the case study of the Bundelkhand situation, further up north, the community radios in the Himalayan state of Uttarakhand struggle with the issue of gender relations in the space of community radio. Community radio, which has been more inclusive and has given programming and management powers to women, has been able to bring positive changes in gender relations. The lesson learnt is that if you are willing to listen, many voices will emerge from the excluded sections of society. Therefore, listening is the most important quality of a sensitive community radio practitioner.

Anjali and Jayasankar also devote a significant section of the book to community video in which they themselves are important players in India. As a professional film-maker, I became a facilitator of community video with my own sense of discomfort with the way rural people, in general, and marginalized sections, in particular, were significantly absent from the media space. One small part of the population, that is, the urban elite, had completely captured the media and become the sole 'producers' of media content. The other part, namely the rural and the marginalized, who constitute 80 per cent of the population, had been consigned to the position of being just 'consumers' of media, with no access to production of media content. Such completely lop-sided media scene cried for corrective action. Answering this call, we started community media, both video and radio. We were probably the first all-rural, all-women from the disadvantaged sections of society, all–non-literate people's media in India. This had its own excitement and frustrations. But after the first few months of the initiation of this effort, the media was completely owned, managed and produced by the women themselves, thereby completely distancing us from the day-to-day affairs of the media. This took away from us the onerous responsibility of 'leading' the community media work and left us the pleasure of watching its growth from a distance and observing the ways it was strengthening itself through emerging as a true platform for female farmers from the poorest sections of the community, mostly non-literate and disadvantaged.

In this volume, Faiz, Anjali and Jayasankar point to the crucial need for participation as a tool of empowerment in the early stages and, once that goal has been accomplished, facilitation of people-to-people exchange, involving other civil society groups, so that the emanating cross- fertilization of thoughts and ideas can produce a vigorous community media.

To the best of my knowledge, this is the first book that puts together a number of writings that reflect diverse thoughts and actions by communication scholars and activists in India and paints a complex but not unrelatable picture of community media in this country. It is a wonderful resource for communication scholars and students.

P. V. Satheesh
Deccan Development Society, Medak, Telangana, India

Preface

One of the key reasons for us to work on this edited volume was to address the gap that we felt existed in the literature on community media in the Indian context. While designing and delivering the Post Graduate Diploma in Community Media (PGDCM) programme at the School of Media and Cultural Studies, Tata Institute of Social Sciences (TISS), we often found ourselves drawing liberally from various disciplines to engage students in serious and reflexive discussions on the contemporary, as well as around the fraught terrain of interventionist, media work. We also worked closely with colleagues within academia, as well as citizens' groups and organizations, to observe ideas in action to further develop an understanding of community media which was sensitive and useful to the rapidly changing political, economic and social realities. This eclectic and collaborative approach allowed us to put together a theoretical toolbox that could be used to plan, implement and critically research and assess community media initiatives in a variety of contexts. This book is an attempt to reflect a particular, though far from comprehensive, view of community media in India.

Much of the mainstream media in the country have either abdicated the role expected of them in democratic societies or, worse, have turned against the citizenry and public interest. Concerted efforts are being made from television studios to drive a wedge between communities. Their advocacy for stripping down all that is public—from education to health to food security—has reached a fever pitch.

In addition to offering criticism, we consider it important to actively work towards strengthening accessible and democratic alternatives that the citizens could use to collectivize and express themselves. A significant part of the motivation behind this volume was to acknowledge and develop an account of the vibrant community media praxes beyond the dominant frameworks that centre on institutions, capital and technology with 'development' as the end goal.

While the volume has been in the works for the last couple of years, it began to assume a concrete form in 2020. This was also the year where not only India but also large parts of the world saw citizens initiating actions demanding social, economic and ecological justice. The COVID-19 pandemic disrupted lives and livelihoods all over. As we write, we still have no clear view of what lies on the horizon. The contributions in the volume mark these difficult circumstances in various ways, in particular through participating in an urgent, public and global conversation about despair and hope.

> To reassure oneself everyday and live; it's getting tough...
> How far does one console oneself; it's getting tough...
> I soothe and put the howling heart to sleep
> Though I see the grain-sack stuffed with sawdust in front of me; to stop; it's tough.
> Live and let live. So, I live: everyday, it's getting tough...
> To deny one's existence; it's getting tough...
> I understand and convince myself, but even after that if I don't fall in line...
> A lit matchstick won't fall into the godown, to guarantee this; it's getting tough.[1]

These lines by acclaimed Marathi poet Narayan Surve invoke the liminal space between despair and hope. As a people's poet in Bombay—then convulsing through violent changes to its most vital neighbourhoods and residents—Surve would take his poetry to the working-class residents of the city to comfort them, to energize them. His words would provide an expression to the conditions most of his listeners thought were uniquely theirs. In doing so, Surve, and many others, brought into common what most considered individual problems. Their work helped create communities exceeding the limiting categories of man and woman, migrant and local, Hindu and Muslim, young and old, and worker and neighbour. It is in this spirit that we hope this edited volume would be considered by the potential readers.

---

[1] Original Marathi poem titled 'Katheen Hoth Aahe' (*Nivdak Narayan Surve [Selected Poetry of Narayan Surve]*, edited by Kusumagraj, Lok Vangmay Griha, Mumbai, 1999, p. 19). Translated by Jatin Wagle for the film *Saacha: The Loom*, TISS, 2001.

Acknowledgements

This book and the many ideas it proposes have been in the making for a long period of time and would not have come to fruition without the unstinting support of many institutions and individuals. The University Grants Commission (UGC) supported our Post Graduate Diploma in Community Media (PGDCM) under its Innovative Programme Scheme between 2012 and 2017. Towards the end of this period, in February 2017, we decided to organize a national seminar on participatory media praxis, with additional support from the Indian Council of Social Sciences Research (ICSSR), with a view to producing an edited volume on the theme. During the 5 years of teaching of PGDCM, we were confronted with a paucity of literature in the Indian context on community media. We thought that based on our 5 years of experience and the fruitful collaborations that we had established with so many community media activists and practitioners, we could address this lacuna as other colleagues in the field were also beginning to do. We are grateful to both the UGC and ICSSR for their support in holding this national consultation in 2017, where the first drafts of many of the chapters in this volume were presented.

Our parent institution, TISS, supported us in this endeavour, and we gratefully acknowledge the help that we received from them. We received invaluable support from the institute's Transforming M Ward project and would particularly like to thank Leena Joshi, Neeraj Kumar and Sabah Khan for facilitating the fieldwork projects of our students. Thanks are also due to Mumbai-based Youth for Unity and Voluntary Action and Pani Haq Samiti (Right to water campaign) for providing our students immersive learning opportunities. Our colleagues at the School of Media and Cultural Studies, some of whom are contributors to this volume, were of tremendous help. We would especially like to thank Nikhil Titus, K. V. Nagesh, P. Niranjana, Debanita Biswas, Barsha Dey, Vrushali Mohite, Sonal Gajaria, Bharat Ahire, Mangesh Gudekar,

Mukund Sawant, Chandu Parmar and Dattaram Patil. The teachers and students of the PGDCM programme, too many to acknowledge individually, helped us hone our ideas and develop a broad understanding of a little-theorized field. We would like to express our appreciation for our alumni Maanvi and Nikhil Ambekar for their editorial assistance in preparing two chapters in this volume.

Our deepest gratitude to Nityan Unnikrishnan for generously permitting us to use his painting *The Half of It*, from his exhibition entitled *It's Getting Louder* (Chatterjee and Lal, Mumbai, 2020).

We will be ever indebted to P. V. Satheesh, for so graciously agreeing to write the foreword to this book. His work in community media has been both inspirational and trailblazing. The critique of the politics of knowledge and the affirmation of subaltern knowledge which his work represents has greatly contributed to a redefinition of what constitutes community media. We are deeply honoured by his participation in our project.

Last and certainly not least, a very big thank you to all our fellow contributors for their cooperation and good humour. It has been a pleasure working with them, and this edited volume is all the richer for the diverse and multiple perspectives that they bring to bear on the complex creature that is community media. We do hope that this multivocality will open up windows and doors to a more nuanced, more politically located and more complex understanding of the field of community media in India today.

We live in times where political and economic power is increasingly becoming centralized, where majoritarian politics is challenging the idea of India and the processes of marginalization are becoming sharper than ever before. Those who resist these flows of power, which impinge on their lives and deny them their right to education, livelihood, citizenship, equality and a dignified life, do so under very adverse conditions. It is to them that we gratefully dedicate this book.

Chapter 1

Introduction
Other Worlds Are Breathing[1]

Faiz Ullah, Anjali Monteiro and K. P. Jayasankar[2]

Another world is not only possible, she's on her way…. [O]n a quiet day, if I listen very carefully, I can hear her breathing.

—Arundhati Roy, World Social Forum, 2003

COMMUNITY MEDIA AND THE DEMOCRATIC NATIONAL IMAGINARY

Communication remains at the heart of the project of democracy for facilitating collective deliberation and decision-making. Democratic ideals require that the means of communication be available and

---

[1] This title of our introduction can be attributed to an eponymous film festival, held as part of the World Social Forum (WSF), 2004, in Mumbai and in 2005 at Porte Alegre, organized by Media Lantern Foundation, India. This in turn draws on writer Arundhati Roy's words at WSF 2003, quoted above.

[2] Our interest in community media developed variously from the ethos of social justice and equity, which is the Weltanschauung of the institution we work with and the particular orientation of the School of Media and Cultural Studies, where we carry out research, teach and produce media. In addition to our flagship MA programme in Media and Cultural Studies, we introduced a Post Graduate Diploma in Community Media in 2012 to contribute towards the community media paradigm in more formal terms. Of the many modest successes of the programme, which we had to withdraw due to lack of funding in 2017, is this volume to which many who were associated with the programme have contributed generously.

accessible to everyone. If in the contemporary moment the idea of democracy in India has been reduced to a certain kind of pride in its size, or the electioneering prowess of political groups, or its increasingly referendum style of eliciting public opinion, it is a strong indication that deliberative spaces and praxes are diminishing and turning more exclusionary. After independence, uneven development, rigid social structures and the erosion of a pluralist ethos, espoused by the founding fathers and mothers of the Indian Constitution, have led to an over-whelmingly large part of the demos being consigned to the margins of society, rendered unheard and unseen.[3] In the post-liberalization era, these inequities became more acute with the withdrawal of the state as a guarantor of social goods. In the prevailing neoliberal regime, not only have the markets extended their reach over non-economic aspects of life, but also democracy is specifically vilified for being slow and inefficient, inasmuch as it retards capital accumulation (Brown, 2019). Simultaneous ascendance of conservative ideologies, mostly as a reaction to the demands of democracy, has sharply fragmented societies, making it all the more difficult to work towards a reasoned consensus on issues of redistribution of power and resources. This is not, for a moment, to suggest that communication is a panacea to problems that are deeply rooted in structural processes, but to underline that having a voice is essential to contest dispossession and injustice. Autonomy and participation in the structures of power go hand in hand in democratic societies—one without the other is meaningless. The arguments in this volume respond, explicitly or implicitly, to the concerns around self-determination and equitable participation in democratic politics, with particular reference to community media.

---

[3] The title of the volume derives from 'Many Voices, One World', the 1980 report of the International Commission for the Study of Communication Problems, popularly known as the MacBride Commission. Following the push from the countries part of the Non-Alignment Movement, a demand for re-hauling of international information flows, in favour of the countries of the Global South, was raised at the United Nations Educational, Scientific and Cultural Organization (UNESCO) in the form of a proposal for a New World Information and Communication Order. The report's recommendations were radical in that they advocated, among other global structural issues, for people's 'right to participate in communication and international exchange of information on the basis of equality, justice, and mutual benefit' (Padovani, 2015, p. 4).

Community media emerged from a deep sense of dissatisfaction with successive paradigms of putting media in the service of democracy in post-colonial India—from attempts at creating an enlightened citizenry through a mix of education and propaganda, towards orienting them to 'development', to deregulating the media sector to establish a marketplace of ideas. While the former treated citizens as passive and unthinking receptacles of information, the latter positioned them as mere consumers. In the way they were organized, the media not only strongly reflected the extant power structures but also became a key instrument of reproducing them. The demands for independent public service media were raised by civil society time and again but were dealt perfunctorily by the state, which was loath to part with the power that centralized control of the means of communication gave it.

The subsequent debates on democratization of media led to the emergence of a vibrant alternative media ecosystem to redress the concerns of representation. While such an approach did indeed manage to shine a light on the concerns that needed wider attention, it did not necessarily carve out any substantive space for the people who had a stake in or were directly impacted by such concerns. Responding to criticism, participatory elements were added to the approach later but only to legitimize what still remained a hierarchical edifice. Moreover, barring some notable exceptions, the paradigm remained couched in the ethos of larger values of developmentalism and contributed towards de-politicization of what are essentially political issues.

The demarcation between alternative, participatory and community media approaches is fuzzy. All of them articulate their commitment, in various ways, to qualitatively improve democracy. However, what sets community media apart from any other media approach is its insistence on recognizing the values of agency, autonomy, self-determination and reflexivity, which translate into practice in the following ways: One, people or communities must be put at the centre of media interventions; two, the means of media production should be owned or controlled by people or communities themselves; three, people or communities should take the lead in designing the objectives and implementing the processes of the media interventions; four, the media apparatus should be subordinated to people or communities, not the other way around; five, facilitators must be reflexive and remain alert and sensitive to the relations of power they work within; and six, though it hardly needs mentioning, everyone involved must share an unwavering commitment to progressive ideals. To be sure, these are normative in nature and are open to interpretations and negotiations within specific material conditions. If we could possibly suggest one more addition to the above, it would be to avoid attempts to reify them and treat them more as a compass and less as a map.[4]

As we write this introduction, on the one hand, we are dealing with the COVID-19 pandemic and the strict policy measures put in place to contain its spread which have had serious consequences for the poor, while, on the other, we are reckoning with a heavy-handed crackdown on the activists associated with the large-scale mobilizations and protests against the Citizenship (Amendment) Act, 2019 (CAA). It is in the context of these two events that we further explore the contested notions of 'community' and community media in concrete forms in the Indian context.

The state, while largely absent when it came to attending to the plight of the migrating workers and the working poor during the COVID-19 lockdowns of the first half of 2020, appeared defiantly unyielding and omnipresent in enforcing its widely protested changes in the citizenship law, also during the same period. The apathy of the state, as well as its brutal might, were brought into sharp relief in both the cases through the images of the force of the law enforcement's lathis[5] on the bodies of those out on the streets, whether trying to survive during the pandemic or protesting for constitutional values to be upheld. Large sections of the mainstream media, in thrall of the incumbent government (Kumar, 2018), doubled down on both the groups and abdicated their basic responsibility to hold the state to account on behalf of the citizens. The Supreme Court of India too, for

---

[4] There have been more radical calls to de-professionalize, de-capitalize and de-institutionalize media initiatives that seek to present themselves as accessible alternatives to the mainstream media (Hamilton, 2000), and even as we recognize them as worthwhile goals to pursue, we remain wary of endorsing them in toto without giving due consideration to the context.

[5] Wooden batons used by the police.

a variety of reasons, did not actively intervene to alleviate the crisis when the besieged (Sruthisagar, 2019) and beleaguered (Ananthakrishnan G, 2020) citizens approached it at the peaks of the respective crises to protect their constitutional rights.

Civil society did mobilize around the concerns of the anti-CAA protestors, as well the working poor, but mostly failed to treat them as political issues or translate them to a generalized political agenda. Civil society functions on the terrain and parameters sanctioned by the state and, over the years, has moved from questions of balancing of power relations and redistribution of resources to those of management of public policy. There is also a large section of civil society which is not quite civil—termed uncivil organizations by Neera Chandhoke (2011)—and has increasingly been weaponized (Hansen, 2017) by ascendant illiberal political powers, raising apprehensions about the churn in the realm and its consequences for the wider democratic and pluralist society. Civil society, inasmuch as it allows itself to be reduced to an instrument of policy implementation or allows its capture by the dominant ideologies that animate the latter, leaves little or no deliberative space in the public sphere for ordinary citizens and potentially paves the way for establishment of an overbearing hegemonic order. Its importance can be gauged through giving some consideration in the present discussion to Antonio Gramsci's (2015) famously vivid imagery of the state–civil society relationship where he sees the state as a forward trench beyond which lie, deep into the territory, the fortresses and emplacements of civil society, suggesting its enduring pervasiveness. Civil society could be an effective bulwark against the excesses of the state or yield to its hegemonic advances and help it fundamentally alter the 'common sense' of the republic. The evidence so far before us suggests that we, as citizens, would do well to remain cautious of the turn contemporary civil society is taking and invest in strengthening alternatives to it.

The passage of the CAA sparked spontaneous protest by Muslim communities and other civic-minded groups across the country. Most notable were the striking images of female Muslim protesters at a sit-in at Shaheen Bagh, New Delhi. These inspired peaceful sit-ins in scores of sites across the country. Though the protests were discrete and loosely coordinated, there was one common thread that bound them together—to uphold the ideals of the Constitution of India and demand that they be realized substantively. In the face of being routinely targeted by large sections of the political class, mainstream media, law enforcement bodies and vigilante groups, and being repudiated by the constitutional court, the sit-ins developed a vibrant repertoire of offline and online protest forms around them: placards, graffiti and murals, slogans, poetry and music, reading and learning spaces, media-making, online communication, mobilization and campaigning, etc. These forms reflected a critical consciousness of the issues among the protestors, drew upon the shared cultural heritage of the communities involved, highlighted the agency and autonomy of the protestors and strongly communicated a resolve to effect desired change. With the crackdown on and arrests of several anti-CAA protestors in the wake of anti-Muslim violence in Delhi in the last week of February 2020, and the discontinuation of the sit-ins in view of the COVID-19 pandemic, the anti-CAA protests came to a grinding halt. However, protesters and engaged citizens continued to create and use media in different ways to keep the protests alive online and demand justice.

The migrating workers, as well as the working poor, made use of mobile phone cameras, often assisted by volunteers engaged in relief work, to highlight their plight in a hope to draw the attention of government authorities. Denied the privileges of political citizenship, they sought recourse in the citizenship of the image, wherein, according to Ariella Azoulay (2008):

> ...the subject of the photograph is a person who has suffered some form of injury, the viewing of the photograph that reconstructs the photographic situation and allows a reading of the injury inflicted on others becomes a civic skill, not an exercise in aesthetic appreciation. This skill is activated the moment one grasps that citizenship is not merely a status, a good, or a private property possessed by citizens, but rather a tool of struggle or an obligation to others to struggle against injuries inflicted on those others, citizen and noncitizen alike. (p. 14)

After these videos began to circulate first among the activist networks and thereafter on social media platforms, many professional journalists were alerted to the seriousness and scale of the crisis. Part of the earliest coverage of the crisis was characteristic of the larger orientation of the mainstream media that either do not give adequate space to the issues of the marginalized sections of society or simply treat them as 'human interest stories' stripped of context. But as more and more such videos began to emerge, especially the ones that depicted large number of people converging at transportation hubs and state-border crossings, initiating online conversations and sparking outrage, the mainstream media were forced to cover the crisis, albeit without any significant critical perspective, and elicited a response from the state.

As civil society was found wanting, several spontaneously formed collectives stepped up. Lawyers, medics, students, academics, information technology (IT) professionals, communicators, artists and volunteers, bringing in a wide variety of knowledge and skills, began to support the anti-CAA protests and distressed workers in various ways. Largely self-organized and lacking hierarchies, these 'communities' began to make visible the contours of what alternatives to traditional civil society might look like—associational forms that are symbolically constructed, that is, through communication and shared meanings and concerns. Though not new, such forms do not fit into the modernist or developmental approaches that are more interested in remedying the problems of 'folk', 'natural' or 'traditional' communities. They also sit uncomfortably with *au courant* postmodernist discourses of 'mob', 'crowd' or 'swarms' which privilege contingency. They emerge, as in the context of the current discussion, through considered and strategic responses to the changing and challenging social, political and economic circumstances. This has also meant that what seemed like irreconcilable differences at one point of time have now begun to be articulated in hyphenated forms. In the case of the working classes, for example, there have been many instances where larger solidarities were being forged across categories of workers and sectors. Pressure from rank and file have pushed trade unions to pay more attention to intersectional issues of gender and caste and re-imagine their roles as social movement unions.

Community media can be thought of in a manner that they are not just media used by localized or limited communities but are actually media practices that serve to affirm the rights and demands of national communities, particularly those sections that have been marginalized and seen as less than citizens. If the nation has been defined as an 'imagined community' (Anderson, 1983) created through discourse, participation in the realm of media representation and media–making becomes an essential condition to participate in its imagination. If indeed one were to think of citizens using media to rè-imagine national communities as being based on cultures of constitutionalism, then such media practices constitute nation-building by the citizens themselves.

This edited volume is thus an invitation to rethink the space of community media, enabling it to respond to the present context, marked by relations of power which seek to disenfranchise and exclude large groups of citizens. As the various chapters in this volume bear out, the practice of community media emerges from a multitude of spaces and processes, challenging more traditional notions of community media which regard it as an extension of development communication practice that seeks to move from a 'top-down' model to a more 'participatory' one. We have tried to be as representative of the range of issues or community media practices in this volume as resources and circumstances allowed for the moment. We are acutely mindful of the exclusions[6] and hope that with the continued support of the wider researcher and practitioner community we would be able to cover more ground in future collaborative endeavours.

WAVES OF FREEDOM: COMMUNITY RADIO AND ITS DISCONTENTS

If one asks what most people understand by the term community media, chances are community radio would figure quite prominently in their responses. That the two terms have come to be regarded as

---

[6] For instance, the range of rural communities and their diverse communication practices have not been adequately covered. The powerful transformative praxes of the LGBTQIA (lesbian, gay, bisexual, transgender, queer, intersex, asexual) communities across the country find no mention. The media practices that emerge from those at the margins of the nation state, in the places such as Kashmir and many states of the north-eastern region of India, subject to draconian laws, the might of the armed forces and deprivation of Internet access, have also not found place in this volume.

so closely associated speaks to the efforts of the those involved in the sector and the space that they have been able to carve for third-sector broadcasting in the dense contemporary media ecologies despite regulatory and market challenges. The advocacy for community radio in India built a compelling case for citizens to claim access to broadcast spectrum, essentially a public resource, and lobbied with various stakeholders to convey the importance of democratization of communication in the processes of empowerment of the historically marginalized communities, albeit with mixed results. The chapters in the first section of the book critically look at the institution of community radio in India, a decade and half after the first community radio station was established, from the perspectives of political autonomy, gender, caste and indigenous identities.

In the second chapter, Vinod Pavarala and Kanchan K. Malik offer a sobering assessment of the community radio movement, holding it to scrutiny for sidestepping the political questions in its brief but significant growth trajectory. Envisioned as a political project—to make what was hitherto inaudible not only audible but also meaningful—the advocacy for the community radio sector couched its demands in the rhetoric of development, as opposed to communication rights, to make it more palatable to the political elite, as well as the easily alarmed bureaucracy in Delhi, who are ever reluctant to cede even a modicum of power from their desks. While the strategy worked in the corridors of power, which eventually opened up to the idea of community broadcasting, it effectively shut doors to the radical possibilities of community participation and autonomy. In *Development as Freedom*, Amartya Sen (1999) considers political autonomy, particularly as it manifests in abilities to voice one's choices, as an essential element of individual, as well as collective, well-being. He writes that '…the general enhancement of political and civil freedoms is central to the process of development itself. The relevant freedoms include the liberty of acting as citizens who matter and whose voices count, rather than living as well-fed, well-clothed and well-entertained vassals' (p. 288). Thus, even while the project of community radio was conceived in India as a vehicle for development, it is worth asking: To what extent did the stakeholders attempt to resist this capture of the medium by the state and, later, by civil society?

Pavarala and Malik parse the archive of exchanges between community radio enthusiasts, campaigners, practitioners and researchers and bring to fore the sense of unease and disappointment they collectively shared as the policy began to assume concrete forms. From 'taking the government to court' to 'electronic civil disobedience', several tactics were put forth and debated, only to result in a few stray legal challenges focused on specific aspects of the community radio policy. A real—or, as the authors call it, missed—opportunity to resist the overbearing sway of the state over and creeping influence of non-governmental organizations (NGOs) on the sector presented itself in the form of tinkerers who, as the authors note, combined 'DIY technological innovation and a happy legal naivete' and took matters literally in their hands to reclaim 'public property' they were told belongs to them. As expected, these experiments were short-lived and were nipped in the bud. At a time when the national policy landscape is rife with the chatter of unleashing animal spirits, stories of mythical entrepreneurial derring-do and catch-all buzzwords, like disruption, it is disappointing to reflect on the irony of the situation where such tendencies are curbed among the citizens and instead public resources are readily made available to those seeking to make a quick buck at the expense of collective development.

While it may seem like a formidable task to persuade the state or take on the market and strengthen the communication commons and secure communication rights for the most marginal citizens in the prevailing circumstances, attempts should continue to be made towards sensitizing civil society institutions to the democratizing potential of community broadcasting and hold them accountable to higher standards of transparency and participation than what are mandated by the law and policy. Even while stations have been set up and broadcasting has begun, the continuous task of the community radio movement should be to empower communities to ask, nay demand, those on the console to *pass the mic*.

The next two chapters by Bidu Bhushan Dash and Shweta Radhakrishnan in the section on community radio help us move from the capital-P Politics of Political Economy and Policy to small-p politics, or, if you will, micro-politics of everyday life—of participation and representation (Jank, 2010). But before going ahead, the term participation, invoked several times earlier, needs to be briefly interrogated, for its instrumental use, on the one hand—the add-participation-and-stir approach—and uncritical celebration, on the other, which have deeply compromised the radical and democratic ethos of community media. One simple way to do this would be to observe the process of participation in its specificities and ask questions that those of us working in the realms of cultural studies consider de rigueur—Participation in what? Who can participate? Are there any impediments to participating? Who remains excluded and why? What are the terms of participation? What are the ends towards which participation is oriented? What follows after participation?—and so on. To those who do not usually raise these questions, the answers, in all likelihood, would appear to be patterned neatly on the extant power relations in the community and their differentiated interests. N. C. Saxena (1998), writing in the context of rural development, offers the following comprehensive definition of participation:

> Participation should include the notions of contribution, influencing, sharing, or redistributing power and of control, resources, benefits, knowledge, and skills to be gained through beneficiary involvement in decision-making. Participation is a voluntary process by which people, including the disadvantaged (in income, gender, caste, or education), influence or control the decisions that affect them. The essence of participation is exercising voice and choice and developing the human, organizational and management capacity to solve problems as they arise in order to sustain the improvements. (p. 111)

Both Dash and Radhakrishnan bring to bear this framework while assessing community radio initiatives based in northern India with which they have had associations in different capacities. In the third chapter, Dash carries out an ethnographic study of two community radio stations in Bundelkhand region of Uttar Pradesh (UP), with an emphasis on delineating participation of Dalits and adivasis and representation of their concerns. Bundelkhand is one of the most deprived regions of the country, with significant concentrations of Dalit and adivasi communities. It is also a region that has remained at the focus of civil society organizations engaged in welfare and development work with funding support from the government, as well as large national and international agencies. The two community radio stations under study have been functioning for almost a decade now, with both, in Dash's assessment, falling short at providing adequate participation opportunities to Dalits and adivasis in management, operation and programming functions. Dash's assessment also indicts the larger community radio network in Bundelkhand as being 're-feudalized by NGOs' that seem to cater to the 'emerging middle-class bourgeois' at the expense of marginalized communities.

Dash raises two important questions. One, why cannot community radio stations try to prioritize the needs of the marginalized sections of society instead of trying to reach out to everyone in their geographic catchment area? He cites some exceptions to this norm by identifying stations in India, as well as the neighbouring Nepal, which work dedicatedly with marginalized communities. And two, how can the oppressed people negotiate a representational space for themselves when even community media continue to exclude them? While the liberal desire of civil society to be free of identity politics—others', not theirs—could approximate some sort an answer to the first question, the second one is definitely knotty.

Earlier in the chapter Dash highlights how the victory of the Bahujan Samaj Party (BSP) a political outfit formed to represent the oppressed castes and communities, in UP in 2017 translated into a 'democratic upsurge from below' for Dalit and adivasi communities in the state. But the gains were reversed with its loss of power in 2012, with things taking a turn for the worse for marginalized communities in 2017 with the conservative, right-wing Bhartiya Janata Party (BJP) assuming power. What is perhaps worth noting here is the exclusionary nature of civil society which remains entrenched irrespective of changes in the political realm. Suryakant Waghmore (2013), however, views civil society as 'a space for critical and complex public conversations influencing the goals and values of governance and for reforming not just state and society but civil society itself' (p. 4). Civil society organizations, he further argues, may potentially create spaces for wider collaborations to aid local movements.

In the fourth chapter, Radhakrishnan presents a participatory account of a community radio station in the hilly North Indian state of Uttarakhand while foregrounding the gender relations in the larger community, as well as the station. She outlines the various challenges women face in the process of associating with the station in both voluntary and professional capacities. Restrictions on physical mobility, a variety of risks to personal safety, social norms of respectability, and the non-negotiable responsibilities of care work at home mean that even nominal participation in their community radio remains a difficult proposition for most women. Read along with Dash's insights on exclusion or participation deficit on the basis of identity, it is not very difficult to imagine what an intersectional analysis of women's participation may look like in the larger realm of community radio.

Radhakrishnan highlights that the organization behind the station recognized the issues faced by women soon and took decisive steps to make the workspace, as well as the organization structure, more responsive to their needs and concerns. With increased and sustained participation of women in programme production and management, positive changes began to reflect in the programming as well. For illustration, the idea for a show focused on women's health, where a doctor responds to listeners' health issues collated by the field producers, was conceptualized and executed by the female members of the station team. This goes on to show that the organizations that support or facilitate community radio initiatives can foster participatory cultures by *listening* to the members of the community and demonstrating an openness to addressing their concerns. Writing in the context of carrying out qualitative research among women, Ghazala Jamil (2017) argues that most of the time what is lamented as 'lack of voice' is only 'the lack of will to listen' by those in positions of power.

The respect women who work with the station receive in the community, the sure-footedness with which they negotiate various public and personal relations and the confidence in their own selves are indicative of the broader realization that they are being heard: feeling heard at the workplace, feeling heard in the community and feeling heard as women. As Susan Bickford (1996) suggests, the ways in which we listen have a bearing on how others feel they can speak or be heard.

To a large extent, community radio still holds strong potential to emerge as a truly people's medium. The technological infrastructure it requires, at both the production and reception ends, is no longer complicated or expensive. But as long as the policy stranglehold does not ease over the medium, it will keep moving away from the reach of the ordinary people. For now, the pragmatic task before those invested in the community radio movement should be to stridently challenge the ventriloquism of the civil society organizations in control of the sector, commit to foster intra-community democracy and enable communities to think creatively about mobilizing available alternatives to audio broadcasting.

IN THEIR OWN MOVING IMAGE: COMMUNITY VIDEO PRACTICES

In the second section of the volume, we turn our attention towards the work on community video initiatives and practices in varied contexts. The use of video for mobilization in India, particularly the documentary film, has been discussed extensively in both academic and popular literature (Basu & Banerjee, 2018; Jayasankar & Monteiro, 2009). What was till the 1970s largely a vehicle for state propaganda was cast anew in the crucible of the tumultuous Emergency era as a counter-hegemonic political form. Independent film-makers began to use it to critically interrogate the skewed relations of power with a hope to move the viewers to question their perspectives and get involved in activism. With the arrival of more affordable, convenient and mobile video acquisition and manipulation technologies in the next few decades, the independent documentary film practices proliferated not only in quantitative terms but also in as many ways as it was challenged by the questions of ethics of representation, agency of the 'subjects' and reflexivity of the film-maker, among others, raised primarily by the gender and caste movements. While the films were definitely political in content and their objectives, little attention was paid, barring a few exceptions, to the conditions under which they were made and exhibited. What was the role of the people in the production process with whom, or rather *on* whom, the films were made? Who were the films really made for? Was producing films an end in itself? These and many other questions alerted many of the film-makers to contend with their own notions of what constituted the political in the first place—to read the politics off the backs of the marginalized people much like the political elites and present it before largely concerned but powerless proxies living in islands of affluence or to create conditions for the communities they worked with to learn, think, express and act autonomously. The idea of what has been variously called community video or participatory video[7] or collaborative video took shape as a response to this ferment, where the figure of the film-maker gradually ceded ground to that of an organizer or facilitator who enabled the marginalized communities to develop their voices.[8]

Community video, however, has its roots in participatory development communication, and many regard the Kheda project of Satellite Instructional Television Experiment (SITE), conducted in the mid-1970s, as the first community video initiative (Dutta & Anamika Ray, 2017). This was followed by the work of Centre for the Development of Instructional Technology (CENDIT) of using video in communities, which took place in the mid-1980s (Dutta & Anamika Ray, 2017). Around the same time, the Self Employed Women's Association started its work in Gujarat, in 1984; the female video makers of SEWA have produced hundreds of videos, which have been used for advocacy, and still continue their work.[9] Another very significant and sustained community media initiative is that of Deccan Development Society (DDS), Telangana, which began its video work in 1998;[10] the women working

---

[7] For a brief overview of participatory video, see Lunch and Roberts (2015).

[8] Banks (2001) and Pink (2001), among others, make a distinction between collaborative video, which involves relatively less participation, and participatory video, which hands over the control of production to the community, with the external community worker playing a marginal role.

[9] SEWA, or Self Employed Women's Association, is a trade union of female workers at several sites across India, with a concentration in Gujarat, started by the Gandhian activist Ela Bhat. Video SEWA started in 1984, 'with one set of production equipment and three weeks of training from Communication for Change, formerly Martha Stuart Communications. Of the twenty SEWA members and workers who participated in the training, one third were illiterate and another third had less than a high school education. They included women of all ages, Hindus and Muslims, craftswomen and vendors and women from many arms and levels of SEWA including three senior organizers. A second instalment of equipment, including editing equipment, and training were given in 1987' (http://www. communicationforchange.org/about/videoSEWA.html).

[10] 'The Deccan Development Society (DDS), is a three and half decade old grassroots organisation working in about 75 villages with women's Sanghams (voluntary village level associations of the poor) in Sangareddy District of Telangana. The 5000 women members of the Society represent the poorest of the poor in

in radio and video formed the DDS Community Media Trust in 2001 (discussed in the sixth chapter). At one point, in the early 2000s, there were many community video projects being run by a range of NGOs, including Laya in Andhra Pradesh, Drishti in Ahmedabad and Hamari Aawaz (Our Voice) of Youth for Unity and Voluntary Action (YUVA) and Apna TV of Akshara, both in Mumbai, among others.[11] Due to lack of funding, among other reasons, many of these gradually shut down.[12] More recent initiatives in participatory video include Ektara Collective from Madhya Pradesh and Chalchitra Abhiyan from UP.

The chapters in this section engage with community video praxes in a range of contemporary contexts that allow for a critical and comparative assessment of how they negotiate with the underlying principles of community media processes—reflexive engagement with the communities and building of their capacities to express themselves—and the concrete form they assume. In the sixth chapter, Madhavi Manchi presents a compelling ethnographic account of her engagement with the DDS' community video initiative, which focuses on creating visual narratives around the issues of biodiversity, gender justice and community knowledge. Learning to produce these narratives enhances the

---

their village communities' (http://www.ddsindia.com/www/default.asp). The organization works on issues of food security, sustainable agriculture, education and health, among others, with women at the forefront of all work.

[11] Refer to Dutta and Anamika Ray (2017), for a description of many more community video projects operating in the first decade of this millennium.

[12] There are other initiatives, such as Video Volunteers, which started off as a community media initiative but currently functions in a more structured and codified mode as an activist news platform, under the rubric of India Unheard:

> With the goal to have a network of community correspondents in each of India's 650 or so districts, India Unheard identifies young activists who are employed part time or not at all and they train them in video making and storytelling for two weeks and supply each new correspondent with a Flip Cam. Generally, these community correspondents shoot a story or two each month (for each story they publish they are paid on a sliding scale based on the quality of work, the type of video made, years in the organization, etc). Each correspondent accesses a computer, downloads their footage, burns it to a CD and sends the CD along with notes/storyboard via postal mail to Goa, where it is eventually edited, put on both YouTube and the India Unheard web- site and often screened informally at home in the community as well. (Lenzner, 2014, pp. 98–99)

capacities of those participating, mostly women from the rural Dalit Bahujan communities, to represent themselves without any intermediaries and also to join in collectively and meaningfully in the spheres of debates and discussions where significant decisions concerning their identities, culture, habitat and livelihood are made.

As mentioned earlier, a large part of the early community video projects and the literature associated with them subordinated or, at best, appended the form to the larger and worthier goal of development (White, 2003). They primarily seemed to be concerned with how the community video form could aid in bringing about attitudinal and, more problematically, behavioural change among the community members so that they are better disposed towards finding or crafting solutions, using available resources, to their problems of underdevelopment. While it seemed clear to many that participatory video could potentially empower communities, the contours of such processes of participation qua empowerment were rarely ever fully chalked out, particularly the weightier political issues of whether the development goals were mandated by the communities in question or were worth aspiring for in the first place. Manchi disentangles some of these issues in the fourth chapter by clearly outlining how the community video practice of the DDS initiative emanates from and builds upon the community's experiences as agriculturalists who gainfully practise biodiverse farming and have a well-grounded critique of the mainstream notions of development which privilege a universal notion of market-demanded productivity.

While at the local levels the production and exhibition of such narratives have a bearing on intra-community power relations, Manchi shows, using the metaphor of a rhizome, how they relate in various, and differentiated, ways with regional, national and global institutions and networks.[13] The community retains and exercises their autonomy tactfully while navigating these connections. For instance, while their films are often broadcast by state and private television networks, in a telling instance, they refused to part with the folk songs they recorded, as they did not want 'private companies [to] co-opt what they had

---

[13] The significance of global dimensions of what are essentially seen as local movements needs a larger space within the study of community media, especially learning and transference of strategies and tactics around communication.

spent years collecting and building' and asserted 'ownership over their inheritance'. In bringing out this dimension, Manchi opens up space for discussion on exceptionalism ascribed to or foisted on community video, or community media in general, which requires it to be insulated against exchanges with civil society, the state and the market. The DDS example shows that rather than prematurely foreclosing the possibilities of such exchanges, more emphasis should be placed on ensuring that the communities have substantive freedom to exercise the choices they deem empowering and valuable.

Nina Sabnani, in the fifth chapter, presents edifying reflections on her experiences of a participatory video project in a non-development context—an animation video project with tribal artists which sought to preserve and popularize the community's intangible heritage in the face of relentless erasure. The chapter affords a clear view of the processes of participation which are given a short shrift in the work on development communication or Information and Communications Technologies for Development (ICT4D) projects in favour of their larger objectives. Working with the Bhil artists of Madhya Pradesh, she and her colleagues reflexively negotiated with layers of asymmetries of economic and cultural capital which existed between them and the collaborating 'other' and remained cognizant, throughout the process, of the fact that while such power differentials cannot ever be adequately resolved, their effects could be mitigated to a large extent.

Earnest curiosity, transparency, self-doubt, sensitivity to difference, respect, generosity and dialogue, as Sabnani shows, can go a long way in reassuring communities that their heritage is not under any kind of threat. This assumes much more significance at a time when cultural engagement, exchange and larger possibilities of social and cultural transformations have become acutely vulnerable to infringing expressions of dominant communities, on the one hand, and charges of cultural appropriation, on the other hand, levelled by those at the receiving end. It is imperative that the work of fostering intercultural trust and understanding, under such testing circumstances, must necessarily be carried out with great care, though without fear or favour. The larger responsibility of creating conditions for such work—where, as Sabnani notes, 'each participant feels secure enough to have their ways of seeing questioned, and where they may explore other perspectives'—which exceed mere 'interventions', lies with the community media practitioners, where broader disciplinary traditions of anthropology and the politics of knowledge production need to be questioned and decolonized (Smith, 2012).

The opportunities to employ community media practices are often passed over by those working in the realms of social and cultural change through dismissing them as too local or specific. In doing so, they fall short in recognizing the form's potential for effecting deeper and wide-ranging possibilities of progressive change. From the interactions between Sabnani and her colleagues and the Bhil artists, aside from exchange of skills, the former gained newer ways of seeing, and the latter obtained positive terms of recognition. The critical value of their coming together though is held out in the narrative they created through which, as Sabnani point out, 'we learn to see our world as a composite of many worlds. And sometimes, the stories told by the other can help us learn something about the world that we share with them'. The interpretation, visualization and animation[14] of one of the origin myths of the Bhil community related to the human–nature relationship, which they collaboratively worked out, constitute not only a project of cultural preservation on the part of those directly involved but also an invitation to those contemplating and working on similar concerns elsewhere.

Shweta Ghosh's critical reflections, in the seventh chapter, on the process of workshopping with film-makers with disabilities as part of her doctoral research work, raise sobering questions for community video and its promise and potential for democratizing access. Building on her analysis of marginalization of persons with disabilities at multiple levels—wider ableist society, hierarchies within the disability groups and socio-economic status—she notes that community media initiatives are not often adequately disability-sensitive and intersectional in their approach, resulting in situations where the 'needs and experiences of

---

[14] The collaborative animation film *Hum Chitra Banate Hain* (We Make Pictures) was awarded the Rajat Kamal for the Best Animation Film at the 64th National Film Awards in 2017.

disability groups tend to be subsumed into those of the wider "community", and the resulting representations of disability (if any) in the stories that emerge, are often ableist and/or Inaccessible'. Three broad questions emerge from Ghosh's participatory research engagement: one, to include disability in the broader conversations for diversity within film-making; two, to identify and address specific challenges and barriers that film-makers with disabilities, across the physical, sensory and cognitive spectrum, face in their quest to make films—as she reminds us, 'the off-screen participation and engagement of Deaf and disabled film-makers is absolutely crucial if we are to question and change problematic on-screen representations'; and three, to not essentialize film-makers with disabilities in terms of their identities or welcome them only for their 'marginal' narratives but to appreciate them for how they contribute towards reflecting our shared social life. Ghosh elaborates:

> FwDs need to make films not just because we need more stories of disability across our multiple and diverse communities, but also because in its most basic sense, films and video strive to tell stories that are multi-layered, well-rounded and fresh on perspective, to be interesting, engaging and enjoyable.

The community media practitioners and researchers also need to reckon with some of the latent assumptions that were built in or have crept over the years into the vocabulary we use, particularly the ways in which ideas of agency and empowerment are discussed, which seem premised upon an individual's or communities' ability to *use* technology or *think* rationally (Capstick, 2012). Ableist constructs and language abound in much of community media training manuals and literature—including the current volume that we have resisted revising so that it may remain as an index of the prevailing discourse—in which the imagination of the ideal participant is largely articulated in terms of their bodily and mental abilities. Little affordances are made for approaches that enable participants *of all kinds* to negotiate with, for instance, the barriers identified by Ghosh in her work. Community media practitioners and researchers are better placed than those in other domains of media practices to reflect on and redress the concerns around access by ensuring their methodologies respond sensitively to the realities of the participants rather than perfunctorily following abstract principles.

It bears repeating once again, drawing on Ghosh's reflections on allyship, that one needs to take the concerns of access and accessibility in community media practices seriously not only for the sake of those who find the terrain uneven and daunting but also for those of us privileged enough to not ever have had to consider these concerns in a world shaped in and by our images so that our practices do not ossify and become a hindrance to progressive change. As allies, we must resist the habit of putting the weight of the responsibility of educating us on those who are already burdened by structures of injustice and marginalization which all of us are complicit in in various ways. The work required to develop ourselves as worthy allies must be put in by us earnestly before we step into the collaborations where, as pointed out earlier as well, we stand to gain as much as the other(s) we engage with.

As things stand, though, the responsibility of sensitizing, educating and mobilizing the larger society to act and put an end to entrenched processes that reproduce inequality and injustice falls disproportionately on those most affected. In the eighth chapter, Raees Mohammed, founder of the popular anti-caste media initiative Dalit Camera, records that while online and mobile technologies have enabled Bahujan communities to raise consciousness, engage in intra-community discussions and influence dominant mainstream media and intellectual discourses, little seems to be changing as far as systemic oppression of the communities is concerned. However, the change Dalit Camera and several other web-based initiatives have been able to effect in a relatively short period of time is not insignificant for the sizeable, heterogenous and spatially dispersed Bahujan communities. One would argue that it is unfair to transpose the objectives, strategy and organizational work expected from collective social movements onto community media initiatives with meagre resources. Without going into the detailed aspects of debates around movements and their relationships with Internet interfaces, it would perhaps be sufficient to point out here that the platforms like Dalit Camera perform a crucial role in what Paolo Gerbaudo (2012) calls *choreography of assembly*, which according to him involves emotional scripting and scene setting for further action. Dalit Camera performs this role primarily through the direct or minimally obstructive approach of documenting important events, perspectives and performances, through its network of volunteers in several parts of the country, and making the material available to its audiences through YouTube, forging, in the process, a sense of togetherness or community and making available a live repository of political resources (Paul & Dowling, 2018, p. 7). Gerbaudo elaborates on this dimension by underlining that without such prior work, the task of organizing would be difficult even with all the tools of technology at one's disposal:

> The success of popular movements still lies to a great extent in the organisational skill of its activists and in their capacity to create a compelling sense of togetherness capable of initiating the coalescence of a disparate constituency. Arguably, contemporary movements could get by well enough without the tactical affordances offered by social media. But what they cannot do without (or what they do better with) is the capacity of such media to become the instruments of an emotional narration capable of motivating individuals to take to the streets. (p. 162)

The work of Dalit Camera assumes particular importance in the times of increasingly motivated and blunt atrocities against all kinds of marginalized communities across the world. As the #BlackLivesMatter protests rage on in the United States, hundreds of cases of organized state and vigilante violence against the anti-CAA protestors have been reported in India. One of the ways in which these instances of violence have come in front of the public eye is through ordinary citizens bearing witness to and documenting them on their mobile phone cameras. These videos are the only evidence of violence against citizens, as law enforcement agencies, who otherwise place great importance on surveillance, switched off their body cams or smashed public and private closed-circuit television (CCTV) cameras.

Such user-generated videos, according to Gabriel Dattatreyan (2020), 'more generally disrupt (and police) the sensible[15] in a way that mainstream journalistic, artistic, or social scientific accounts cannot precisely because the user-generated footage it is comprised of—in its shaky, grainy, amateurish presentation—appeals to the idea one can

---

[15] 'Sensible' in noted political philosopher Jacques Rancière's work broadly means what is deemed acceptable in terms of presence/visibility and speech in a particular context.

experience an unmediated real' (p. 2). Though such videos trigger outrage and sympathy and lead to wider public conversations, they have not been very successful in ensuring justice for a variety of reasons. However, this sousveillance[16] (Mann et al., 2003), many continue to believe, has become a 'powerful fuel for social movements demanding racial justice and fairer policing' (Zuckerman, 2016).

Community video holds particular importance in contemporary media ecologies, especially in urban areas, where more and more people are being drafted into the rapidly developing smartphone-centric infrastructures that prop up the service economy, e-governance and creative industries. Among documents of identity and other material objects that people deem essential to make claims on the urban and to live a full urban life, the smartphone has come to occupy a very high rank. If one is looking for a job, wants to remit or receive money, needs to apply for a government permit or certificate, wants to have a private conversation with family and friends or simply wants to follow the news, listen to music or watch a film, having a smartphone today makes it easier. It is precisely because of this commercial and policy and consequently need-driven ubiquity that the smartphone emerges as a key plank in the contexts of community media as well, without for a moment being fully detached from the crucial issues of affordability, literacy and data protection and surveillance. Smartphone manufacturers, moving in tandem with online publishers and social media platforms, have pivoted sharply and decisively in favour of video. They seem to be competing with each other in not only packing smartphones with more processing power, storage, multiple cameras, better resolution—HD is now almost a default—and a bevy of image manipulation tools but also offering them at aggressive prices.

DURABLE MARGINS: ASSERTING CITIZENSHIP

Nikhil Titus, in the ninth chapter, offers a sharp analysis of the deep social, economic and spatial inequities in media-saturated urban India.

---

[16] A play on the word 'surveillance'. 'Sous' in French means subordinate, under or below. Sousveillance is translated by authors to mean 'inverse surveillance' or watching from below.

It is a matter of cruel irony that in a city like Mumbai, the largest hub of media and entertainment production in the country, there are spaces and populations that still do not have access to basic media infrastructures. While their homes and livelihood are routinely destroyed in the name of (re)development, they seldom get to enjoy its fruits. When the textile-mills district of central Mumbai was being taken apart by real estate developers in the 1990s to pave way for living, working and leisure spaces for the burgeoning middle classes, ignoring the rights of the workers who had built and enlivened the city through their labour, the fate of the city was sealed insofar as the poor may get to stake a claim on it. A report published by Lokshahi Hakk Sangathana (Organization for Democratic Rights) and Girangaon Bachao Andolan (Movement to Save the Mill Districts) had struck warning bells, alerting how the land grab was going to shape the future of the city:

> ...today a group of corporate and multinational financiers and entertainment promoters, in league with millowners, state and civic authorities, claim to lead Bombay into a new era of leisure and prosperity—in pursuit of which they have quietly swept aside legal norms, financial propriety, social justice and the legal and democratic rights of workers. All this to develop the mill areas into a destination for corporate investment and middle-class entertainment, in the process dispersing the organised working-class, their productive activities and livelihoods, their history of struggle and the culture that has been the heart of all that Bombay was once proud of. This destruction of a class of workers, an entire urban lifeworld, holds untold consequences for the city. (Krishnan, 2000, p. 3)

The reel narratives capture this accelerated pace of dispossession quite well. Several cultural commentators have drawn connections[17] between the national award–winning film *Saleem Langde Pe Mat Ro* (Mirza, 1989) and the critically acclaimed and commercially hit film *Gully Boy* (Akhtar, 2019), also India's official entry to the Oscars. Made three decades apart, the films link the unrelenting and violent transformation of the lifeworlds of Mumbai's underclasses; the mills in which an earlier

---

[17] See Pragyan (2019) and Amaal (2019). Also see Jayasankar and Monteiro (2009) for a critique of the reductionist representation of Mumbai's slums in mainstream cinema.

generation worked have now turned into hyper-consumerist spaces where their children hustle for recognition. While such narratives are lapped up by the middle-class and elite audiences in upmarket malls, particularly for their unalloyed realism, substantive media representation continues to elude their 'subjects'. As Titus notes, 'while such traditional mass media tools have produced engagement with a range of socially relevant topics, these instances lack community participation at levels of content, finance, and ownership, and act more as aberrations to hegemonic purchasing rhythms in society'. These questions are often relegated to the bottom of the priority list of both the state and the non-state actors who, in good faith, make substantial developmental interventions in such neighbourhoods. More often, the media dimension of such interventions, if at all there is one, includes production of sensitizing material for the larger society or simply documentation of the projects themselves.

However, there are murmurs on the ground. Several young people from neighbourhoods, such as the one Titus refers to, have begun to engage in media making at the crossroads of hip hop and TikTok, churning out a wide variety of cultural productions that are not immediately reducible to 'issues' or 'complaints', even as they face very real risks of being co-opted by the commercial mainstream (Border Movement, 2018). And indeed, as Titus points out, university students are playing important roles in such emerging cultures as 'learners, interpreters, reviewers and critics' and creating space for 'much-needed dialogue in the public sphere around issues of marginalized persons and alternative media, pushing them beyond frames that offer merely production quality, legal and moral counterpoints'. Possibilities of such alliances need to be explored widely, not only within the context of the existing taught curricula—such as documentary film, journalism or social work practice, which has a long tradition of 'programme media'— but also at the institutional level through engaged co-curricular activities and community outreach programmes.[18]

---

[18] The School of Media and Cultural Studies has been doing this through networking and collaborating with community-based organizations in Mumbai, crowdsourcing multimedia materials that point to alternative narratives of the city. See 'Divercity: Visual Mumbai Archive' at http://divercity.tiss.edu/

In terms of the urban context, with the tenth chapter we move to one that explores the role of news publications in community formation and mobilization. Mahtab Alam profiles two popular English-language news publications—*The Milli Gazette*, a hybrid print–online publication, and *TwoCircles.net* (hereafter *TCN*), a native online outlet—that primarily cater to Muslim communities in India, or those who have an interest in the concerns of the communities, by locating them in historical, as well as contemporary, sociopolitical contexts. Creating a discursive space for Muslim communities, which are either not afforded the space and seriousness they deserve in the mainstream media or rendered in broad strokes of stereotypes, these publications address a crucial and still under-serviced need for minority communities to participate meaningfully in the public sphere. For a long time, this task was being discharged primarily by Urdu-language media, which did not find much traction among the Muslim communities outside North and Central India. The choice of publishing in English, while also excluding a large number of potential readers, managed to address this linguistic chasm to some extent. It is a trade-off that the publishers were ready to make to extend their reach spatially, if perhaps not numerically, and make their publications more representative of the sheer diversity among the Muslim communities in India. It becomes important in this context to consider the importance of translation in enabling intra- and cross-cultural exchanges. *The Milli Gazette* and *TCN* regularly translate and republish relevant content from Urdu and other-language publications, and, as Alam points out, much of their original material, in turn, freely finds its way onto other platforms.

Their quest for a more representative character did not end with making the significant choice to publish in English but extended to the way they framed their editorial policies. Both the publications, over the years, have consciously focused on Muslim communities rather than the religion Islam. Instead of following a narrow conception of community, defined by sacred and legal texts or the perspective of intellectuals and religious elites, their decision to focus on the popular, local and everyday experience has made possible inclusive and progressive debates, as Alam documents, on various intra-community issues.

Alam wraps up with critical reflections and some prescriptive arguments, clearly identifying issues that need to be addressed if *The Milli
Gazette* and *TCN* desire to have a lasting presence in and influence on
their readership. They emanate mostly from ownership and editorial
control, which is concentrated in a few individuals. Alam additionally
highlights the problems of funding to cover the operational costs, as
well as to compensate the journalists and contributing writers. These
are without doubt serious concerns but ones that could be addressed
through putting in place a strategy to encourage participation of the
communities in ownership and funding structures—through long- or
short-term and formal or informal means—as well as through opening
up the publications to their readership in more participatory terms. One
of the strategies for the latter issue, particularly relevant in text-oriented
community media projects, could be to conceive and promote writing
as part of social literacy. There are several models available before us—
writing fellowships,[19] writing centres and workshops,[20] wiki hackathons
(Kashif-ul-Huda, 2015), etc.—which have made possible participation
of constituencies that have so far been designated only as readers in the
realms of cultural production and exchange.

The next two chapters in this section focus on community theatre in
different contexts. Madhura Dutta, in the 11th chapter, presents a case
study of Contact Base, a West Bengal-based NGO that works closely
with the state in strengthening its delivery of rural development programmes through education, capacity building and community-based
research using the street theatre form, along with elements of forum and
folk theatres. In the subsequent chapter, Dakxinkumar Bajrange shares
the evolution and objectives of Budhan Theatre of Gujarat—a theatre
collective run by young members of the denotified Chhara tribe that
primarily makes use of the street theatre form for its agitprop potential.
The approaches of both the groups, while using broadly the same form,
are quite divergent. Contact Base uses theatre to work professionally
with rural communities to empower them through awareness and

---

[19] Laadli Media Fellowships for Journalists: http://populationfirst.org/
laadli-media-advocacy-initiative/

[20] Cybermohalla: https://sarai.net/projects/cybermohalla/

capacity building to be able to deal collectively with their local and internal concerns, as well as those that arise in their encounters with the state agencies. The Chhara youth who constitute Budhan Theatre represent themselves before whom they call the 'mainstream society' and use material drawn from their own lifeworlds to sensitize their audiences to the plight of the denotified tribes of the country.

Contact Base's work unfolds mostly on the turf of the state and, as Dutta shows, follows a functionalist approach. The organization believes that sustainable development of the communities it works with requires active involvement of the state, particularly its agents charged with ensuring efficient last-mile delivery of citizen services. Conversely, it also engages the agents in similar processes, so that they are better placed to respond to the needs and demands of the communities. Their interventions are designed to get various actors in the system to: one, develop an understanding of the greater whole; two, to 'own' their individual or collective roles; and three, to work in tandem with others so that the system works like a well-oiled machinery. While the processes they use may empower individuals or communities in specific ways—as the evidence indeed demonstrates—the overarching approach does raise some concerns precisely about the claims of sustainability in the event the machinery does not function in expected ways. Or, to put in a different way, what kind of theatre does one resort to when the state does not respond to the legitimate demands of the citizens?

In early 2018, more than 30,000 farmers from various parts of Maharashtra staged a 5-day march in Mumbai. The large-scale mobilization was organized for them to express their anguish with the lack of response from the state to their long-standing concerns and demands (Parth M. N., 2018). In the tradition of radical street performance, which includes rallies, marches, vigils, etc. (Cohen-Cruz, 1998), it was a powerful one. For its sheer size, density and duration, the moving sea of humanity captured the public imagination across the country.

NGOs cannot match the might and scale of political mobilizations or social movements, but in the context of community theatre—a space where actors develop capacities that they may perhaps use in real-life situations—it would be pertinent to consider the horizon of such exercises. What kind of conceptions or relationships of power do the actors rehearse to deal with? Do they have the space to improvise if the play veers off-script? Can they script it anew, if they wish to do so?

As Dutta shows, most citizens have to inevitably negotiate with state power in the course of their everyday life for crucial services and resources. It is a power that can be overwhelming, and if community theatre supplies people with the skills and confidence to contend with it, it is a worthwhile Act One. Dutta concludes by noting that community theatre, as it is practised by Contact Base, 'facilitates access and internalization of intellectual inputs, knowledge, and attitude of questioning one's existing social reality, which leads to internal changes reflected in increased confidence, leadership, and capacity to break free from a state of marginalisation enforced by socio-political institutions'.

For Budhan Theatre in Ahmedabad, Gujarat, resisting marginalization is unrelenting work. The stigma associated with belonging to a denotified tribe, marked as 'habitual offenders', means that the Chharas, even today, remain extremely vulnerable to social discrimination and state violence. The central theme in their work is the experience of atrocities they have been subjected to for generations, which they present in an austere but powerful form using only their bodies and voices. Most of their plays speak truth to power forcefully, to the extent that they have been accused of being 'anti-police' for their productions on police violence and have been targeted for their transgressive approach in this regard.

Their plays are remarkable for their ability to clearly convey how crime and criminals are produced by the very system that should work to curb them. They lay bare how power works and, more importantly, how it could be resisted. Budhan Theatre enjoys widespread support of the larger community for its role in bringing attention to the problems of denotified tribes and the opportunities of mentorship it offers to the Chhara youth. Through being involved in theatre work, the young adults are protected not only against the risk of being drawn into a life of criminality but also from being indoctrinated by religious fundamentalist forces (Talukdar & Friedman, 2011). Bajrange counts this among Budhan Theatre's major achievements.

Budhan Theatre makes interventions at various levels. In its neighbourhood, Chharanagar, it runs a library and a cultural space. It performs plays to stall impending demolition of local *bastis* or to protest beatings and torture of the community members. It engages with various networks and institutions, including the police force, and tries to sensitize them towards the concerns of denotified tribes. Lastly, it is an important node of a national advocacy campaign for denotified tribes, through which it envisages that other groups too may get the resources and opportunities to revive their cultural heritage and shed the identities forced on them. The weight of the past hangs heavy on Chharas, but instead of denying or abandoning it, they have been able to turn it into a potent resource to shape their present.

TRAJECTORIES OF CHANGE: SPACES OF HOPE

For any kind of community, cultural heritage is the repository of resources which its members draw on to give values to their thoughts and actions. It includes not only material artefacts or sites of historical and cultural importance but also the contestations around creation of historical and cultural meanings. It has to be reiterated that cultural heritage is not an unchanging tradition or thing of the past. It is deeply connected to the present practices of memorializing, recounting and articulating group identities and culture. Its tangible and intangible constituents are not timeless or inherent but are actively constructed by groups and communities. Culture, then, is by no means static; it rather takes shape over time as a result of deliberation and exchange between people. The chapters in the last section look at a range of such processes as they play out among rural communities, self-organizing urban groups, online feminist collectives and social contexts of technology and help provisionally diagram the wider shifts in community media praxes.

In the 13th chapter, Monteiro and Jayasankar reflect on a significant part of their body of documentary film work among various rural communities engaged in marginal agriculture, animal husbandry and crafts in Kachchh region of Gujarat, and they bring into relief the ways in which the communities mobilize their rich and diverse cultural heritage, primarily poetry and music, as a resource to lead meaningful lives in the contemporary times. The communities have been engaged in a cultural revival, documentation and preservation initiative, facilitated by an NGO that, among other activities, has anchored a community radio project in the region for over two decades where some of the community members first performed for a wider audience. The analysis of this particular community media initiative assumes particular importance in the context of the edited volume, as it holds out invaluable lessons in repairing the fraying social fabric—not by stitching on ungainly swatches cut from elsewhere but by darning it with threads taken from within.

Historian Romila Thapar's seminal work *The Past as Present* (Thapar, 2014) points to how our position in the present shapes our view of the past. The attempt of Hindutva historians has been to reinvent the past and rewrite history from a unitary, communal standpoint that reifies a certain moment in history as the starting point of 'Indian culture/ tradition', which exacerbates the fault lines of religion, by representing certain religious minorities as non-Indian, inherently barbaric and violent conquerors. This needs to be countered with alternative ways of encountering our 'traditions'. It is here that the little, marginal traditions practised by many communities in Kachchh, which Monteiro and Jayasankar's film work has documented and which the community radio initiatives seek to keep alive, gain special significance. These wellsprings of hope and compassion, which draw on the subversive and anti-essentialist work of medieval poets, such as Kabir and Shah Abdul Latif Bhitai, and which have been passed on over generations, through oral traditions of storytelling, poetry and music, in Kachchh and all across the Indian subcontinent, become all the more relevant in the present context. The contemporary moment is marked by a situation where, over the years, there has been an erasure of 'vernacular practices' (Scott, 2012) by a universal national politics that draws on 'a North Atlantic crossed dressed vernacular masquerading as a universal' (p. 56):

A huge variety of languages and dialects, often mutually unintelligible, were, largely through schooling, subordinated to a standardized national language—often the dialect of the dominant region. This led to the disappearance of languages; of local literature, oral and written; of music; of legends and epics; of whole worlds of meaning.

A huge variety of local laws and customary practices were replaced by a national system of law that was, in principle at least, everywhere the same. (Scott, 2012, p. 54)

Open-ended plural and subversive traditions, such as those represented by the work of Kabir, Bhitai and many others, have faced a double-edged cultural genocide from, on the one hand, the nationalist project of a scientific modern certainty and, on the other, the reinvented muscular 'tradition' of the Hindu right, which has been dubbed as a perverse mirror image of scientific modernity (Nandy, 1997). Today, further decimated by neoliberalism, they continue to live on in the cultural spaces of marginalized communities that are recent entrants into the nation state's post-colonial project. Monteiro and Jayasankar point to the need to use these cultural spaces, which community media communicators enter, to interrogate their own location in modernity, in the process also questioning the normalized relations of power which obtain in community media contexts:

There is hence a need to critically interrogate and rethink the relationship between communicators and the communities they work with. Can one work towards building relationships based on trust and mutual respect, on sharing of knowledge and ways of seeing, making it possible to participate in a dialogue that has the potential to problematise these relations of power, transforming both 'us' and 'them'? In many ways, community media initiatives could open up these spaces for mutual learning, given their focus on the 'intangible heritage' of local communities.

In the 14th chapter, Faiz Ullah explores the same dynamic of power relations and the spaces for local self-expression, in a very different context. Starting with a critique of the notion of the public sphere, as it plays out in an inequitable, uneven society with sharp fault lines between the rich and the poor, the rulers and the ruled and the upper and lower castes, the chapter points out that the space for expression of subaltern interests and aspirations is continually thwarted by the mainstream media, whether state-controlled or owned by the private, for-profit sector. This co-opting of the media by those in power further reproduces and makes invisible the exercise of power by them:

'Instead of facilitating and encouraging an expansion and enrichment of the public sphere, the mainstream media wish to replace it, assimilate diverse people, and centralise power. Encroaching upon political processes and spheres is one of their strong tendencies'.

While the emergence of digital technologies has helped democratize access to the media and create alternatives to the mass mainstream media, this process has not been without limitations. The chapter differentiates between the public sphere and civil society, where the latter, which uses the space of alternative media to voice its concerns, is not essentially democratic and participatory. The notion of participation, as actualized by the alternative media itself, is fraught with contradictions and limits, set by sponsorship of costs, top-down development paradigms and a reluctance to hand over control of technology to the community itself. Added to this is the state's co-opting of civil society itself, in order to further its neoliberal agenda.

The present juncture is also characterized by the fluidity of populations and their extreme precarity, due to the policies of the neoliberal state, the vagaries of the globalized world order, migration and the nature of work in the gig economy and information technology–enabled workspaces. The disastrous consequences of this precarity have been witnessed in the wake of the lockdown following the COVID-19 pandemic. The chapter points out that the alternative media circulated by civil society do not reach or serve the interests of this precariat (Standing, 2011), this multitude of citizens, who are often denied their rights as citizens[21] and regarded as enmeshed in 'illegality', in their everyday lives and even in their consumption of media. With affordable access to technologies of communication (e.g., cheap smartphones and data packs) the possibilities for these citizens to voice their concerns is increased:

A new public culture is taking shape where people, freed of socially inherited roles and obligations, are creatively engaging in media criticism and creating their own media. The difficulties that prevented a vast majority of people from joining knowledge and political spheres

---

[21] Standing characterizes their status as one of denizens rather than citizens.

remain—literacy, social restrictions, and unreliable infrastructure—but people have started to work around them, drawing on their own strengths.

It is in this context that Ullah explores the dynamics of self-expression and self-organizing that the new media ecologies facilitate, which begin to expand the space of community media, of what we consider as community media. For too long, community media have been seen as media that are initiated by NGOs in order to help communities help themselves and even 'improve' themselves (in the likeness of an external normative framework, e.g., no child labour or marriage, literacy and education for girls and women, etc.). Without going into the merits of these normative frameworks, the point remains that these may not be the priorities of these communities themselves, but they become targets through which community media demonstrate their efficacy in order to secure support from funders. In many ways, the various examples of diverse communities using the media, which this volume explores, begin to problematize this model of community media.

The two examples that this chapter discusses do not belong to the body of practice of what is generally considered as community media. The first case is of the Honda workers, under attack from the management, using social media to create their own narrative of events and counter the dominant images of violent and destructive workers circulated by the mainstream media. The second case is of an informal settlement, Ambujwadi in Malvani, Mumbai, which, like most other such settlements, faces severe problems in access to the basic amenities like water due to its 'illegal' status in the eyes of the local government. The use of video technology by a local youth group, in collaboration with a group of students of community media, resulted in the production of a series of videos that the group then used for its advocacy work.

The two cases, while different from each other, are similar in that they seek to create space for the articulation of political voice, rather than focusing on the creation of an end product or an institutional structure. As the chapter points out, 'In general, such initiatives do not take the form of an institution - the emphasis is on building the capacity of the people who are involved'. The emphasis on the creation and sustenance of institutions, which often becomes the raison d'être of many community media projects, perhaps needs to be interrogated, in order to explore more fully the transformative possibilities of community media.

In the last decade, notably since the Arab Spring of 2010, the online space in general and social media in particular have become crucial spaces for mobilization, communication and dissemination for a diverse range of social movements and campaigns by marginalized sections of society, so much so that governments that want to clamp down on dissent often shut down the Internet. It is this space that Shilpa Phadke and Nithila Kanagasabai explore in the 15th chapter, through looking at feminist communities in the online space. The four feminist groups that the chapter engages with—Girls at Dhabas (GaD), Pinjra Tod (PT), Blank Noise (BN) and Parcham—enact their politics in urban spaces and seek, in various ways, to claim the right of women to occupy public space in towns and cities. Some of them are middle-class initiatives, which do not usually get included in the ambit of community media.

The claim to space, which these groups work to extend, involves an interweaving of offline and online performance, such that the collectives view 'the online and the street as contiguous and co-constitutive spaces'. For instance, GaD, which started off as a hashtag when a woman posted a picture of herself at a dhaba in Karachi, became a popular hashtag that elicited participation from women across South Asian cities, allowing them to re-imagine themselves in hitherto 'male' spaces in their cities. The act of inscribing one's gendered physical presence in public space and then affirming this performance through indexical images that begin to circulate in online space becomes a powerful assertion of the right to space. Jurgenson (2019) speaks of how in our contemporary social media–ted world the vast archives of images produced and circulated no longer signify a documentary function but rather have become 'units of communication'. In other words, we use images not so much to memorialize our lives as to construct and perform our identities and to speak to one another through images. The deployment of social photos is a powerful strategy, as the GaD and BN initiatives would suggest, used by online feminist initiatives to build solidarities and widen the ambit of communities. The engagements, however, go far beyond social media, allowing for new kinds of political linkages and the formation of communities around similar concerns, across diverse geographies. The online space also allows groups that are geographically located, such as Parcham, to use social media to share their initiatives and concerns and to work towards challenging stereotypes about Muslim women and the 'othered' spaces they live in. These communities also seek to work with new models of organization which are fluid, non-hierarchical and hence somewhat messy. As Phadke and Kanagasabai point out, 'These communities then appear to approximate the values that community media holds—the desire for democracy, a flat structure, a space where different people find voice and are able to publish and put out ideas'. The collectives are well aware of the limitations of social media, with its attendant dangers of surveillance, trolling and co-opting. They are also aware of the ephemerality of their efforts, of their collectives, and many of them are committed to changing the discourse around the notion of women's presence in public space, and not so much to continuing within a particular organizational form.

In the ultimate analysis, all the feminist communities spoke of the building of friendships and relationships as an important part of their work. In their concluding reflections, one of the editors of the volume *Friendship as Social Justice Activism: Critical Solidarities in Global Perspective* notes

> how social justice lies in our efforts to build communities outside and within normative modes of belonging and togetherness. Friendship provides relief at a time when telling truth about self, determines who will be bestowed with the coveted prize of recognition. Friendship is transformative social justice when we're are able to be together through an ethic of responsibility toward the other (including its fail- ure), share a language of critique, and nurture the social bonds that emerge within the struggles to endure oppressive spaces and benevo- lent norms. (Banerjea et al., 2018, p. 271)

This perhaps is an important insight that needs to find a place in our understanding of community media.

Another significant contribution of this chapter is to push for

> the expansion of the conception of a community to include those that are *ideologically chosen rather than geographically contained.* These scattered feminist communities might challenge the idea that there is

a community out there which is always already in existence and to which technological capabilities can be imparted to produce 'community media'. Instead, we argue for the possibility of re-imagining the idea of community as *implicitly partial and in a constant state of becoming*. (...) Rather than thinking of communities as fixed and stable entities that aspire to upscale or grow in one direction, we ask if it is possible to allow for *ephemerality and shape shifting....*

Perhaps the contemporary moment, with its multitude of challenges, calls for a re-imagination of communities as more contingent, non-hierarchical entities with a commonality of interests which could work collectively to contest the dominant relations of power and work towards changing the discourse around a theme. It is with this spirit that this volume includes several such initiatives that would generally not be seen as belonging to the domain of community media.

If the first three chapters in this section are a call to inflect our notions of community media somewhat differently, the last chapter, 'Divided We Stand, United We Fall: The Newfound Wisdom of Digital Age Communication Technology' by Babu, provokes us to question the very bedrock of technology on which community media in the 21st century tends to be based. Taking the case of the 2019 Hong Kong insurrections, it looks at how young people are eschewing the data-hungry corporate-based social media platforms, which are prone to arm-twisting by the state, and creating their own local, home-grown solutions, based on open-source software, which fly under the radar of state and corporate surveillance. The chapter explores many such examples, created by individuals driven not by the profit motive but by the desire to provide independent and secure platforms to those who seek to resist the power of states and corporations the world over.

The lessons that these fascinating accounts teach us are, first, to question the primacy of technological determinism. As the author puts it,

The idea of technological determinism has been seen, for quite some time now, as a major impediment to equal access and democratic usage of communication technology. (...) Given that technological innovation, at least in the popular perception, is controlled and directed by capital, it has always led to the generation of surplus capital rather than being a catalyst for human development.

The emerging examples of people's creative and subversive use of digital technologies on the ground point towards the paradigm of social construction of technology, where it is human action that shapes technology and not the other way round, as Babu points out:

> These events essentially tell us that the meaning of communication technology is not derived or fixed by its design or original intention, but it arises through an active interaction between technology, its users and their dynamic social and political circumstances. That the transformative power of technology is vested in its users and their interpretation rather than in its design and original intention is a thought that holds the power to transform the popular notion of technology itself.

Second, this also implies the imperative to remain curious and questioning about both the larger constructs within which our digital practices are often located—the technological policies of the state—and the technological affordances given to us by corporate-owned online networks. Rather than seeing them as essentially liberating and empowering, one needs to be wary of the insidious ways in which they impinge on our everyday lives and to realize that there are technological alternatives, based on open source, that are beyond the state and the market, which we could possibly explore.

Third, social theory in general, and media studies in particular, needs to take the questions of infrastructures of mediatization very seriously. Just as those working in the realms of science and technology today make use of the critical social sciences perspectives, those of us who are involved in understanding social phenomena and are working to question dominant social relations of power using media, including community media, should also endeavour to acquaint ourselves with a working knowledge of what is under the hood of the platforms and apps we use and develop the abilities to tinker with them. One of the most astute critics of technology, its potentials and consequences, Paul Virilio (2001), noted that much like the artistic and literary cultures, development of 'democratic technological culture' is essential for citizens to realize 'practical ideals of democracy', without which

> the hype generated by the publicity around the Internet and so on is not counter-balanced by a political intelligence that is based on

a technological culture...techno-scientific intelligence is presently insufficiently spread among society at large to enable us to interpret the sorts of techno-scientific advances that are taking shape today. (Virilio, 2001, p. 194)

Lastly, any deployment of technology by people and in people's interest, as community media aims to do, must be based on a larger understanding of the ways in which state policies and programmes position technology and use it for their own ideological and political ends.[22] An understanding of the political history of technology in India, the dilemmas that it creates for the government in power and the way the government shapes the public's relationship with technology would help strategize how community media could relate to this process in their attempt to democratize communication technologies.

RETHINKING THE SPACE OF THE POLITICAL

In many ways, the themes discussed in this volume have come out of dissatisfaction with contemporary community media practice, primarily community radio, and the somewhat cocooned existence that it has been pushed into, through restrictions imposed by the state which seek to divest it of any taint of the 'political'. Yet, as we realize, the political is omnipresent and emerges in covert ways, through gender, class and caste relations of power. In the meanwhile, given the easy accessibility of digital technologies and the Internet, there is a flourishing of various modes of subaltern communication, beyond the space of the NGO or the university, which have in many cases been the catalysts of community radio and video initiatives. What are the implications of considering these perhaps less structured, more political processes under the ambit of community media? We certainly do not see this as a means of domesticating them. Rather, we propose that the space of community media should be conceptualized as a diverse, at times contradictory, force field that responds in various ways to the contemporary sociopolitical–economic context. There is the potential for different kinds of initiatives to learn from each other if the aim of all community media is to extend the

---

[22] Refer to Sukumar (2019), for a provocative account of the state's relationship with technology over seven decades of post-colonial India.

claim to citizenship and voice to the most marginalized inhabitants of this country.

Second, the implicit privileging of an external facilitator or catalyst and the setting of targets and measurable outputs which often underlie community media initiatives need to be questioned. As many of the initiatives discussed in this volume bear out, community media could also be seen in more process-oriented, organic terms, where mobilization through the media takes place when called for by the situation. It may not always take the form of an institutional structure. This means a rethinking of what 'sustainability' means in these conditions. Many development communication initiatives are focused on 'sustainability', 'replication' and 'scaling up' of successful initiatives. This would certainly be a more managerial approach to communication, which runs counter to the spirit of community media.

Third, we would like to propose that community media and cultural studies have a shared agenda. Both are concerned with understanding dominant relations of power. Both position communicators or subjects or researchers as reflexive, questioning beings enmeshed in processes of resistance to taken-for-granted, normalized ways of seeing the world. Both see culture as a fluid terrain of struggle over meanings. Community media has much to gain from adopting a cultural-studies approach to its own texts and processes. As Stuart Hall puts it:

> It is only through the way in which we represent and imagine ourselves that we come to know how we are constituted and who we are. There is no escape from the politics of representation, and we cannot wield 'how life really is out there' as a kind of text against which the political rightness or wrongness of a particular cultural strategy or text can be measured. (Hall, 2004, p. 261)

In summation, we seek to locate, through a broader and critical reading, the increasingly ubiquitous practices of community media within the discussions around citizenship and democratization of power. The contributions in this volume respond, from different contexts and perspectives, to the rapid erosion of public power and engage with the question of how it might be checked and restored. Promises of *roti, kapda, aur makaan*[23] (food, clothing and housing) or the catchall term 'development' does not quite fully respond to the substantive demands of overwhelmingly large sections of society. Their demands include all these, of course, but more. As all the contributions clearly demonstrate, the questions of autonomy and substantive participation in social, economic and political structures form the larger horizon of contemporary struggles.

REFERENCES

Akhtar, Z. (2019). *Gully boy*. Excel Entertainment and Tiger Baby Films.

Amaal, A. (2019). *'Gully Boy' and the legacy of 'Salim Langde Pe Mat Ro'*. https://www.thehindu.com/entertainment/movies/apna-time-aayega-gully-boy-and-the-legacy-of-salim-langde-pe-mat-ro/article26951915.ece

Ananthakrishnan G. (2020). Can't stop or monitor their movement of roads': SC rejects plea seeking relief for migrant. https://indianexpress.com/article/india/supreme-court-on-migrant-workers-movement-on-roads-covid19-lock-down-6411143/

Anderson, B. (1983). *Imagined communities: Reflections on the origin and spread of nationalism*. Verso.

Azoulay, A. (2008). *The civil contract of photography*. Zone Books

Banerjea, N., Dasgupta, D., Dasgupta, R. K., & Grant, J. M. (2018). *Friendship as social justice activism: Critical solidarities in a global perspective*. Seagull Books.

Banks, M. (2001). *Visual methods in social research*. SAGE Publications.

Basu, K., & Banerjee, D. (Ed.). (2018). *Towards a peoples' cinema: Independent documentary and its audience in India*. Three Essays Collective.

Bickford, S. (1996). *The dissonance of democracy: Listening, conflict and citizenship*. Cornell University Press.

Border Movement. (2018). *The commodification of Hip-Hop in India*: A discussion http://www.bordermovement.com/the-commodification-of-hip-hop-in-india-a-discussion/

Brown, W. (2019). *In the ruins of neoliberalism: The rise of antidemocratic politics in the west*. Columbia University Press.

Capstick, A. (2012). Participatory video and situated ethics: Avoiding disablism. In E.-J. Milne, C. Mitchell, & N. De Lange (Eds.), *The handbook of participatory video* (pp. 269–282). AltaMira Press.

Chandhoke, N. (2011). Civil society in India. In M. Edwards (Ed.), *The oxford handbook of civil society* (pp. 122–134). Oxford University Press.

---

[23] *Sadak, bijli, paani* (roads, electricity, water) and the latest, *naukri*, degree, Wi-Fi (jobs, education, Internet access), are a couple of the other various updated versions of the popular slogan.

Cohen-Cruz, J. (Ed.). (1998). *General introduction in radical street performance: An international anthology.* Routledge.

Dattatreyan, G. E. (2020). Policing the 'sensible' in the Era of YouTube: Urban villages and racialized subjects in Delhi. *Television & New Media, 21*(4), 407–419. https://doi.org/10.1177/1527476419870511

Dutta, A., & Anamika Ray. (2017). Democratic and participatory potentiality of community video in India. *Asian Journal of Distance Education, 12*(2), 20–36.

Gerbaudo, P. (2012). *Tweets and the streets: Social media and contemporary activism.* Pluto Press.

Gramsci, A. (2015). *Antonio Gramsci: Selections from the prison notebooks.* Aakar Books.

Hall, S. (2004). What is this 'Black' in black popular culture. In J. Bobo, C. Hudley, & C. Michel (Eds.), *The black studies reader* (11 pp.). Psychology Press.

Hamilton, J. (2000). Alternative media: Conceptual difficulties, critical possibilities. *Journal of Communication Inquiry, 24*(4), 357–378. https://dx.doi.org/10.1177/0196859900024004002

Hansen, T. B. (2017). *On law, violence, and jouissance in India.* Member Voices, *Fieldsights,* November 1. https://culanth.org/fieldsights/on-law-violence-and-jouissance-in-india

Jamil, G. (2017). *Muslim women speak: Of dreams and shackles.* SAGE Yoda Press.

Jank, H. (2010). *Literacy and power.* Routledge.

Jayasankar, K. P., & Anjali, M. (2009). *Jai Ho Shanghai: The invisible poor in Slumdog Millionaire.* In K. Ashwani, J. A. Scholte, M. Kaldor, M. Glasius, H. Seckinelgn, & H. K. Anheier (Eds.), *Global civil society yearbook* (pp. 14–15). LSE and SAGE Publications.

Jurgenson, N. (2019). *The social photo.* Verso Books.

Kashif-ul-Huda. (2015). *Activism meets Hacktivism for Dalit history month.* http://twocircles.net/2015apr06/1428322812.html

Krishnan, S. (2000). *Murder of the mills: A case study of Phoenix mills.* Lokshahi Hakk Sangathana and Girangaon Bachao Andolan.

Kumar, R. (2018). *The free voice: On democracy culture and the nation.* Speaking Tiger.

Lenzner, B. (2014). *Emerging forms of citizen video activism: Challenges in documentary storytelling & sustainability.* In R. Hudson Moura (Ed.), Proceedings of the Interactive Narratives, New Media & Social Engagement International Conference, University of Toronto, October 23–25.

Lunch, C., & Roberts, T. (2015). *Participatory video. International Encyclopaedia of digital communication and society.* John Wiley and Sons.

Mann, S., Nolan, J., and Wellman, B. (2003). Sousveillance: inventing and using wearable computing devices for data collection in surveillance environments. *Surveillance & Society, 1*(3), 331–355. https://doi.org/10.24908/ss.v1i3.3344

Mirza, S. A. (1989). *Salim Langde Pe Mat Ro.* National Film Development Corporation.

Nandy, A. (1997). The twilight of certitudes: Secularism, Hindu nationalism, and other masks of deculturation. *Alternatives, 22*(2), 157–176. https://doi.org/10.1177/030437549702200201

Padovani, C. (2015). *New world information and communication order (NWICO)*. The International Encyclopaedia of Communication. https://dx.doi.org/10.1002/9781405186407.wbiecn013.pub2

Parth M. N. (2018). Why tens of thousands of Maharashtra's farmers are marching their way to Mumbai. https://thewire.in/agriculture/maharashtra-farmers-protest-march-mumbai

Paul, S., & Dowling, D. O. (2018). Digital archiving as social protest. *Digital Journalism, 6*(9), 1239–1254. https://dx.doi.org/10.1080/21670811.2018.1493938

Pink, S. (2001). *Doing visual ethnography*. SAGE Publications.

Pragyan, M. (2019). *Before Murad, Saeed Mirza's Salim Langde was the OG Gully Boy dreaming of 'Apna Time Aayega'*. https://www.arre.co.in/bollywood/saeed-mirza-salim-langda-gully-boy-apna-time-aayega/

Saxena, N. C. (1998). What is meant by people's participation? *Journal of Rural Development, 17*(1), 111–113.

Scott, J. C. (2012). *Two cheers for anarchism*. Princeton University Press.

Sen, A. (1999). *Development as freedom*. Oxford University Press.

Smith, L. T. (2012). *Decolonizing methodologies: Research and indigenous peoples*. Zed Books.

Sruthisagar, Y. (2019). *Supreme court to Tis Hazari: How the judiciary responded to CAA protests and police action*. https://scroll.in/article/947770/supreme-court-to-tiz-hazari-how-the-judiciary-responded-to-caa-protests-and-police-action

Standing, G. (2011). *The precariat: The new dangerous class*. Bloomsbury.

Sukumar, A. M. (2019). *Midnight's machines: A political history of technology in India*. Penguin Random House.

Talukdar, S., & Kerim Friedman, P. (2011). *Please don't beat me, sir*. Four Nine and Half Pictures Inc.

Thapar, R. (2014). *The past as present: Forging contemporary identities through history*. Aleph Books.

Virilio, P. (2001). The Kosovo W@r did take place. In J. Armitage (Ed.), *Virilio live: Selected interviews*. SAGE Publications.

Waghmore, S. (2013). *Civility against caste: Dalit politics and citizenship in Western India*. SAGE Publications.

White, S. A. (2003). *Participatory video: Images that transform and empower*. SAGE Publications.

Zuckerman, E. (2016). Why we must continue to turn the camera on police. *MIT Technology Review*. https://www.technologyreview.com/2016/07/11/70642/why-we-must-continue-to-turn-the-camera-on-police/

Section I

Waves of Freedom: Community Radio and Its Discontents

Chapter 2

Negotiating 'the Political' in the Community Radio Sphere
Historical Choices, Contemporary Predicaments

Vinod Pavarala and Kanchan K. Malik

The two-decade-old community radio (CR) movement in India, right from its inception, has had to contend with the political question.[1] Advocates and activists campaigning for the opening up of airwaves in India for third-sector broadcasting, independent of the state and the market, were cautious to eschew an argument based on communication rights, something that would have surely been construed as overtly political by the government in power in Delhi which was wary of the demand for CR. Instead, campaigners deployed an already prevalent paradigm of communication for development which seemed somewhat benign and acceptable to the state.

---

[1] We use the term 'political' not only to include state policy for regulating the media but also to refer to the 'micropolitics' of various stakeholders engaging with the state, what one may, perhaps, call the social flows of power. Our notion of the 'political' invokes, implicitly, Foucault's notion of 'governmentality' that incorporates rational systems of governance—the management and administration of power—as well as ways in which the governed negotiate with that rationality of rule, in this case in the domain of broadcasting. See Gordon (1991) for a coherent introduction to the concept of governmentality.

Not only did this strategic decision by the movement turn into a trap, but it was also compounded by other originary sins, such as the policy prohibitions placed on broadcast of news and 'political' content by CR. During the past 10–15 years of their existence, many CR stations, while trying to deliver on their mandate to use CR as a tool for enhancing people's participation in development, have had to muddle through the political question. In the process, the CR sector[2] has fallen short of its own campaign expectations that CR would help reverse the hierarchy of access, promote alternative voices, support social movements, revitalize neglected cultural forms, build solidarities among and empower the marginalized and propagate the right to communication for all.

In this chapter, we provide a review of the historical context in which broadcasting policy in India evolved from the patronizing and authoritarian colonial control to the post-colonial period when the state swung schizophrenically between autonomy and regulation. In the second part of the chapter, we offer a ring-side view of the campaign for CR in India by dipping into the archive and analysing some of the early posts on cr–India, an online mailing list that was set up by media activists and scholars who initiated the movement for CR in India in 2000. The latter allows us to understand the paradigmatic choices made by (mostly urban) media activists and advocates to graft an older media technology (radio, albeit in its new frequency modulation [FM] *avatar*) on to an equally settled discourse of development communication and, more hesitantly, on to ongoing political and social struggles in Latin America and elsewhere.

Finally, we also discuss the complex ways in which the CR sector in India has been negotiating the 'political' in their programming, as well as through their engagement with the state. We consider some key

---

[2] Throughout this chapter, we use 'movement' and 'sector' interchangeably to refer to community radio (CR) in India. A loose coalition of media activists involved in the initial campaign for democratization of media in the country did not themselves set up stations after the policy was announced but remained as a pressure group of sorts; meanwhile, the stations that were set up since 2003 have gradually coalesced into a sectoral body seeking a favourable deal from the state. The former called itself the Community Radio Forum (now disbanded), and the latter operates as the Community Radio Association of India.

challenges of the sector—content restrictions, state funding, monitoring and surveillance and NGO-ization—in order to analyse how this complex web of patronage and surveillance results in keeping CR stations, from the state's perspective, at a safe distance from the potential ravages of the political.

BROADCASTING LANDSCAPE IN INDIA—THE POLITICS OF REGULATION AND REFORM

In post-independence India, the regulatory ecology of broadcasting may best be described as one of policy dissonance, by which we imply that the concerns that determine the normative underpinnings of government legislations on broadcasting are in conflict with each other. These have been crafted essentially as politically motivated knee-jerk reactions or fixes to governing exigencies posed by the exponential advancement in broadcasting technologies and infrastructure. They do not form part of a comprehensive agenda of reform for broadcasting in India which would suitably address the techno-social or techno-commercial realities on the ground.

This dissonance is reflective of the tug of war between the state's imperative to retain statutory control over broadcasting, on the one hand, and its obligation towards constitutional guarantees of freedom of expression, as well as to the emerging international consensus on people's access to communication technologies, on the other. The state also seeks to find an enduring balance between the pressures from the corporate sector that seeks private and commercial use of broadcasting, vis-à-vis the political compulsion to generate content that blends with the larger schema of nation-building and development goals.

Thus, it is not surprising that the state still retains the means to control broadcasting in India derived from the antiquated Indian Telegraph Act, 1885 (and its subsequent amendments), which gives absolute power for the establishment, maintenance and working of wireless apparatus to the central government, complemented by the Indian Wireless Telegraphy Act of 1933, which makes possession, without a license, of wireless receivers or radio equipment a transgression (Pavarala & Malik, 2007).

Also, the programming by All India Radio (AIR), the state broad-caster, has not been able to break the mould of its embarrassing reputa-tion of being a channel for government propaganda. The production of content remains highly centralized, and bureaucratization stands in the way of production of innovative or quality programmes that contend with politically contentious themes or civic issues.

However, just when this may appear to be a classic case of an authoritative and narrow regime, there is a bag full of broadcasting bills and policies in India formulated to facilitate functional autonomy for the broadcasting sector, assist decentralization of programming and endorse liberalization of media. Even though there still may be a gap between policy and practice, the 2003 and 2006 policies[3] allowing for community-owned non-profit broadcasting are progressive initiatives by the state. This opening up of airwaves to communities could be seen as a step towards providing media access to citizens and the much-awaited and anticipated democratization of broadcasting.

Even preceding this, the government had made a start to the dis-mantling of the state's monopoly over radio by giving in (probably reluctantly) to the liberalization and privatization wave initiated by the satellite television era. In 1999, it announced a policy for private agencies to set up FM radio stations on a licence fee basis. With the completion of FM Radio Phase III Auction in 2018, private FM radio broadcasting will cover all the 29 states and six of the seven union territories.[4]

Hence, while navigating the chequered historical trajectory of the Indian broadcasting landscape that now boasts three distinct tiers of broadcasting—public, commercial and community—one can identify two contradictory pulls that emerge. These, as will be explained fur-ther, serve separate constituencies and a cross-section of stakeholders, and the final outcome is an uneasy compromise that accentuates the need for a comprehensive reform of the broadcasting sector in India.

---

[3] Called 'Policy Guidelines for setting up Community Radio Stations in India', this was first announced in 2003, opening a window for 'established educational institutions' to apply. In 2006, the same guidelines were amended to add community-based organizations to potential applicants.

[4] See https://www.livemint.com/Consumer/wx62mIJLipvVF7OiW0Ow3J/Govt-approves-auction-of-683-private-FM-radio-frequencies.html

LEGACY OF BROADCASTING IN INDIA—STATE CONTROL AND NATION-BUILDING BURDENS

India set out after Independence to achieve total government control over broadcasting. This may be looked upon as part of the paternalistic Reithian[5] and colonial legacy of regulation and control, as well as the fervour to tap the power of mass media for fulfilling the national targets of large-scale development. Over the years, with allocation of funds made in all subsequent Five-Year Plans (FYPs), AIR, as the national broadcaster, has become

> one of the largest broadcasting organisations in the world in terms of the number of languages of broadcast, [and] the spectrum of socio-economic and cultural diversity it serves. AIR's home service comprises 420 stations today located across the country, reaching nearly 92% of the country's area and 99.19 % of the total population. AIR originates programming in 23 languages and 179 dialects.[6]

The earliest official appraisal of the functioning of the state-owned media by the Ministry of Information and Broadcasting (MIB) was carried out in 1964 by a committee headed by Ashok K. Chanda, a former auditor general. The committee's terms of reference mentioned that there was a need for an evaluation, as 'there had been persistent criticism both in parliament and the press of the deficiencies of AIR', and that it had not succeeded in eliciting people's 'cooperation in fulfilling the plans of social and economic development' (MIB, 1966, p. 2). The report submitted by the Chanda Committee in 1966 observed that broadcasting was being treated as a routine function of the state, and it recommended that radio (and television) must be used creatively to accelerate the pace of development. It pointed a finger at the political considerations and regional arm-twisting that led to the choice of unsuitable locations of transmitters and selection of sources for their procurement. The committee was also critical of AIR being employed as an instrument of the government and that an infrastructure

---

[5] The adjective 'Reithian' relates to Lord Reith, Director General of the British Broadcasting Corporation (1927–1938), and his principles, especially his belief in the responsibility of broadcasting to enlighten and educate public taste.

[6] http://allindiaradio.gov.in

created with public funds was being misappropriated for propaganda and political mileage. It noted the existence of a culture of conformity and that AIR's recruitment pattern fostered obedience and silent acquiescence. The talks and discussions were hogged by elites, and even there, those unsympathetic of governmental programmes were circumvented (MIB, 1966).

AIR's rural broadcasts sought to educate, inform and entertain villagers by use of regional languages and local dialects, and provisions were made for community listening sets in villages (Chatterji, 1991). There was no endeavour to seek people's feedback, until an experiment in farm radio forums was conducted in 1956 by the United Nations Educational, Scientific and Cultural Organization (UNESCO) in 150 villages of Maharashtra. For the first time, a two-way communication was established between village audiences and programme makers. Between 1959 and 1964, the farm forums project gained popularity, but AIR failed to capitalize on the lessons learnt and the project remained just an experiment (Mathur & Neurath, 1959).

The Chanda Committee report evokes the success of farm radio forums to validate that 'given the right approach and the opportunity to discuss and find solutions to local problems, the farmer is receptive to new ideas and techniques' (MIB, 1966, p. 11). AIR's 1966 broadcasts from Trichinopoly station, in the fertile rice-growing areas of Tamil Nadu, helped persuade farmers to adopt high-yielding varieties of rice that came to be known as 'Radio Paddy' (Page & Crawley, 2001). The blatant misuse of AIR during the national emergency from 1975 to 1977 propelled the debate around autonomy for the electronic media, and a working group led by former newspaper editor B. G. Verghese was assigned in 1977 to look into the possibilities for autonomy. Ascribing the unplanned progression of broadcast media to the lack of a 'wider perception of a national communication policy or philosophy', the group recommended the establishment of an autonomous National Broadcasting Trust, 'Akash Bharati', with a mandate to democratize media through a 'web of vertical and lateral communication designed to facilitate the transmission of informational, educational, and cultural messages not merely from government to people but from people to government, masses to decision-makers, rural to urban, the young to the rest and so on' and also for this cross-cultural exchange to include 'dissenting voices and minority voices' (MIB, 1978, p. 18).

The 1982 working group on software for Doordarshan (often referred to as the P. C. Joshi Committee) was also critical of the repeated use of national communication set-up to represent 'a Delhi-centric view of India'. Its report mentioned systematically how 'communication should help to create a participatory model of development, a participatory rural community in which information flows not only downwards, from governments to the people but also upwards from people to the government' (MIB, 1985, vol. 2, p. 30).

DEMOCRATIZATION OF AIRWAVES IN INDIA—FREEDOM OF EXPRESSION AND MEDIA PLURALISM

The Akash Bharati report was revisited in 1989 and produced as the Prasar Bharati bill in the Parliament. Prasar Bharati was envisaged as an autonomous corporation, but the terms still reproduced earlier notions of servicing rural, illiterate and underprivileged populations, promoting regional language and culture, addressing issues concerning women's equality and engaging with the youth, minorities and tribal groups (Thomas, 1990). Parliament approved this bill, but the government fell before it could be notified. This act languished for 7 years from August 1990 to July 1997, when it was finally notified. The act was brought into force on 15 September 1997, and Prasar Bharati (Broadcasting Corporation of India) was established on 23 November 1997 (Pavarala & Malik, 2007).

However, autonomy for broadcasting remains an unimplemented good intention until today, as the working of Prasar Bharati continues to be controlled by government cadres. With the effects of globalization and commercialization posing challenges, the role of Prasar Bharati as a broadcaster could have been vital, but the lack of political will appeared to be thwarting its public-service function. Attempts to invigorate the role of Prasar Bharati were made through setting up the Prasar Bharati Review Committee that submitted its report on 20 May 2000 (Pavarala & Malik, 2007). The committee was of the opinion that:

The public service broadcaster plays a key role in any society, especially, in a large and thriving democracy. It must be a part of 'civil society', independent of and distinct from the government. In fact, the public service broadcaster must act as one of the bedrocks of society and seek to continuously enlarge the so-called 'public sphere'. It must play host to informed debate, provide space for alternative and dissenting viewpoints, be a voice of the voiceless and give substance to the phrase participatory democracy. (MIB, 2000, p. 16)

The committee also recommended giving serious consideration to '[…] the franchising of local radio stations by Prasar Bharati to selected local community and voluntary groups on an experimental basis. Now that FM radio has been privatized, we do hope that the long-standing opposition and aversion to such a worthwhile step will fade away' (MIB, 2000, p. 37).

During the period of the deliberations around autonomy for the broadcasting sector, there were other forces (private and civil society) at work demanding their share of the airwaves (as is discussed later). The Supreme Court (SC) delivered a celebrated judgement in February 1995 (*Ministry of Information and Broadcasting v. Cricket Association of Bengal*), pronouncing that 'Airwaves constitute public property and must be utilised for advancing public good'.

The core of the judgement was to curtail the government's control over broadcasting. However, it did not favour deregulating the airwaves solely for operation by the private companies. It specified that

> no individual had a right to utilise them (airwaves) at his choice and pleasure and for purposes of his choice including profit….The broad-casting media should be under the control of the public as distinct from government. This is the command implicit in Article 19(1) (a). It should be operated by a public statutory corporation or corpora-tions…. (as cited in MIB, 1997)

The judgement ordered the central government to 'take immediate steps to establish an autonomous public authority to control and regu-late the use of the airwaves'. While the 1995 Supreme Court judgement opened the gates for private commercial broadcasting to be introduced in India, community broadcasting still had to go through a long struggle before it became a reality.

The above account offers valuable insights into the governmentality that shaped the evolution of broadcasting policy in India. Fear of a fully autonomous electronic media, the desire to retain substantive control over broadcasting infrastructure, suspicion of citizen access to means of electronic communication and a subsequent confidence that it could effectively domesticate any citizens' media that may emerge define the state's approach to broadcasting. In the following section, we shift the fulcrum of our discussion on the broadcasting policy of the state to that of civil society, especially in the context of the movement for CR. As Marc Raboy (1990, p. xi) points out, debates over media policy 'frame and situate the public politics of communication'.

THE CAMPAIGN FOR COMMUNITY RADIO IN INDIA—PARADIGMATIC OPTIONS AND CONSTRAINTS

It was in the year 2000 that about 50 people who had assembled in Hyderabad for a UNESCO conference on CR, including some senior UNESCO officials, activists and advocates from other parts of South Asia and elsewhere in the world, took the roughly 3-hour journey to village Pastapur in Medak district of what is now Telangana. The purpose was to listen to rural women who articulated with great passion and conviction the need for their own media, to tell their own stories, in their own voices. They already had some basic equipment and were involved in community audio production and narrowcasting through the village-level *sanghams*. The Pastapur Declaration that was signed by civil society organizations and activists during that visit became a sort of manifesto for the CR movement in India, coherently expressing, for the first time, a demand for a three-tier system of broadcasting in India (public, private and community).[7] The inspiration drawn from this declaration and the women's articulations spurred the long-drawn-out campaign for CR in the country.

---

[7] UNESCO Chair on Community Media, http://uccommedia.in/news/the-pastapur-initiative-on-community-radio-broadcasting/

Further, when the initial version of the CR policy was announced two years later (and a modified one permitting NGOs in 2006), this was the first case of a media policy in the country which emerged out of grassroots advocacy and years of community audio production, not something imposed suddenly and abruptly from the top by policy-makers. The policy was a good example of deliberative democracy in action, an outcome of intense consultations among various stakehold-ers combined with hard negotiations with well-meaning bureaucrats.[8]

Today, a decade after the opening up of the airwaves, we have over 200 CR stations across the country. As the number of stations grows, there is a visible heterogeneity in terms of ideologies, interests, degrees and varieties of community participation, broadcast durations that vary from 3–22 hours a day, content ranging from the pedagogical to the musical, formats and styles that reflect those of AIR, while others create innovative genres, ownership ranging from universities to engineering colleges to agricultural institutions to well-funded NGOs and not-so-well-funded community-based organizations.

The CR movement in India is now a little over two decades old, if we consider the ferment caused by the airwaves judgement of the Supreme Court in 1995. A study of the early discourse of CR in India, through an examination of the archives of the cr-India mailing list, allows us to not only understand some key historical choices that were made but also identify the complex ways in which those choices impinge on our contemporary predicaments.[9]

INTERPRETING 'COMMUNITY' IN COMMUNITY RADIO

First, even a cursory glance at the policy guidelines is adequate to suggest how smug the policy was about the term 'community' in 'community radio'. It was in effect defined by the geographical limits

---

[8] See Raghunath (2018) for a detailed analysis of the negotiated nature of CR policymaking, with emphasis on its deliberative aspects, in the South Asian region.

[9] This section of the chapter draws from an analysis of the cr-India archive presented by Vinod Pavarala as a keynote address at the National Conference on 'Questioning Community Radio in India: Looking Back to Look Forward', organized by Savitribai Phule Pune University, 5–7 March 2017.

placed by the technology. In practice, though, stations and organiza-tions seeking to set up stations have dealt with the issue in fascinating ways. Some stations have been proactive in opening their doors to multiple publics, with the recognition that the community out there is not a homogeneous entity. Some others, especially CR stations run by educational institutions, meanwhile, seem to be in search of that mythical community—represented by images of poor farmers or fish-erfolk with haunted looks or rustic women in colourful saris with *bindis* on their foreheads and holding microphones. When we asked why no one in the campus seemed to be listening to their radio station, the director of a prominent educational institution in western India with a large residential community said with a swish of his hand that the station was meant for those *gaon wale* (people of the village) out there. He obviously missed the irony!

As the campaign for opening of airwaves to communities was gain-ing momentum, the then Minister of Information and Broadcasting, Ms Sushma Swaraj, said in an interview to the Media Watch website *The Hoot*, 'I will not use the word community because in India the word community is not automatically linked to geographical regions. I prefer to use the term "Narrowcasting" which clearly defines that the radio station is for people living within a small radius' (Interview by Bandana Mukhopadhyay, *The Hoot*, as reproduced in cr-India, January 2002). Apart from the fact that she mixes up a conceptual understand-ing of the term with a mode of content delivery ('narrowcasting'), her definition was perfectly in sync with the one incorporated in the Pastapur Declaration, which saw 'community' as a 'territorially bound group with some commonality of interests'. It is quite apparent that the government was anxious about the potentially unruly interpretations of 'community' and that the campaigners were eager to assure, strate-gically, that theirs was in compliance, contained and confined by the technological possibilities of FM. In the same interview, the minister emphasized the linguistic diversity of the country and suggested that it was linguistic affinity (dialect spoken within a 30-km radius) that bound people together in a culture dominated by orality. The cam-paign's stress on the 'local'—local culture and identities, language and issues—echoes this understanding of 'community'. This was a some-what problematic understanding that assumed a degree of homogeneity and cultural coherence, glossing over hierarchical structures of religion, caste and gender. It is only in practice that CR stations in the country are realizing that 'community' is a malleable concept—it is something that station personnel and listeners construct intersubjectively through constant interaction with each other. As Tucker (2013) emphasizes, CR upholds the ideal of public deliberation by promoting conversation and dialogue. Invoking John Dewey, she suggests that community is something that is constructed through such dialogic communication.

A second issue that strikes us as significant when we go through the cr-India archives is the particularly schizophrenic character (rivalling the schizophrenia of the state discussed above) of the justification provided for CR in the early 2000s, arguments that swung between development, on the one hand, and communication rights, on the other. In the interview that we just mentioned, Sushma Swaraj clearly had education and development on her mind when she suggested that educational institutions could be the first to receive CR licenses. In an interview given for the same online conference on *The Hoot*, the first author of this article, even as he urged moving away from the top-down community development paradigm, seemed to have asserted that radio can be a catalyst for social change in the Third World and that CR could be an extension of grassroots development work being done by well-meaning NGOs. Elsewhere in the interview, however, he had called for keeping up sustained pressure on the government to yield to the democratic aspirations of the voiceless for a 'right to communicate'.

In many ways, this linking of CR in India with development was evident in one of the original documents of the CR movement, the Bangalore Declaration (September 1996).[10] After the one reference to the airwaves judgement, the document is replete with terms like 'development', 'education', 'social change', 'welfare', 'decentralized village governance', etc. One of the founders of the cr-India mailing list, while sharing news about CR advocacy in neighbouring Bangladesh in

---

[10] About 60 people, including representatives of All India Radio, academics, journalists and members of civil society organizations, met in Bangalore during 11–14 September 1996 to discuss an autonomous structure for public service broadcasting. The declaration that emerged at the end of the consultation articulated, among other things, the need for a community broadcasting sector in India.

July 2002, had firmly located the aspiration for CR in the region within the then emerging information and communications technologies (ICTs) discourse by saying, 'Radio could play a key role in harnessing ICTs for development' (cr-India, July 1, 2002). A leading Bangladeshi spokesperson for democratization of communication in the country followed up with an advocacy document, which among other things stated unequivocally that 'NGOs could run a Community Radio station to serve the communication needs of their development projects' (cr-India, July 10, 2002). The seeds for the de-politicization of CR in India were sown in these early definitions of CR and its mandate both by members of a security-conscious government and by eager activists seeking to crack open the door in the name of development.

When in January 2002 the Deccan Development Society (DDS) received a letter from MIB rejecting their application for setting up a CR station, there was much indignation on the cr-India mailing list set up in the wake of the Pastapur Declaration. One of the founders of the list declared, 'We need to make this into a *right-to-communicate issue*' (emphasis added; cr-India, January 24, 2002). An Australian scholar on the list invoked Lawrence Soley's (1999) phrase 'electronic civil disobedience' and reminded people that in 1932 the Indian National Congress had used radio to broadcast protest messages against the British (cr-India, January 24, 2002). One former member of a communication advocacy group urged the activists to take the government to court even as she firmly located the civil-society demand for CR as a means to promote 'education, social development, and cultural expression' (cr-India, February 8, 2002), reflecting the CR movement's foundational dilemma. A representative of the Telangana-based NGO DDS had commented strongly that the struggle was about the 'right of communities to have a radio of their own' and questioned 'the right of the government to auction people's right to broadcast' (cr-India, February 9, 2002). Another astute commentator on the list wrote a lengthy opinion cautioning that the constitution did not guarantee the people's right to broadcast. He pointed out that a legal case could be made out only if it can be shown that the government's regulation of the FM space constituted an unreasonable restriction on the freedom of speech (cr-India, February 9, 2002). Of course, this group of well-meaning campaigners were too dispersed and too inchoate a group to ever be able to mount a legal fight to secure the communication rights of the people. It took over a decade for advocate Prashant Bhushan's organization, 'Common Cause', to file a public interest litigation (PIL) in 2013 in the Supreme Court questioning the government's ban on broadcast of news on private FM radio and CR precisely on the grounds of 'unreasonable restrictions'.[11] We will return to the issue of news ban a little later, but now let us turn to something that has perplexed many external observers of the Indian CR scene.

TECHNOLOGICAL ADVENTURISM: A TALE OF MISSED OPPORTUNITIES

In many countries where CR is a reality, especially in the United States, Europe and Latin America, there is a long history of amateur groups using technological developments, such as miniaturized transmitters and mobile recording devices, to run pirate radio stations outside the ambit of legal licensing, as an expression of free speech (see, e.g., Klinger, 2011; Langlois et al., 2010; Murillo, 2003). Variously called 'bootleg radio', 'free radio' and 'secret radio', these transgressive activities have not only challenged the boundaries of citizens' communication rights but also forced governments to legalize such initiatives through policy change.

India is one of the few countries in the world where technological adventurism (or what someone had called 'electromagnetic deviance') of this kind did not precede the legal opening of airwaves to communities. Many of the middle-class, urban professionals who were part of the early CR movement in India were understandably reluctant to take on the law. There was simply too much at risk in terms of their own personal positions in society, but also, despite occasional bluster ('all that we need is a boat and a transmitter'), there was considerable hesitation to place poor communities, on whose behalf they were speaking, in the crossfire of the law enforcement machinery. In May 2002, however, we were taken aback to come across a news story headlined, 'Orissa police unearth illegal radio stations'. It said:

---

[11] See a report of the case in the Live Law News Network, https://www.livelaw.in/ban-on-news-broadcast-on-private-fm-radio-questioned-by-supreme-court/

After detection of clandestine broadcast [*sic*] from two low power transmitters in Orissa's coastal belt this week, police have come to know
that five more such unauthorized radio stations were functioning in
the region. These five transmitters, which operated from Kendrapara
and Bhadrak districts, had gone off the air following the police crackdown, official sources said.[12]

The story went on to allude that Bangladeshi immigrants may have
been behind the illegal activity, although it clarified helpfully that
'no anti-national content' could be found in the material seized. A
technological activist questioned why the cr-India list was silent on
the issue: 'I have seen no response on this list, rather to my surprise.
Are we silent about the concept of village level low power transmitters being used by local villagers to broadcast their own selections of
entertainment and features to their neighbors?' (cr-India, May 19,
2002). While an independent journalist from Chennai saw 'salvation
for us in this obscure event', an international contributor pitched in,
saying: 'Pirate activities have influenced opening up of broadcasting
elsewhere in the world [...] will such activity in India spread do
you think?' (cr-India, May 21, 2002). No such activity, amounting
to what Shukaitis (2008) in a different context referred to as 'minor
cultural politics', ever took off in India, unleashing the liberatory and
radical potential of radio. However, in 2002, a 21-year-old freelance
journalist wanted to know on cr-India what the punishment would
be for someone caught running a pirate station; he then went on to
suggest a plan:

> I would like to initiate a small battle, if you will. I believe that by
> pooling in our resources and investments, a group of people can run
> a pirate radio station off the coast of India. If you gather about 100
> odd people, from different parts of the country, doing just one really
> large pirate radio station, I will feel that we've not only won the battle
> but shoved the sword of free speech into the candy bottoms of the govt
> [*sic*]'. (cr-India, September 2002)

---

[12] See https://timesofindia.indiatimes.com/india/Orissa-police-unearth-illegal-
radio-stations/articleshow/10361113.cms

He might not ever have managed to mobilize the '100-odd people', but there were other individual efforts already under way, combining do-it-yourself (DIY) technological innovation and a happy legal naivete.

Christina Dunbar-Hester's (2014) book *Low Power to the People* draws our attention to the intersection of technical practice and political engagement. She makes the point that 'tinkering' with broadcast technologies has historically aligned itself with a commitment to participatory politics, democratization of media and demystification of technology. The story of Raghav Mahato in eastern India should be seen as an example, albeit a minor and transient one, of media activism that challenged the hierarchy of knowledge around electronic media technologies. As far back as 2001, even before all the activist debates had picked up, Raghav, who ran a small electronic repair shop in Vaishali district of Bihar, rigged up a transmitter for ₹50 and started broadcasting Bhojpuri songs, jokes and interesting local information. Raghav FM was India's own 'Radio Favela',[13] and as his station's popularity increased, he even raised the range of his broadcast. He seemed to have done all this under the radar, so to speak, for several years until sudden national and international coverage made him a heroic figure. The authorities got wind of his illegal operation and closed it in 2006. Soon thereafter, the government found a way to widen the ambit of CR by allowing other players, such as NGOs, who operated within apparently safer institutional spaces.

Another instance of aborted technological activism in CR in India was Radiophony's project in village Orvakal, off the highway from Hyderabad, the capital of Telangana state, to Kurnool—a low-power FM station called Mana Radio (Our Radio), broadcast at about 98 MHz, with a 40mW transmitter within a range of less than 500 m. It went on air in October 2002 before CR became a legal reality with the full knowledge of the Society for Elimination of Rural Poverty (SERP), a World Bank-funded programme, whose chief patron was the state chief minister who saw in it a way to involve one of the self-help groups in the area. This is also an ironic case where state authorities

---

[13] A 2002 Brazilian film directed by Helvécio Ratton about four friends who start a pirate radio station in an urban slum in Rio de Janeiro.

actively colluded with an experiment that would still be considered a violation of the Telegraph Act of 1885. The initiators were told by enthusiasts that the station was so small that the government would not come after them. Of course, as is known among those of us who rummage in the footnotes of CR history in India, the project was shut down soon by the local police on the instructions of the Ministry of Communications and Information Technology. These projects must surely be seen as experiments that bravely sought to test the limits of the law and to assert people's communication rights against colonial-era prohibitions (cr-India, September 17, 19, 20, 2002).

In hindsight, one wonders whether these disparate attempts were lost opportunities for CR activists and advocates to rally around this technological adventurism and reclaim the radio commons, which by then was already under siege by privatization of the spectrum.

NGO-IZATION OF CR AND ITS DISCONTENTS

Civil society organizations and media activists who ran a campaign for democratization of airwaves had emphasized the potential of using CR for development, rather than foregrounding the more radical framework of communication rights. Many of these groups and individuals had themselves emerged in the crucible of the post-Emergency civil society ferment and had strong belief in the power of non-governmental action in articulating an alternative vision of development from that of the state. Further, in sheer strategic terms, pushing for a CR policy based on a development agenda appeared to be a more prudent lever to use with an overly suspicious government. This more benign approach led to the government permitting NGOs to apply for CR licenses in 2007. During the past decade, the funding imperative, the policy specifying NGOs as the eligible applicants, and the overall developmental framework led to the growth of CR in India, largely through the efforts of NGOs. While some of the best examples of genuine grassroots CR in India come from NGO initiatives, some organizations are beginning to enter the arena solely to further organizational objectives, and they take to less-than-participatory methods under pressure from donors to 'scale up' operations and to demonstrate 'impact' on behaviour change. The implications of this incipient NGO-ization of

CR in India are beginning to be felt across the sector. Many scholars have critiqued the de-politicization of development and the taming of the radical impulse in people's movements through systematic co-opting and incorporation within a dominant paradigm of development (Ferguson, 1990; Kamat, 2001).

The developmental lens through which CR in India was forged becomes evident from the restrictive content guidelines for CR, especially about broadcast of news and political material, which we believe is a consequence of the vacillation over communication rights more than a decade ago. *Policy Guidelines for Community Radio in India*[14] clearly suppresses the political dimension by suggesting that programmes broadcast over CR stations be relevant to 'the educational, developmental, social and cultural needs' of the community (clause 1d). In clause 5(i), it further mandates stations to lay emphasis on 'developmental, agricultural, health, educational, environmental, social welfare, community development and cultural programmes'.

RESTRICTIVE CONTENT GUIDELINES AND THE IMPULSE TO MONITOR

The vision of CR stations as de-politicized entities becomes apparent when the content guidelines draw the proverbial line in the sand: 'The Permission Holder [the CR station] *shall not* broadcast any programmes, which relate to *news and current affairs* and are otherwise *political in nature*' (5(vi); emphasis added).

When the CR policy was finally announced with these caveats, there was hardly any murmur of protest, with everyone seeing it as a welcome opening to do development programming. The security mindset and anxieties over the sovereignty of the nation had held back opening of the airwaves for far too long, and the same anxieties govern the continued ban on broadcast of news on private radio and CR. In the ongoing PIL[15]

---

[14] See https://mib.gov.in/sites/default/files/c1_0.pdf

[15] *Common Cause v. Union of India* (through Ministry of Information & Broadcasting), 2013. Common Cause, a Delhi-based citizens' rights group, contended that excluding commercial radio and CR stations from the right to broadcast news 'violates the fundamental right to freedom of speech and expression and flies in the face of the ruling of the Supreme Court in Ministry of I & B Vs Cricket

in the Supreme Court of India challenging the ban, the government submitted to the court in 2017 that it is hesitant to permit news because 'anti-national elements' within the country and abroad could misuse it for propagating their radical agendas. The government has suddenly discovered that news and current affairs have 'the inherent capability to manipulate the minds of the people', and hence the decision to keep them out of the pale of private broadcasters.[16] It seems it would rather retain state monopoly over 'mind manipulation'! In more than a decade of the existence of CR in India, no significant violations by stations have come into notice except for some minor raps on the knuckles received by a couple of stations in northern India for alleged on-air infractions unrelated to broadcast of news.[17]

The impulse to monitor, however, runs deep within the security apparatus of the state in India, leading to all kinds of ideas, ranging from the ludicrous to the preposterous, for surveillance of CR stations spread across the length and breadth of the country. Some years ago, the Ministry of Information and Broadcasting issued a diktat to a number of CR stations in the National Capital Region to provide compact disks (CDs) of all their programmes of the previous 3 months. With some of the stations broadcasting for several hours a day, a procession of box loads of CDs arriving at the ministry witnessed. One order issued from Shastri Bhavan, the Delhi headquarters of the ministry, in 2015 commanded all stations to 'provide recordings of all programmes broadcast on a daily basis [...] along with the logbook and the Q sheet [cue sheet]'.[18] If all the 200 operational CR stations in the country had taken the injunction seriously, the ministry's servers would have been severely stressed! No

---

Association of Bengal, 1995'. The organization filed a public interest litigation (PIL) in the Supreme Court asking it 'to quash the unreasonable and unconstitutional provisions in the relevant policy guidelines and grant of permission agreements'.

See https://www.commoncause.in/latest-pils.php

[16] See newspaper report. https://www.tribuneindia.com/news/nation/allow-community-radio-to-broadcast-already-published-news-bulletins-sc-to-centre/364021.html

[17] See https://www.indiatoday.in/pti-feed/story/iandampb-min-warnings-to-2-community-radio-stations-over-content-653259-2016-11-25

[18] See https://www.thehindu.com/news/national/community-radio-stations-in-a-fix-over-govt-bid-to-monitor-content/article7949615.ece

wonder the order was withdrawn shortly after it was issued. In 2016, the Ministry of Information and Broadcasting came up with something even more Orwellian, informing a parliamentary standing committee that it proposed to use its Delhi-based Electronic Media Monitoring Centre (EMMC) to keep track of CR broadcasts across the country.[19] It was amazing how the centre that has scores of employees sitting before television screens round the clock to watch satellite television (TV) content would monitor FM radio stations in remote rural areas when very few of them had the bandwidth to live-stream their broadcasts. Of course, the challenge of finding staff who would understand Kutchi, Bundeli and the many other languages and dialects in which CR stations broadcast completely escaped the bureaucratic watchdogs. Perhaps realizing the futility of this exercise, the following year the ministry asked state governments and union territories to use the existing district-level committees for monitoring of television content for also listening in on CR broadcasts. A news report helpfully pointed out that over 300 districts across India already had such committees and urged local governments to set up these bodies where they did not exist.[20]

The fears that CR could potentially threaten national integration, manifest as they are in the news ban, as well as in the reluctance shown in issuing licenses in so-called conflict zones, need to be addressed directly. Here again, historical arguments serve us well. In September 2001, at a National Seminar on Community Radio in Jakarta, Indonesia, Wijayananda Jayaweera, the then Regional Communication Advisor of UNESCO, one of the most sensitive and engaged observers of the communication ecology of South and Southeast Asia, took on the question of whether CR can contribute to national disintegration. His resounding answer was that 'the argument has no empirical or conceptual validity and is based mostly on wrong assumptions'. An integrated nationhood, he argued, depended on the extent to which democracy is promoted and practised at the grassroots level and the degree to which nations build relationships of trust with various marginalized and disadvantaged communities, especially in multicultural

---

[19] See http://www.radioandmusic.com/biz/regulators/others/160119-electronic-media-monitoring-centre-cover-all

[20] See https://indianexpress.com/article/india/monitor-content-of-pvt-community-radio-stations-centre-asks-states-uts-4785198/

societies. Looking directly at the anxieties of national governments about violent conflicts in the region, Jayaweera suggested:

> There is no empirical evidence that armed groups have effectively used community radio to promote their own separatist agenda. No armed group will venture to acquire a community radio that belongs to the community as a whole and risk of facing the community wrath. This is more so because such an attempt will immediately expose the authoritarian nature of the armed group. The community will interpret it as [an] act of another dictatorial group who has no concerns of community affairs other than dominating the community will. In any case no listener can be forced to subscribe to unilateral viewpoints propagandized by such a radio. (Jayaweera, *The Hoot*, as reproduced in cr-India, March 4, 2002)

In a telling commentary on inadequate or incomplete democratization in the countries of South and Southeast Asia, many of which enjoy systems of constitutional democracy, Jayaweera pointed out:

> A nation consisting of empowered communities is more secure. Only empowered communities can make an equitable contribution to nation building. Disempowered communities are the ones that often threaten national integration and alienate themselves from the nationhood.

Jayaweera's brilliant dismantling of the unreasonable fear of nation states that anarchic use of the airwaves would result in national disintegration deserves our attention today, as the slow progress of CR in India is often marred by the state's desperation to monitor and domesticate its content. It all comes down to a trust deficit in modern democracies where people's representatives seem to be wary of trusting people to do the right thing. In a long post in cr-India in May 2002, an activist who was then engaged in democratization of communication technologies had this to say about monitoring the potentially unruly CR:

> As regards questions of monitoring for anti-national activity, why not a local radio council consisting of all the broadcasters, content producers and people earning their living partly or fully from the activity, that adopts a voluntary code of content regulation, and also deals with violations? Why can't the government trust people to do the job themselves? (cr-India, May 21, 2002)

However, this appears too complicated. It might be easier, as Bertolt Brecht wrote in his caustic 1953 poem called *Die Lösung* (The Solution): 'Stating that the people/Had forfeited the confidence of the government/And could win it back only/By redoubled efforts/Would it not be easier/In that case for the government/To dissolve the people/And elect another?'

CONCLUSION

In conclusion, we would like to suggest that even as CR stations in India are coping with umpteen existential problems of improving participatory parity in terms of religion, caste and gender, sustaining the enterprise without compromising on core principles, expanding continuously people's capacities to deploy their voices more effectively and learning to negotiate the minefield of cooperation/co-opting with the state in the best interests of the communities they represent, it is the history of the CR movement in India and elsewhere that ought to show us the path ahead.

As in many democratic countries worldwide, CR must be integrated into the larger mandate of broadcasting policy reforms that look at strengthening the sector, making it pluralistic and encouraging the freedom of broadcasters. The Supreme Court judgement has recommended setting up an independent Broadcasting Authority of India, and this has also been articulated in the reports of committees set up to examine the situation of broadcasting in India. While the prospect of an independent broadcasting authority remains a work in progress and a comprehensive media policy to enable democratization of media stands out as unfinished business till today, efforts must be made to stay alert that political and corporate interests do not overpower the spectrum and wish away the CR sector. There are warning signs alerting us to the need for rebooting the efforts to revive the movement for CR and bringing back the vibrancy of voices and the colours of diversity that ought to symbolize broadcasting in India.

REFERENCES

Chatterji, P. C. (1991). *Broadcasting in India*. SAGE Publications.
Dunbar-Hester, C. (2014). *Low power to the people: Pirates, protest, and politics in FM Radio Activism*. MIT Press.

Ferguson, J. (1990). *The Anti-politics machine: 'Development', depoliticization and bureaucratic power in Lesotho.* University of Minnesota Press.

Gordon, C. (1991). Governmental rationality: An introduction. In G. Burchell, C. Gordon, & P. Miller (Eds.), *The Foucault effect: Studies in government rationality* (pp. 1–52). University of Chicago Press.

Kamat, S. (2001). *Development hegemony: NGOs and the state in India.* Oxford University Press.

Klinger, U. (2011). Democratizing media policy: Community radios in Mexico and Latin America. *Journal of Latin American Communication Research, 1*(2), 1–20.

Langlois, A., Sakolsky, R., & van der Zon, M. (Eds.). (2010). *Islands of resistance: Pirate radio in Canada.* New Star Books.

Mathur, J. C., & Neurath, P. (1959). *An Indian experiment in farm radio forums.* UNESCO.

Ministry of Information and Broadcasting (MIB). (1966). *Report of the committee on broadcasting and information media.* MIB.

Ministry of Information and Broadcasting (MIB). (1978). *Akash Bharati: Report of the working group on autonomy for Akashvani and Doordarshan.* MIB.

Ministry of Information and Broadcasting (MIB). (1985). *An Indian personality for television: Report of the working group on software for Doordarshan.* MIB.

Ministry of Information and Broadcasting (MIB). (1997). *The broadcasting bill.* MIB.

Ministry of Information and Broadcasting (MIB). (2000). *Prasar Bharati review committee report.* MIB.

Murillo, M. A. (2003). Community radio in Colombia: Civil conflict, popular media and the construction of a public sphere. *Journal of Radio Studies, 10*(1), 120–140.

Page, D., & Crawley, W. (2001). *Satellites over South Asia: Broadcasting, culture, and the public interest.* SAGE Publications.

Pavarala, V., & Malik, K. K. (2007). *Other voices: The struggle for community radio in India.* SAGE Publications.

Raboy, M. (1990). *Missed opportunities: The story of Canada's broadcasting policy.* McGill-Queen's University Press.

Raghunath, P. (2018). *Deliberating community radio in South Asia: A critical policy ethnography* (Unpublished PhD Thesis). University of Hyderabad.

Shukaitis, S. (2008). Dancing amidst the flames: Imagination and self-organization in a minor key. *Organization, 15*(5), 743–764. https://doi.org/10.1177/1350508408093651

Soley, L. (1999). *Free radio: Electronic civil disobedience.* Westview Press.

Thomas, T. K. (Ed.). (1990). *Autonomy for the electronic media: A national debate on the Prasar Bharati Bill.* Konark Publishers.

Tucker, E. (2013). Community radio in political theory and development practice. *Journal of Development and Communication Studies, 2*(2/3), 2305–7432.

Chapter 3

Dalits and Adivasis in Community Radio
Understanding Representation and Participation in Bundelkhand

Bidu Bhusan Dash

Bundelkhand, a historically significant divisional region, is sandwiched between northern Madhya Pradesh (MP) and southern Uttar Pradesh (UP) of India. It is a land belonging to heterogeneous social groups, including Dalits and adivasis. These social groups are marginalized in various spheres across the Indian subcontinent, including the Bundelkhand region. They are also on the margins of mainstream media. When mainstream media fails to raise the voices of those silenced by the power relations in society—notably Dalits and adivasis—community media hypothetically emerges as a panacea to address these erasures. There are a few community media initiatives in Bundelkhand which are active and vibrant in some locations. Hence, this chapter seeks to critically understand how community media, especially two community radio stations in the region, works as an alternative space for Dalits and adivasis. This chapter is an ethnographic account of participation and representation of Dalits and adivasis in the various activities of these community media initiatives.

BUNDELKHAND: A REGION IN CENTRAL INDIA

Bundelkhand is beautiful, as depicted by poet Indra,[1] a beauty that is reflected through its murals and paintings, texts and dances (Upadhyaya & Dehejia, 2019). It does not only have a mythological (Hiltebeitel, 1999) and historical (Jain, 2002) significance, but it is also important as a sub-national geopolitical region. Such regions are defined by the labyrinth of relations existing among geography, polity, people and their commonalities in terms of folklore, culture, language and regional identity. This section discusses the history, polity, language and culture, development and divisiveness of the region. Administratively, the land comprises seven districts of southern UP and six districts of northern MP. There has been a demand for separate statehood since independence, though it seems that this political movement has been silent for a long time. The former chief minister of UP, Mayawati, had announced plans in 2007 to make smaller states by dividing UP into four parts, out of which Bundelkhand was one. It was the election agenda in 2007 that helped Mayawati win a larger percentage of votes and assembly seats from the region. Later, different political parties, including the Aam Aadmi Party, demanded separate statehood for Bundelkhand. Raja Bundela initiated the Bundelkhand Mukti Morcha and later floated a political party named Bundelkhand Congress to fuel the demand for statehood. However, nothing came to fruition.

According to the Human Development Report Bundelkhand 2012, the region is one of the most deprived areas in India as far as human development indices are concerned (NITI Aayog, 2015). The real challenge of underdevelopment in the region is of identifying vulnerable groups and their level of vulnerability (Suthar, 2018). The majority of the population in the region are Dalits, adivasis and landless workers. The high concentration of Scheduled Caste (SC)/ Scheduled Tribe (ST) population, low wages and low productivity are

---

[1] Poet Indra depicts Bundelkhand as beautiful in a poem referring to its mountains (Vindhya ranges), rivers (Betwa, Dhasan, Ken), pilgrimages (Kalijar, Sonagir, Orchha, Unnava), mythology (Chitrakoot—dwelling place of Rama), legends (Chandelas, Bundelas) and art (Khajuraho). See Upadhyaya and Dehejia (2019) for the poem.

some of the reasons that result in the districts being labelled as 'backward'. In addition to that, the area recurrently experiences droughts, and the population has limited access to water resources, which has a direct impact on the lives of Dalits and adivasis (Verma, 2011). In contradiction to this, the region is rich in the natural resources like rivers, forests and minerals. Drought is engineered by human beings in Bundelkhand (Perspectives, 2010). Due to the long-term structural problems like intimate correlation of caste and land ownership in the region, Dalits are deprived of the basic resources like drinking water and state welfare schemes like public distribution system and the Mahatma Gandhi National Rural Employment Guarantee Act. It gives a clear picture of the imbalanced and inequitable human development in the region. Though the region was a political and economic backwater under the Raj, its ecological vulnerability contributed to the existing caste problem. Due to underdevelopment, supplemented by drought, the so-called lower-caste community became financially dependent on economically prosperous so-called upper castes. In return, the bonding and collusion among landowning caste communities became more pronounced, and the dependent caste communities became weaker in adverse situations.

Though there are heterogenous caste communities in Bundelkhand, the region is known for the warrior castes, Rajputs—Bundelas and Thakurs. Rajputs have asserted and reinforced their status, power and position in the region since the pre-colonial era. There are instances of Rajputs having targeted lower-caste settlements to assert their community status and caste hierarchies during the Raj (Kasturi, 1999). Jain (1979) also writes that osmosis between regional and local political systems in British Bundelkhand was based on the clan-based structure of indigenous polity. Violence is used in and has become part of Rajput culture and identity. It is also exercised to augment resources and power and to reinforce Rajputs' honour. These power relations were a constant from pre-colonial to colonial times and continue in independent India. Locally, landowning Rajputs are socio-politically and economically dominant in the communities. Though there are a few Rajputs who are comparatively weaker, still they are powerful because of their symbolic assertion of kinship. Nevertheless, it strengthened the caste system in the region.

According to the Linguistic Survey of India, Bundeli is one of five dialects of Western Hindi. It is spoken in Bundelkhand, Gwalior and the adjoining districts of Central Provinces. The dialect spoken in Jhansi district may be considered as the standard form, as the district is situated in the heart of the region. Standard Bundeli has three sub-dialects—Pawari, Rathora and Khatola—which are spoken in different parts of the region. There are also a few more mixed dialects (Grierson, 1916). The dialect has crossed the geopolitical boundary of the region and influenced neighbouring dialects. Though the dialect has influenced other dialects, Grierson (1916) laments that the literary culture of Bundelkhand and this important dialect is neglected historically. Bundeli folklore is full of narratives of chivalry and bravery of Bundelas and Chandelas. There are also many narratives of brave deeds of, whether Alha (Sahai-Achuthan, 1987; Tewari, 1989) or Jhalkari Bai, lower-caste women (Narayan, 1998).

DALITS AND *ADIVASIS* IN THE REGION

According to Census 2011, the SC population in India is 16.6 per cent of the total population. In the cases of MP and UP, the SC population is 15.6 per cent and 21.14 per cent, respectively, of the total population of the states. What is noteworthy is that the Dalits are concentrated largely in the rural areas of MP Bundelkhand[2] and UP Bundelkhand.[3] Nationally, the literacy rate among SCs is 66.1 per cent, whereas in MP it stands at 66.2 per cent. Adivasi population

---

[2] Madhya Pradesh (MP) Bundelkhand includes five districts of Sagar division and one district of Gwalior division. According to the 2011 census, Scheduled Caste (SC) and Scheduled Tribe (ST) populations in these districts are present in Chhatarpur (23% and 4.18%, respectively), Damoh (19.5% and 13.15%, respectively), Datia (25.5% and 1.91%, respectively), Panna (20.5% and 16.8%, respectively), Sagar (21.1% and 9.33%, respectively), Tikamgarh (25% and 4.7%, respectively), etc.

[3] Uttar Pradesh (UP) Bundelkhand includes three districts of Jhansi division and four districts of Chitrakoot division. According to the 2011 census, SC and ST populations in these districts are present in Banda (21.6% and 0.6%, respectively), Chitrakoot (26.9% and 0%, respectively), Hamirpur (21.8% and 0%, respectively), Jalaun (27.7% and 0%, respectively), Jhansi (28.14% and 0.9%, respectively), Lalitpur (19.7% and 5.9%, respectively), Mahoba (25.2% and 0.1%, respectively), etc.

in UP Bundelkhand is negligible except in Lalitpur district. A high percentage of Dalits and adivasis also reside in the locality of two community radio stations. In most of the villages under study, it is found that hamlets of either Dalits or adivasis coexist with caste Hindu communities. There are also a few villages that are exclusively either of Dalits or of adivasis.

The power structure in rural India depends upon numerical superiority, economic dominance and social or ritual rank (Oommen, 1970), which reveals that groups like Dalits and adivasis are less powerful compared to caste Hindus. They are the oppressed groups, who have been engaged in a struggle for power. The role of the state in their empowerment has remained as mere tokenism. It is based on an idea of patronage, rather than power redistributed through social processes (Mohanty, 1995). Dalits and adivasis are two of the most neglected communities in the community power structure in Bundelkhand. Hence, it is pertinent to discuss the historical debate about caste dynamics in the region, specifically those related to Dalits and adivasis. Dalits constitute the poor and marginalized sections of the society and are still looked down upon by both the so-called upper castes and most other backward castes too. Due to the democratization of polity, sociocultural movements and state's development programmes, a post-independence, educated, upwardly mobile, identity conscious and politicized generation has emerged (Pai, 1997). This generation has minimized absolute dependence on landowners and patron–client relations. Due to community mobilization, urbanization, presence of civil society and education, Dalits have asserted their identity and rights, which has impacted society and polity in India. Studying Dalit assertion in UP, Pai (1997) cites that this assertion helps create a new Dalit identity and break the existing upper-caste assertion and social system, ergo introducing change. As an offshoot, it also creates more significant social fragmentation, jealousy, caste tensions and alienation in the society. Though there is a considerable improvement in the socio-economic condition and political position of Dalits in parts of UP, there is scope for further improvements too.

The Congress-led government in MP and Bahujan Samaj Party (BSP)-led government in UP had formulated agendas for Dalit upliftment, with the aim of gaining political support (Pai, 2004). Regardless of the hidden agendas, the various welfare schemes and identity politics engineered by them were not mere symbolism. During the BSP government, led by Mayawati, in the first decade of the 21st century, Dalit and adivasi groups were able to speak in front of caste Hindus (Dash, 2016). As Ninan (2007) points out, the public sphere began to reflect the democratic upsurge from below. Slowly and gradually, untouchability became less manifested, as people had access to education and employment in the government sector. The government in the state changed in 2012, and again in 2017. The Samajwadi Party (SP), which claims to be a democratic socialist party, won the 2012 elections. However, in 2017, the Bharatiya Janata Party (BJP), a right-wing conservative political party, won. The so-called upper caste—Yadavs and Thakurs—regained political power and disturbed the changed social structure. This affected negatively the lives of Dalits and adivasis in the region. In Bundelkhand, change has been slower; mobilization and spread of the electoral process underlie Dalit assertion. Correspondingly, relations with the so-called upper castes range from repression in remote areas and tolerance in better-off regions. Clashes centre around the installation of Ambedkar statues, common village resources and distribution of governmental benefits. The situation of the marginalized sections has been getting worse since BSP, the political party of the dynamic Dalit leader Mayawati, lost the election.

MANUWADI[4] MAINSTREAM MEDIA

Dalits and adivasis are not only marginalized in the backward regions of the country but also neglected and marginalized by the mainstream media. Media can play a significant role in questioning the existing power structure in a democratic society, strengthening democratic alternatives fostering equality, inclusiveness and social change. Therefore, demanding the inclusion of Dalits in the media should

---

[4] The reference here is to Manusmriti or a Vedic law book propagated by some sections of the upper castes, which is based on the ideologies of casteism and patriarchy, in contradistinction to the constitution, which stands for secularism and gender and caste equality.

not be merely regarded as a plea for jobs but rather as a demand for democracy (Ravikumar, 2007). Vivek Kumar (2006) highlights the inability of the Indian media to understand the problems of Dalits, atrocities committed against them and the politics of exclusion. This urbanized Indian media reports the concerns of Dalits as victims and remains silent about the assailants, mostly the Brahminical middle class. Even when the mainstream media reports violence against Dalits, it is termed as coverage of caste, and ironically, it is still under-reported if compared to the cases of crimes against Dalits (Anand, 2005). Similarly, Dutta (2016) argues that adivasis are always neglected by the mainstream media, even by the alternative media like community radio, though they have the abilities to negotiate and even develop their own media. Adivasis have unique strength from cultural, communicative and credibility perspectives. One particular tribe inhabits any particular locality with its own culture, beliefs and language or dialect. Their culture helps adivasis have community feelings, which helps trust what they communicate among themselves in their own language or dialect and create a discourse on their own local issues. If any media, including community radio, is applied in this context, it can achieve its objectives.

The marginalization of Dalits is reinforced through various modes of media representation. One such instance is when newspapers do not carry Dalit stories unless there is some spectacular violence or restrict themselves to issues related to reservation from an upper-caste point of view. This is because Dalits are not present in the newsrooms, press clubs and journalism departments. The paucity of adequate qualifications is often given as a reason for the absence of Dalit reporters, sub-editors and editors. Newspaper managements have no policies for recruiting or encouraging Dalit journalists. Therefore, the stories concerned with Dalits lack the insights that only Dalits themselves can provide (Jeffrey, 2000). The invisibility of Dalits' representation in print media is a cause, as well as a symptom, of their oppressed position in today's India. Dalits are also not in the mental maps of the people who design India's newspapers. Siddharth Varadarajan (2006) argues that if media coverage of the anti-reservation agitation is indulgent and one-sided, the lack of diversity in the newsroom is undoubtedly a primary culprit. Like any other media, radio is also afflicted by the exclusion of

Dalits from its domain. If the management of radios is removed from the hands of governments, it may offer cheap ways to reach scattered Dalit audiences. However, the Indian government shows little inclination to deregulate radio. Dalits would need to gather setting-up costs and expertise (Jeffrey, 2001), which is difficult to come by.

It was also found that inclusion of Dalits in radio farm forums in Indian villages during the early 1960s was minimal, though the state had instructed the organizers to include members from all the social groups present in villages (Neurath, 1962). The dominant Brahminical media becomes the space of caste ideology (Patil, 2011). The subaltern classes rarely have access to the channels of communication, their access very often mediated by those who exercise control over the means of communication (Das, 1990). Regarding the temple entry issue of Odisha in print media, Dash (2013) argues that media is articulating the caste Hindu agenda, though it has been reporting the same issue for the last 100 years. The technology of communication, which is often projected as socially neutral, was, in reality, ideologically charged and politically moulded (Das, 1990).

B. R. Ambedkar once said that the untouchables have no press, in *Plea to the Foreigner*. Studies across the length and breadth of India, including in the Hindi heartland, have found that Dalits are reported in a sympathetic manner and are under-reported if the issue concerns Dalits and not the so-called upper castes. Once, Kanshi Ram had articulated that mainstream media is *manuwadi*, which cannot be trusted. Political leadership has changed, and political power has shifted from upper-caste politicians to backward castes and even Dalits. However, media power is still confined to the upper-caste, upper-class, urban English-language journalists (Ninan, 2007). Whether regular employees at editorial desks or part-time stringers on the ground, most of them are *manuwadi*. It is not only the staff structure in media houses and classroom structure in journalism schools but also the social structure in a feudal, casteist society that decides which and whose story would be disseminated and who would participate in the process of content creation. Though the process of inclusion has started slowly, it has miles to go. There may be hope in community media to accelerate this inclusion process.

REGIONAL COMMUNITY MEDIA MAP

Though the Bundelkhand region is neglected in both development and media maps, it is prominent in the community media map. There is a history of three decades of community newspaper experiments in the region, commencing from *Mahila Dakiya* in the early 1990s to *Khabar Lahariya* and its digital platforms up to recent times (Dwivedi, 2015; Naqvi, 2007; Sinha & Malik, 2020). There are three community radio stations—Radio Bundelkhand, Lalit Lokvani and Radio Bundeli—in the state-defined Bundelkhand region and one more—Chanderi Ki Awaz (established on 27 March 2010 in Ashok Nagar district of MP)—in the historically defined region of Bundelkhand. Another one—Radio Dhadkan—in Shivpuri district of Gwalior division of MP is cultur-ally connected with Bundelkhand. These community radio stations formed a network called Bundelkhand Community Radio Network (BCRN). Except Radio Dhadkan, the other radio stations have been functioning sustainably for more than a decade. Bundeli Radio in Chhatarpur district of MP has been recently added to the community media map of Bundelkhand. However, this chapter's scope is limited to Radio Bundelkhand and Lalit Lokvani. Hence, these two stations are discussed in detail.

Radio Bundelkhand is not only the first community radio initiative in the region but also an early non-governmental organization (NGO)–led initiative in India. It was initiated at TARAgram near Orchha in Tikamgarh district of MP on 23 October 2008 by Development Alternatives (DA). DA, a prominent NGO, has its global headquarters in New Delhi. The organization is known for its contribution to social entrepreneurship and sustainable development. It has been working in Bundelkhand for the last 25 years, focusing on the environment, energy, livelihood and sustainability. After intervening in the com-munity for more than a decade, the organization felt that there was a need for alternative communication to bring balance in development in the drought-prone region. The decade-long community work had already prepared the ground for Radio Bundelkhand to connect with the community. With the tag line *Apna Radio Apni Baatein* (Our Radio, Our Conversations), Radio Bundelkhand has been working uninter-rupted for the last 12 years and broadcasting programmes for 11 hours every day, from 7 a.m. to 6 p.m. There are 21 members as part of the community radio management committee (CRMC), which includes listeners, social workers, people's representatives and local experts from the sectors of health, agriculture, forestry, etc. There is a core team to manage everyday activities of the station, including community reporters and volunteers. Though Radio Bundelkhand claims that it is managed and run by the community and DA jointly, there are many national and international organizations, such as the World Bank, United Nations Educational, Scientific and Cultural Organization (UNESCO), Swiss Development Corporation, Climate Development Knowledge Network, Sesame Workshop India, Government of India, local governments and so on, which extend partnership for content creation and other activities.

Lalit Lokvani claims that it is the first rural community radio station in the state of UP. It was established in Alapur village of Lalitpur district on 3 September 2010 by Sai Jyoti Gramodhyog Samaj Seva Samiti, popularly known as Sai Jyoti. Sai Jyoti, a local NGO, was registered in 1989 and started working with the community in 1998. Similarly, the parent organization had prepared the ground in the community to set up a community radio initiative. With the tag line *Jan ki Vaani* (Voice of the People), it has been working with the marginalized sections from the very beginning. Its work is not limited to livelihood but extends to advocacy and rights. Most of the development work of the organization is project-based and depends on external funds, though it tries to address the organization's mission and vision. Before starting the community radio station, the organization had conducted a research to understand issues and concerns of the communities in the locality. The primary issues and concerns included child marriage, instilling of values in children, domestic violence, family planning, folk art, agriculture, behavioural change for better hygiene, government schemes, migration, women empowerment, local art and culture, dowry, illiteracy, village empowerment, superstitions, malpractices, exploitation, discrimination and untouchability. Lalit Lokvani broadcasts for 12 hours in three slots nowadays. Its broadcast starts from 7 a.m. and concludes at 8 p.m. It used to broadcast for only 3 hours in 2010. There is a core team and a 13-member management committee to provide managerial guidance. A few international and national organizations have supported this station in various stages, including United Nations Children's Fund (UNICEF), ActionAid, Government of India, Ideosync Media Combine, Development Alternatives, etc.

As per the Policy Guidelines for Setting Up Community Radio Stations in India, Ministry of Information and Broadcasting, Government of India, a legal entity should be a non-profit organization and should have a proven record of at least 3 years of service to the local community (Government of India, 2006). Both the stations have been on the ground for long in their respective localities and satisfy the minimum requirements of the government. They have the same frequency, that is, 90.4 MHz, as there is only around a 98-km aerial distance between them, and either radio station's reach is limited to 15 km. Both the stations produce not only thematic programmes but also some audience-centric programmes. While the thematic programmes are generally based on religion, culture, heritage, local governance, the environment and development, the audience-centric programmes may include women, children, Dalits and adivasis. Many times, thematic programmes and audience-centric programmes overlap. The audience-centric programmes of a community radio station are decided based on the issues like backwardness, exploitation and marginalization prevailing in the field, for groups that are misrepresented and under-represented in mainstream media. Both the thematic and audience-centric programmes are meant to address the development and empowerment of the communities concerned. These community radio stations produce programmes in Hindi and Bundeli, the local dialect. The community radio stations in the Bundelkhand region address several issues and themes in their programmes. The programmes of the community radio stations are moulded not only by the funding agencies but also by the parent organizations. The community radio stations start the day with religious notes. Though they produce programmes on science and technology, the environment and climate change, they also promote local customs, traditions, culture, heritage, history, language and folk music. Apart from language, culture, history and heritage, the community radio stations also produce programmes on local governance, livelihoods, the environment and climate change. While these two initiatives and their parent organizations claim that they work with the marginalized communities and their social inclusion, it is necessary to understand how Dalits and adivasis are portrayed, involved and represented in the community media in the Indian subcontinent across time and space.

DALITS AND ADIVASIS IN ALTERNATIVE MEDIASCAPES

The Times, the oldest daily, once had declared that it was going to offer 'something suited to every palate' (Whale, 1977, p. 82). When a few mainstream media houses with noble intentions aspire to address issues and concerns of a heterogeneous society, they either fail or display tokenism towards the marginalized sections. Therefore, an alternative mediascape sprouts and tries to sustain itself in adverse conditions. The question arises: How does this alternative mediascape address the issues and concerns of the marginalized communities? If community radio can be considered as an alternative mediascape, how does it address the issues and concerns of the marginalized, especially Dalits and adivasis in the Indian subcontinent? The mission of mainstream media and its achievement brought uncertainty around the mission of alternative media, and a pertinent curiosity emerged: Can a community radio produce something that would be suited to all, that is, to a lord-like Thakur, Ahirwar daily worker or a landless Sahariya? Thakur is a so-called upper-caste landowning caste community, Ahirwar is a Chamar sub-caste of the Dalit community, and Sahariya is a so-called primitive tribal group. Hence, to know 'what suits whose palate', this section reviews the literature on Dalits and adivasis in community media.

As mentioned by Dahal (2013), many community interventions have experimented with introducing inclusive programming not only in India but also in Nepal, which has provided a stronger collective voice to marginalized communities and empowered them. There are also a few community radio stations in Nepal which address the issues and concerns of particular marginalized communities, such as Dalits and indigenous communities. Radio Jagaran is one such station in western Nepal that publicly fixed its mission and vision to work with Dalits. Hamro Lumbini, another community radio station, is inclusive through presenting the voices of the socially marginalized, such as the so-called lower-caste people in the community (Martin & Wilmore, 2010). The United Nations Development Programme (UNDP) (2009) reports that around one-fourth of functional community radio stations have programmes in the languages of the indigenous communities, but most of them are either musical programmes or broadcast during the graveyard slots. UNDP also expressed its concern that though there is a strong network of community radio stations in Nepal, it has not been used for empowerment of indigenous communities. These stations inadequately cover and often politicize issues and concerns of indigenous communities. Martin and Wilmore (2010) also question the legitimacy of media production by both the corporate and NGO-owned media units in Nepal.

Very few community radio stations in the Indian subcontinent involve Dalits and adivasis in the process of programme production and station management. Sangham Radio is one such community radio station that is owned, run and managed by Dalit women in Machnoor village of Telangana state. Almost 95 per cent of the producers and reporters are Dalits in Sangham Radio. Dalit women produce programmes and disseminate them through broadcast and narrowcast. They are engaged in dialogues and discussions on various issues and concerns, such as organic farming, plant-based healthcare, ethno-veterinary practices, childcare systems and a host of other issues, in the radio station. They open up their treasure of knowledge and experiences for the listeners to learn from and hone their practices. It is genuinely a horizontal learning system that rejects hierarchical expertocracy (Chittoor, 2011). Though Deccan Development Society (DDS), a leading local NGO, has parented the station, the doubly excluded community is its face, and a few projected leaders have emerged among them as poster children of the initiative. As Saeed (2010) argues, that the community that has historically existed on the outermost margins of society is able to shake off the fetters of patriarchy and caste and dares to tell its stories is an expression of freedom and justice.

Pavarala (2003) studied *Chala Ho Gaon Mein*, a community radio project in Jharkhand, a tribal state in eastern India. Though the author has critically discussed the project as a case study, he could have focused more on the participation and representation of adivasis in the programmes. Further, the caste profile of the community reporters is not revealed. The author suggests providing identity cards to the community reporters to enhance their credibility and accord some prestige to their hard work at the grassroots without seriously disrupting the existing social hierarchies in the villages. The author may have given this suggestion looking at the ethics of the organization. However, it would seems problematic and against the philosophy of community media if it cannot succeed to shake off the fibres of Indian society, which are feudal, patriarchal and casteist.

Dutta (2016) states that community radio stations in India include adivasis to co-create the media discourse. However, such inclusion is negligible, if the number of tribal communities, their populations and their problems are considered. Another concern is also that there are very few community radio stations in the country. Most of these functional stations are either in the cities or in the developing rural set-up. From the Community Radio Compendium for 2019 and previous years, it was found that only a few stations, such as Radio Milan in West Bengal, Brahmaputra CRS in Assam, Vanya Radios in MP, Tilonia Radio and Radio Madhuban in Rajasthan, Radio Muskan in Odisha and Radio Mattoli in Kerala, address tribal issues. Similarly, a few, like Radio Namaskar and Radio Sanskar in Odisha and Loyola CR in Tamil Nadu, out of around 200 reported community radio stations talked about caste discrimination and social exclusion. It seems that most of the community radio stations have emerged as a re-feudalization of NGOs and the media and address the issues and concerns of the emerging middle-class bourgeois at the local level if they are silent about the issues and concerns of the marginalized communities. Against this background, I explore programmes, participation and representation of Dalits and adivasis in two community radio initiatives in Bundelkhand.

PROGRAMMES, PARTICIPATION AND REPRESENTATION

Media programmes can be broadly divided into two categories: (a) theme- or issue-based; and (b) audience- or people-based. Most of the community radio stations across India produce programmes in this way. Though most of the stations try to address various themes to cater to the infotainment needs of different sections of the community holistically, a few of the themes are pretty close to the core of their parent organizations' mission and vision. They try to fulfil these mandates through their programming. Both Radio Bundelkhand and Lalit Lokvani have produced several thematic programmes, which may cater to different sections. The thematic or issue-based programmes are outstanding because of their more extensive reach, appreciation by the audiences, reception and effect on the lives of the people. As both stations claim that they work with the marginalized communities, they also produce a few audience-centric or people-centric programmes. If a few lead programmes are briefly discussed, it would paint a coherent picture of what major themes are addressed and for which marginalized communities.

There are a few community radio stations in India which address global concerns, like climate change, in local dialects and local contexts successfully. One of them is Radio Bundelkhand. Its programme *Shubh Kaal—Badli Jalvayu ke Liye Taiyar Hum* (Better Tomorrow— We are Prepared for Climate Change) is an outstanding contribution. The programme has continued for several years. Undergraduate and professionals-by-practice community reporters talk about science, politics and the effect of climate change on the lives of local people for hours. *Hum Honge Kaamyaab* (We Shall Overcome) is another popular programme of the station, which empowers the rural youth, women of self-help groups and local entrepreneurs.

Similarly, Lalit Lokvani has a good number of thematic programmes on agriculture, health, livelihood and entertainment. *Suno, Meri Behena* (Listen, My Sister) is a 370-episode programme to address health and nutrition problems of women and adolescent girls. *Ajivika* (Livelihood), a 100-episode programme, talks about farming and small industry. As the station manager shared, it caters to all sections of society, including landless households. There is also another 50-episode programme called *Jeevan ke Anmol Pal* (Precious Moments of Life) which talks about child marriage. According to census and National Family Health Survey (NFHS) data, Lalitpur is one of the infamous districts of the country for child marriage. For entertainment purposes, *Bundeli Jhalak* (Bundeli Glimpse) is broadcast, which is a half-an-hour interview-and-song programme of one Bundeli artist in each episode. There are over 100 episodes in this series. *Bundeli Bidha* (genre of Bundeli songs) is an entertainment programme of Radio Bundelkhand which discusses the genre of songs in detail. Both Radio Bundelkhand and Lalit Lokvani also produce a few target group–centric programmes, looking at a few specific audience groups. Lalit Lokvani broadcasts several series for children, as the station was financially supported by UNICEF, an international organization working primarily for children. Such children's series are *Baal Sabha* (Children's Assembly) and *Gyan Vaani* (a quiz programme), each having around 50 episodes. The station has also broadcast two content-sponsored programmes, namely *Galli Sim Sim* by Sesame Workshop India and *Meena ki Duniya* by UNICEF. As the parent organization is working with livelihood issues and the radio station is in rural set-up, there is a well-designed and structured series for farmers, called *Khet Khalihan* (Agricultural Fields). Radio Bundelkhand also broadcast the *Khet Khalihan* programme to address the issues and concerns of farmers. *Stree, Ek Kahani Meri Bhi* (Woman, a Story of Me Too) is a women-centric programme of Radio Bundelkhand that narrates everyday stories of women.

It is seen that thematic programmes have dominated over audience-centric programmes. Though both the stations claim that they work with the marginalized communities, the idea of marginalization is limited to farmers, masons, women and children. When I asked the question of who is marginalized, many from the core committee of Lalit Lokvani said they were women and children, whereas for Radio Bundelkhand it is farmers and masons. It gives a clear indication that both the stations are influenced by parent organizations, funding agencies and their work mandate. Radio Bundelkhand works with these communities (farmers and masons), cutting across caste, class and gender. However, it hardly includes Dalits and adivasis. One of the community reporters of Radio Bundelkhand defended this in the following manner:

> Our station consciously avoids mentioning caste in any of the programmes, as it is indicative. Nevertheless, we are inclusive. We have a popular name called *Baari Hamari Gaon Ki* [This time, Our village]. We go to a particular village, record about the village, its problems and concerns. There are many multi-caste villages in our jurisdiction. We include people from all the hamlets, whether it is Kushwah or Chamar. Everybody has equal rights to say, and we ensure it.

The programmes of community radio stations for production and dissemination are explored from the standpoint of the local issues and concerns that make the programmes people-centric. Lalit Lokvani has a mission to develop means of livelihoods to bring equality in society through focusing on the underprivileged communities of adivasis and Dalits. Hence, this radio station has started a programme called *Dalit Mahola ki Kahani* (Story of Dalit Mahola). After a few brainstorming sessions by the leaders of the community radio station this programme was started, but it could not be continued. A dalit community reporter said:

> It is challenging to produce such programmes. Dalits and adivasis, who are subjugated for centuries, have lost their voices. Moreover, we expect that they will share their stories in front of the recorder immediately, which is mostly impossible. After motivating them, even if they start speaking, what will they speak? They will either share their stories of harassment or out of anger use slang to scold or cry because of frustration. They will keep ranting on their problems, problems of their neighbours and hamlets. How can I produce a programme out of it? If the programme is not good, who will listen to it? Will Pandit ji allow me to broadcast such a rubbish programme the next day morning? It is challenging when the leaders are brahmins.

The community radio reporter indicated at the end that leadership and the leaders' orientation mattered in this regard. In both the stations, so-called upper-caste people are in leadership positions, such as station manager, assistant station manager and programme producer. Therefore, there are hardly any specific Dalit- and adivasi-centric programmes. However, their issues and concerns are general and are addressed by both the radio stations. The programming of the community radio stations also resolves a few of their issues. Thus, people from the periphery connected with these stations are genuine active listeners. As programmes for these listeners are less, it is difficult to analyse their representation.

Lalit Lokvani produces programmes on issues, concerns, lives and rights of Dalits and adivasis, though few in number. Radio Bundelkhand does not produce any such programme. Prachi, one of the former community reporters of Radio Bundelkhand, said, 'Radio can produce programmes in this line. Radio can produce such programmes, which can reduce caste prejudices. Radio reporters can go to the village and invite both the parties—dalits and caste Hindus and have discussions on the issue'. When she was asked whether her radio station should produce such programmes or not, she answered,

> There are no such issues in my area. If there are a few issues, there is no content on the issue. If there is a little content, there are no experts on the caste issue. If there are experts, people will listen. Then we can have debates and discussions; people will listen to the experts.

Who is this expert? As Escobar (1995) rightly questioned, 'who can speak, from what points of view, with what authority, and according to what criteria of expertise'. It is necessary to scrutinize who has expertise on caste issues. It is problematic if there is this understanding among the community reporters that expertise on the caste issue from external 'experts' is needed more than experiences of people themselves to produce programmes on Dalits and adivasis. If community radio stations search for experts to talk on caste, finally they would invite so-called upper-caste people to talk on caste, like any mainstream media. If community radio mediates expert discourse, there would no more be a discourse on marginalization. This dependency on experts would create an 'expert community' in the locality, whose voices only would be heard in community radio stations. As most of the community reporters are caste Hindus, there is a need for an orientation towards a zero-tolerance environment to casteism in the community radio stations. There is an urgent need to go beyond tokenism, to involve Dalits and adivasis in the day-to-day activities of radio and management committees in a representative manner.

Dalits and adivasis are mostly active listeners in the region. During my visits to the villages, I found that a great number of Dalits and adivasis listen to radio compared to other caste communities. Maybe they do not have modern gadgets of communication except either a cheap radio set or a cheap China-made mobile phone. Group listening, especially among the adivasis, still exists in the community. During my frequent visits to Ramapura, a Sahariya adivasi village 14 km from Lalit Lokvani, I observed that tribal children, women, youth and aged people listen to radio, either individually or in groups, using either radio sets or mobile phones. Though there was electricity supply to the village, due to frequent power cuts and economic deprivation, there were only two sets of television in the village. Interestingly, the television sets do not have a cable connection. Hence, people use these sets to play compact disks for the purpose of watching Bundeli folk song videos, mythological series and old Bollywood movies. It can be seen otherwise that the community radio stations have served the mandate of *antyodaya*,[5] citing Gandhi and his exhortation to look after the needs of the last man. Bringing in gender balance, the last man may be a woman too. However, if the marginalized people's participation is limited to listening to other voices, how community radio stations can be different from any other mainstream media may be questioned. The idea of prosumer, which is the objective of community radio, fails in this case.

In a personal interview during her visit to Lalit Lokvani, Alka Malhotra, programme communication specialist of UNICEF, said that community radio stations should include all members who are within the catchment of the stations, be they Dalits or adivasis. The mission and vision of the parent organizations also state the need to be inclusive. In the programming and staffing of community radio stations, participation of Dalits and adivasis is ensured as tokenism. In a few programmes, a few representatives of the marginalized communities have a voice. They are not only part of content creation but also part of programme production and dissemination. In terms of representation, both Radio Bundelkhand and Lalit Lokvani have appointed community reporters from marginalized communities. During times of sufficient funding support from the funding agencies, there were eight community reporters in Lalit Lokvani, out of which two were Dalits. They contributed to the station for around 4 years. Due to fund crunch, there is only one community reporter running the station nowadays. Similarly, there were five community reporters in Radio Bundelkhand, of whom one was from a tribal community. Now, there are only three community reporters. While both the Dalit reporters lost their jobs in Lalit Lokvani due to the funding crisis, the tribal reporter could sustain his job in

---

[5] M. K. Gandhi thought that *sarvodaya* (development of all) would be possible through *antyodoya* (development of the weakest person in the society).

Radio Bundelkhand. These community reporters are as competent and efficient as others. However, they are identified by their caste in the community, for instance, 'Ahirwar'. This reflects the social stigma of caste in the community.

Demographically, Dalits and adivasis have a significant presence in Bundelkhand, especially in the jurisdiction of these two community radio stations. As I have observed, apart from that, they also listen to the radio more, compared to people from other castes. There are also many issues and concerns of Dalits and adivasis in the community. A community radio management committee member of Radio Bundelkhand said,

> There are many problems with adivasis, such as they are not allowed to use forest land. The community radio stations ignore such sensitive issues. They do not address the issues and concerns of dalits and adivasis as there are few people from these caste communities involved in the day to day activities of radio and management committee.

IS CONTEXT ASSIMILATED IN THE TEXTS?

The programme production process is as important as the programmes themselves in any community media initiative. Even though systematic steps are followed in the programme production processes, people's participation in them is still deficient. Participation can be ensured through producing more out-of-studio, field-based programmes, especially in the hamlets and villages of Dalits and adivasis. If more out-of-studio programmes are produced with greater participation of marginalized sections in communities, such as Dalits and adivasis, the texts of community radio stations can address and represent the local context. Otherwise, it would be challenging to communicate the context in the text, which would affect the social change process, which community radio stations claim to do.

Community radio stations are a re-feudalization of the community media world, where the mission and vision of the parent organization and funding agencies are reflected. They produce a good number of programmes by ensuring the participation of a good number of people from the locality. As far as specific programmes on Dalits and adivasis are concerned, the community radio stations are found lacking. Even though Lalit Lokvani produces a few programmes, they are not enough, considering the existence of large populations of Dalits and adivasis in the community. As Saeed (2010) argues, communication rights cannot be ensured for all, and power cannot be bestowed from the top; people should negotiate space for themselves. It would be beneficial to create a critical mass through defeating the idea of re-feudalization of NGOs in the community media world. However, this raises a question: Can the people on the margins, who were socio-culturally subjugated for centuries together, come forward to negotiate without the assistance of the re-feudalized community radio stations?

REFERENCES

Anand, S. (2005). Covering caste: Visible Dalit, invisible Brahmin. In N. Rajan (Ed.), *Practising journalism: Values, constraints, implications* (pp. 172–197). SAGE Publications.

Das, B. (1990). *Communication and power structure: A sociological analysis of an Orissa village* (PhD Thesis). Jawaharlal Nehru University.

Dash, B. B. (2013). Temple entry in Odisha by the Dalit: An ethnographic study of media articulation. *Asia Pacific Media Educator, 23*(1), 63–84.

Dash, B. B. (2016). *Media for empowerment: A study of community radio initiatives in Bundelkhand* (Doctoral Thesis). Tata Institute of Social Sciences.

Dwivedi, A. (2015). *Understanding media work: Experiences of women working in Khabar Lahariya* (Unpublished Masters Dissertation). Tata Institute of Social Sciences.

Chittoor, J. (2011). *Compendium 2011: Community radio stations in India.* CEMCA on behalf of the Ministry of Information and Broadcasting.

Dahal, S. (2013). Power, empowerment and community radio: Media by and for women in Nepal. *Women's Studies International Forum, 40,* 44–55.

Dutta, U. (2016). Adivasi media in India: Relevance in representing marginalized voices. *Intercultural Communication Studies, 25*(3), 213–231.

Escobar, A. (1995). *Encountering development: The making and unmaking of the third world.* Princeton University Press.

Government of India. (2006). *Policy guidelines for setting up community radio stations in India.* Ministry of Information and Broadcasting.

Grierson, G. A. (1916). *Linguistic survey of India* (Vol. 9, Part 1). Superintendent of Government Printing.

Hiltebeitel, A. (1999). *Rethinking India's oral and classical epics: Draupadi among Rajputs, Muslims and Dalits.* The University of Chicago Press.

Jain, R. K. (1979). Kingship, territory and property in pre-British Bundelkhand. *Economic and Political Weekly, 14*(22), 946–950.

Jain, R. K. (2002). *Between history and legend: Status and power in Bundelkhand.* Orient Longman Private Limited.

Jeffrey, R. (2000). *India's newspaper revolution: Capitalism, politics and the Indian-Language Press.* Oxford University Press.

Jeffrey, R. (2001). [Not]Being there: Dalits and India's newspaper. *South Asia, 24*(2), 225–238.

Kasturi, M. (1999). Rajput lineages, banditry and the colonial state in nineteenth-century 'British' Bundelkhand. *Studies in History, 15*(1), 75–108.

Kumar, V. (2006). Indian media and its role in the empowerment of Dalits. *Communicator, 41*(1), 73–97.

Martin, K., & Wilmore, M. (2010). Local voices on community radio: A study of 'Our Lumbini' in Nepal. *Development in Practice, 20*(7), 866–878.

Mohanty, M. (1995). On the concept of 'empowerment'. *Economic and Political Weekly, 30*(24), 1434–1436.

Naqvi, F. (2007). *Waves in the hinterland: The journey of a newspaper.* Nirantar.

Narayan, B. (1998). Popular culture and 1857: A memory against forgetting. *Social Scientist, 26*(1/4), 86–94.

Neurath, P. M. (1962). Radio farm forum as a tool of change in Indian village. *Economic Development and Cultural Change, 10*(3), 275–283.

Ninan, S. (2007). *Headlines from the heartland: Reinventing the Hindi public sphere.* SAGE Publications.

NITI Aayog. (2015). *Human development report Bundelkhand 2012.* Prepared under NITI Aayog-UNDP Project on Human Development: towards Bridging Inequalities.

OneWorld Foundation India. (2019). *Community radio compendium—2019.* OneWorld Foundation India on behalf of the Ministry of Information & Broadcasting, Government of India.

Oommen, T. K. (1970). Rural community power structure in India. *Social Forces, 49*(2), 226–239.

Pai, S. (1997). Dalit assertion in UP: Implications for politics. *Economic and Political Weekly, 32*(37), 2313–2314.

Pai, S. (2004). Dalit question and political response: Comparative study of Uttar Pradesh and Madhya Pradesh. *Economic and Political Weekly, 39*(11), 1141–1150.

Patil, S. (2011). Violence of silence: Brahminic media constructions of caste and gender. *Women's Link, 17*(3), 15–19.

Pavarala, V. (2003). Building solidarities: A case of community radio in Jharkhand. *Economic and Political Weekly, 38*(22), 2188–2197.

Perspectives. (2010). Drought by design: The man-made calamity in Bundelkhand. *Economic and Political Weekly, 45*(5), 33–38.

Ravikumar, D. (2007). The unwritten writing: Dalits and the media. In N. Rajan (Ed.), *21st century journalism in India* (pp. 61–77). SAGE Publications.

Saeed, S. (2010). Negotiating power: Community media, democracy, and the public sphere. *Development in Practice, 19*(4–5), 466–478.

Sahai-Achuthan, N. (1987). Folk songs of Uttar Pradesh. *Ethnomusicology, 31*(3), 395–406.

Sinha, A., & Malik, K. K. (2020). Reimagining community media: A rhizomatic analysis of Khabar Lahariya in Central India. *Media Asia*, https://dx.doi.org/10.1080/01296612.2020.1752433

Suthar, S. K. (2018). Bundelkhand development package, drought and the development question in India. *Social Change, 48*(3), 398–416.

Tewari, L. G. (1989). An elementary reading of the Alhakhand. *South Asia Research, 9*(1), 3–16.

United Nations Development Programme. (2009). *Communication for empowerment in Nepal: An assessment of communication and media needs among indigenous peoples.* United Nations Development Programme.

Upadhyaya, N. P., & Dehejia, H. V. (2019). *Paintings of Bundelkhand: Some remembered, some forgotten, some not yet discovered.* DK Printworld (P) Ltd.

Varadarajan, S. (2006, June 3). Caste matters in the Indian Media. *The Hindu.* https://svaradarajan.com/2006/06/03/caste-matters-in-the-indian-media/

Verma, A. K. (2011). Farmers' suicides and statehood demand in Bundelkhand. *Economic & Political Weekly, 46*(29), 10–14.

Whale, J. (1977). *The politics of the media.* Manchester University Press.

Chapter 4

Understanding the 'Community' in Community Media
Women's Experiences of Leadership in *Mandakini ki Awaaz*

Shweta Radhakrishnan

INTRODUCTION

…the historical philosophy of community radio is to use this medium as the voice of the voiceless, the mouthpiece of oppressed people (be it on racial, gender, or class grounds) and generally as a tool for development. (Mtimde et al., 1998, p. 14)

Community radio has always been understood to be a medium with radical potential, imagined largely as a grassroots media platform that tilts at the mainstream, corporate-owned media windmill—a medium that privileges and promotes local culture and voices local concerns, a medium that destabilizes and decentralizes power through being community-owned and community-run (Malik & Pavarala, 2007; Tabing, 2002).

This chapter tries to understand whether and how this medium, which does provide those traditionally left out of the ambit of mainstream media a voice, engages with the marginalization of the communities it is embedded in, especially in the context of gender. The chapter seeks to understand both the opportunities and challenges women encounter in their engagement with a community radio station, specifically as they occupy leadership roles in the organization. Informed by the framework developed by Pilar Riaño-Alcalá in her work 'Women in Grassroots Communication', the chapter tries to understand what role women play as producers at a community radio station, what facilitates their access to radio stations and defines their decision-making capacities and what impact this engagement has on other facets of their lives. In doing so, the chapter tries to offer insights into how the 'community' in community radio is defined, how gender determines who among the voiceless is granted the privilege of raising their voice through the medium and how the medium might shape the tenor and pitch of their voice.

This chapter draws upon my experiences in the field as part of an organization called People's Power Collective (PPC). PPC is an organization working in the community radio sector in India, helping local organizations and communities set up their own community radio stations. From 2013 to 2015, PPC was engaged in a hands-on, residential training process, in collaboration with the local community-based organization Mandakini ki Awaaz Kalyan Sewa Samiti (MKAKSS), to help the community set up the radio station Mandakini ki Awaaz (MKA) in Rudraprayag District, Uttarakhand. Both organizations worked collectively on various activities, such as procuring MKA's license, sourcing equipment, building a disaster-resilient radio station and running and managing a live broadcasting radio station. Simultaneously, PPC and MKAKSS also worked together to mobilize the community and build community ownership and participation in the radio station to ensure its sustainability, stability and accountability. From 2013 to 2015, the PPC team stayed in Sena Gadsari in Rudraprayag district and worked alongside the MKA team. This chapter draws upon my observations and experiences from that period, as part of the team that set up the community radio station. It broadly discusses the experiences of female colleagues at the radio station. The women who currently work at the station are mostly Hindu, upper-caste, middle-class women, primarily from Rajput communities. While women from other communities participated in training programmes, they did not continue working at the radio station, for stated reasons ranging from the distance of their homes from the community radio station and financial compulsions (since the radio station only paid a small stipend at the time, those who needed money urgently often left to find other work—even working at the radio station on a small stipend is a privilege only certain women have been able to capitalize on) to personal reasons, such as involvement in legal proceedings, disapproval of their marital family, child-rearing, etc.

As mentioned earlier, this chapter is based on my experience and observations during 2013–2015, insights based on the interviews and focus group discussions I conducted with women in the community during my tenure as Communications and Programme Coordinator with PPC, and as part of my film *A Radio of One's Own*, as well as semi-structured telephonic interviews with two staff members of the community radio station for the purpose of this chapter. A key struggle while writing this chapter has been understanding and acknowledging that many insights were possible not because I was a researcher in a specific space but because of friendships that grew in the 2 years that I lived and worked in Rudraprayag. While I have worked to ensure that no details discussed in these personal conversations are shared, these informal conversations with my friends and colleagues from the community, while preparing dinner, over endless cups of tea, during long walks to narrowcasting sites, in the course of disagreements and arguments and while attending all-night weddings and cultural performances, have been significant in helping me sift through my interviews and observations and decide on the issues and themes to highlight and present in this chapter, and the conceptual framework that would be most meaningful in interpreting their experiences as leaders and producers.[1]

---

[1] An earlier version of this chapter was also presented at the National Seminar on Participatory Media Praxis (2017) organized by the School of Media and Cultural Studies, Tata Institute of Social Sciences, Mumbai. The feedback from fellow panelists, organizers and other attendees was also deeply meaningful in reworking key sections of this paper.

A BRIEF OVERVIEW OF THE COMMUNITY

In Rudraprayag, Uttarakhand, the catchment community of MKA is predominantly Hindu, constituted mainly of brahmin, rajput and Scheduled Caste (SC) communities. There are small pockets of Muslim communities in the district, but they are a minority in the community. According to data from the 2011 census (Directorate of Census Operations, 2011a), Hindu communities form 99.1 per cent of the total population in the district. The percentage of SC communities in Rudraprayag district is 18.76 per cent, and the percentage of Scheduled Tribe communities is 2.89 per cent (Directorate of Census Operations, 2011b). Villages and hamlets are organized primarily according to caste and, in villages that have a Muslim population, according to religion as well. The villages are usually divided into the 'General' *basti* and the 'SC' *basti*—the terms used to define the spatial division in the region. In Rudraprayag district, specifically, the main occupations include agriculture, animal husbandry and tourism. Many migrate to cities or plains in search of job opportunities.

In the catchment community, women primarily work on farms, tend to animals and also go to the forest for firewood and grass for cattle, along with managing their other domestic work, such as child-rearing, cooking and cleaning and managing the house. With the proliferation of work under the Mahatma Gandhi National Rural Employment Guarantee Act (MGNREGA), women also work in MGNREGA sites as daily-wage labourers to supplement their families' incomes. In this district, especially post the June 2013 floods, there have been several non-governmental organizations (NGOs) operating in the sectors of health, livelihood and education, and jobs in the NGO sector are also considered desirable—for both women and men in the area.

CHALLENGES TO WOMEN'S PARTICIPATION IN COMMUNITY RADIO

Firstly, Community Radio is characterized by the active participation of the community in the process of creating news, information, entertainment and culturally relevant material, with an emphasis on local issues and concerns. With training, local producers can create programmes using local voices. The community can also actively participate in the management of the station and have a say in the scheduling and content of the programmes. Secondly, it is essentially a non-profit enterprise. In these days of highly commercialized broadcasting, the ethos of community radio remains independence and responsibility to serve the community, not the advertiser. As the station is owned by the community, it also maintains some responsibility in the running of the station. Thirdly, community radio programming is designed by the community, to improve social conditions and the quality of its cultural life. The community itself decides what its priorities and needs are in terms of information provision. (Voices, India, Mtimde et al., 1998; author's emphasis)

The catchment community of any community radio station is expected to participate both in content generation and in ownership and management of the station. In India, given that the process of setting up a community radio station is a long, bureaucratic one (Pavarala, 2013) that requires systematic and sustained engagement with different government agencies and additionally also requires some amount of financial capital, how many people can truly set up community radio stations? Given the restrictions on women's mobility and their involvement in domestic and agricultural work in the region, it becomes doubly hard for many women to occupy public space and lead such movements. As Pavarala, Malik and Cheeli note in their paper 'Community Media and Women: Forging Subaltern Counterpublics':

'Community' has usually been perceived and dealt with as a harmonious collective with equitable internal dynamics. Too often the prevalent hierarchies, differences and conflicts, that are crucial to positive outcomes, are overlooked. It has been observed in numerous cases that community-driven development is not gender-sensitive, and 'the language and practice of "participation" often obscures women's worlds, needs and contributions to development making equitable participatory development an elusive goal'. (Guijt & Kaul Shah, 1998; Pavarala et al., 2005)

Since 2001, community members had been working together to set up their community radio station, although it was only in 2007 that they formally began work as the NGO MKAKSS. Some women were associated with the movement to bring community radio to the Mandakini River Valley. However, most of the women were involved in stand-alone, individual activities, and the few women who were consistently part of the movement were not in higher, decision-making positions. They mostly worked as reporters or narrowcasters. While women were ready resources in terms of content generation, their role in the management of the organization and in leadership seems to have been minimal.

In September 2013, when the PPC training programme began, a concerted effort was made to bring in more women into the decision-making and management aspects of the community radio station and to work with more women to take on leadership roles within the team. While two of the women who had worked with MKA before, during their school and college days, were willing to attend training sessions, persuading married women to be part of the station was more difficult. Their marital families would grant them permission to attend the sessions only if they were convinced that the women would manage all their domestic chores along with the training sessions. Two married women attended the first training programme along with their husbands. While one of them continued at the station (and her husband too continues to be part of the station) and works there till this day, the other had to drop out soon after her husband dropped out. Even though married women have greater responsibilities to juggle than their unmarried counterparts, women who are married into the community (*bahu*) are still seen as more sustainable investments by community members, as opposed to unmarried women (*beti*). The primary idea is that a *bahu* will never leave the community and move away, as opposed to a *beti* who is imagined as a short-term asset by the community— because women in the area are expected to relocate post marriage to their marital home. For example, in the second training programme conducted by PPC, three unmarried girls completed the training, and all of them continued to work at the station until they were either married or engaged, after which they had to relocate elsewhere and were unable to continue working at the station. In 2020, there were four women who were associated with the station full-time. Of them, three are *bahus* and one is a *beti*. Of the three married women currently working at the station, one recently made the transition from *beti* to *bahu*. She has been associated with the station since her school days and, after the founding members, is the most senior person in the team, but despite her seniority and her incredible technical proficiency, she and the team were constantly worried that she would 'have' to move away if her marital home was located in another village/district. The team would often joke with her, asking her to find a husband from her village itself so that she could continue to work at the station. She married into a family that lived in a village that was within commuting distance from the radio station. Additionally, her husband is also supportive of her involvement in the radio station, an important factor that facilitated her transition from *beti* to *bahu* and enabled her to continue working at the station.

Another factor that is often seen as limiting women's access to community radio stations is their limited mobility. In the hilly district of Rudraprayag, transport remains a big point of concern. In Sena Gadsari, where the station is located, the most common mode of transport is shared jeeps. Buses ply twice or thrice a day and at fixed times in the morning and evening. However, jeeps and buses both stop plyiı g after 6.30 p.m. Usually, for field visits, this means that team members are required to stay over in the field one day if they want to mobilize the community. When fieldwork commenced with the newly constituted team at MKA, often women were reluctant to stay over during field visits. Unmarried women were usually more willing than married women, but permissions from natal or marital families were a prerequisite for any woman being allowed to stay overnight. This often required the founding members, who are held in some esteem by the community, to build personal relationships with the families of the women working in the community and often assume paternalistic roles to assure families that their daughters/daughters-in-law would be safe and 'protected'. At some points, male colleagues have also expressed the belief that female colleagues can be 'liabilities' in the field, largely due to the concern that unmarried women will try to use staying overnight as an excuse to meet friends or boyfriends, thereby jeopardizing the trust senior male colleagues had built with their families—a concern that was rarely raised around unmarried men who worked at the station.

For married women with children, the negotiations were different from those for their unmarried colleagues. Working mothers at the station shared how, especially during the early narrowcasting days, they were subjected to barbs about being bad mothers for working and occasionally prioritizing work over their children. They also faced active resistance and criticism from their marital homes and neighbours. The limited and erratic travel options also meant that women who stayed a little away could not come regularly to the station unless they had their own vehicle or a neighbour or family member who could drop them off daily. Additionally, whereas a male colleague who currently works at the station could relocate to Sena Gadsari from his village (which is rather far away), women did not have the same option. Many women who come to the station often commute daily by walking to the station. Often, most women hitch a ride to the station, which sometimes renders them vulnerable, especially if the drivers are not from the community. One woman who worked part-time with the radio station was harassed on her way to work when she hitched a ride in a truck in the morning. She escaped by jumping out of the truck. Specific action points to address the issue of mobility, which systematically prevented women from coming to the station, were drawn up post the incident. For example, while women walked home, reducing to some extent their dependence on jeeps and buses, it also meant that it became more difficult for them to commute once it became dark. While some of the dangers are gender-specific, such as harassment by drunk men along the way (especially if there are alcohol shops on the way), other more gender-neutral fears, such as bear/tiger/leopard attacks and treacherous mountain paths, led the team to decide that for areas from where women were travelling alone, the women would either leave before sundown or the organization would take on the responsibility of dropping them home. If more than one colleague came from the same village, post sundown, a buddy system was employed, so that the colleagues could travel in bigger groups.

The lack of prior institutional understanding of women's concerns around mobility, issues specific to working mothers, exclusionary physical infrastructure, etc. at the community radio station at some level indicated that while founding members most definitely may have wanted to encourage women's participation, women's involvement as permanent decision-making members was probably not part of the active imagination of the group. With more women now occupying leadership roles at the community radio station, institutional changes—from amending station policy to be more gender-sensitive to including sanitary napkins in the medical supplies box—were made at a managerial level to make the station more inclusive and to allow for more women to participate and be part of the station. With women joining the team in leadership and decision-making roles, it can be said that women went from being 'subjects of information' (Riaño-Alcalá, 1994) to active participants in the process, moving the community radio station from a development communication model to a participatory communication model, from the standpoint of gender. The changes this shift has wrought and the opportunities it has provided women in the community are explored in the next section. However, before delving into that, it is important to note that while participation of women has increased at the community radio station, the women who are currently in leadership roles at the station or employed as staff members are from upper-caste, Hindu communities. The active and sustained participation of women from SC communities and minority communities, especially in leadership roles, requires more attention. While women from SC and minority communities participate in content generation, when team members visit their villages, they rarely visit the community radio station. The challenges experienced by women from these communities in accessing the space of the community radio station also need further study and examination.

OPPORTUNITIES AFFORDED BY WOMEN'S PARTICIPATION IN COMMUNITY RADIO

Despite the challenges faced by women, their participation in the community radio station has effected change and created opportunities both for themselves and for other women in the community. At the level of programming and content, the content and communication team leads of MKA are women, and content and timing are often decided keeping the audience in mind. Most women in the community often listen to the radio when they go out to get grass or firewood from the forest, and shows and show timings are often designed to reach out to these women. There are shows that focus on women's daily lives (*Dincharya*), shows based on field interviews with women in the catchment community, special features on inspiring women in the region, which showcase stories of women's leadership, and a weekly programme on Sunday afternoons, titled *Didi Buliyon ka Dagda* (With our Older and Younger Sisters). The weekly women's hour is a composite show that features several things that are of interest to the women in the region, such as health and beauty tips, cooking recipes or tips on child-rearing. Some plays and smaller capsules focus on issues related to gender in the community, often those issues highlighted by the law or the state, such as the ills of dowry, the importance of educating female children, not subjecting women to violence, etc. Another interesting part of the women's weekly show is a segment called *Doctor Didi*. Healthcare is often hard to access in the community, and women especially find it difficult to access gynaecological help easily. The *Doctor Didi* segment is usually based on questions that women from the community send in to the radio station, such as questions related to menstruation, knee pain and stomach issues. Since women are often hesitant to share personal health issues on air themselves, the community radio team collates their questions and then poses these questions (without naming the questioners) to a local doctor who is also a woman. Her responses are broadcast in the weekly *Doctor Didi* segment. The idea for *Doctor Didi* also came from the women who were part of the team, and this innovation is an example of the ways in which having more women in decision-making and leadership roles makes for more gender-sensitive content and programming. Shows like *Didi Buliyon ka Dagda* and the *Dincharya* segment, through their documentation of women's daily lives and practical realities, accord the importance due to women and their labour, and create a virtual subaltern counterpublic that archives and discusses experiences that are often marginalized in the public sphere.

Along with changes in programming, another element of change the community radio station has been able to effect has been with regard to the perception of women working in communication platforms in the region. For example, one of the women currently working at the community radio station used to also work with it in her school and college days. She remembers being harassed, when she was a young girl working with the station, on her way back home in the evening, often being followed by men. These days, she shares, their earlier derisive attitude has been replaced by a new-found respect, in large part because her voice is recognizable from the segments she does on air (Radhakrishnan, 2016). When the radio began its broadcast, it brought with it an air of respectability and credibility to all those associated with it, especially the women who went on air. Along with this, their association with the community radio station has also provided the women with opportunities to travel and present their work to diverse communities and groups. For one of the women working with the radio station, her participation at a national conference was her first journey outside Uttarakhand. The increased mobility of women associated with the radio station and their participation in national and international forums, conferences and other engagements have also earned them additional respect in their communities and even in their families. For example, one of the women currently working at the station became the first from her family to travel internationally, when she was chosen to be part of an exchange programme organized by PPC. Along with Saritha Thomas from PPC, she travelled to the United Kingdom and interacted with female broadcasters from the community radio station Desi Radio, which is run by Punjabi women in Southall, and with broadcasters from the British Broadcasting Corporation radio studios. The increased number of women associated with the radio station, both physically and on air, and the recognition of their hard work by panchayat leaders, district collectors and others who are influential and who mould public opinion, along with the visible increase in opportunities that their association with the radio station has facilitated, have also helped bring more respectability to their association with the community radio medium.

CONCLUSION

The opportunities and changes facilitated by women's participation in the community radio MKA has had an important impact on women in the region. The community radio medium is a participatory communication medium that provides a 'cultural space that mediates the ways in which popular classes make sense of the world. Culture in this view is an important mediation between communication practices and the popular...' (Riaño-Alcalá, 1994). Women's active participation in the community radio station has created attitudinal changes in the community. Their participation in the medium has also actively helped them renegotiate power dynamics in other spheres. As Srilata Batliwala notes in her work on feminist leadership, there are three realms where power operates: the public, the private and the intimate (Batliwala, 2011). The public refers often to agencies of the state, corporations and such entities, the private refers to domestic spaces and important interpersonal relationships, like friendships, and the intimate refers to the realm of the self. Due to their association with the community radio station, the women have clearly felt like they have been able to negotiate power differently than they could before, and they have wrought changes in both the public and private realms as discussed above. Additionally, what is more crucial is that their association with community radio has helped them renegotiate power in the intimate realm in terms of increased self-confidence and self-esteem. As one female staffer notes, when she joined the community radio station, she was uncomfortable even speaking to guests coming into her house. Today, she goes live on air every day, has interviewed the district collector, has represented her organization at national conferences and so on, and all this has given her a confidence she previously did not have. 'The construction of gender identities is linked to concepts of self, personhood, and autonomy by reference to sexual identities and to the ways history, class, and race shape the various cultural definitions of women' (Riaño-Alcalá, 1994). Their association with community radio has helped these women make small changes in the cultural definition of women, for their community and for themselves. In the words of one of the female staffers, 'Khud apne aap ko jaanne ka mauka mila hai' (This gave me the opportunity to know myself).

REFERENCES

Batliwala, S. (2011). *Feminist leadership for social transformation: Clearing the conceptual cloud*. CREA.
Directorate of Census Operations, Uttarakhand. (2011a). *District census handbook, Rudraprayag: Village and town directory*. Census of India 2011. https://censusindia.gov.in/2011census/dchb/0503_PART_A_DCHB_RUDRAPRAYAG.pdf

Directorate of Census Operations, Uttarakhand. (2011b). *District census handbook: Village and town wise primary census abstract (PCA)*. Census of India 2011. https://censusindia.gov.in/2011census/dchb/0503_PART_B_DCHB_RUDRAPRAYAG.pdf

Malik, K. K., & Pavarala, V. (2007). *Other voices: The struggle for community radio in India*. SAGE Publications.

Mtimde, L., Bonin, M.-H., Maphiri, N., Nyamaku, K., & Opoku-Mensah, A. (1998). *What is community radio? A resource guide*. AMARC Africa and Panos Southern Africa. https://web.archive.org/web/20160304023107/www.amarc.org/documents/manuals/What_is_CR_english.pdf

Pavarala, V., Kanchan Kumar, & Cheeli, J. R. (2005). *Community media and women: Forging subaltern counterpublics*. In Gender Perspectives on the Information Society South Asia Pre-WSIS Seminar, Bangalore, 2005. IT for Change.

Pavarala, V. (2013). Ten years of community radio in India: Towards new solidarities. *EduComm Asia, 17*, 2–4.

Radhakrishnan, S. (2016). *A radio of one's own*. YouTube. MurthyNayak Foundation, School of Media and Cultural Studies. https://www.youtube.com/watch?v=TylK0EFevIU&feature=youtu.be

Riaño-Alcalá, P. (1994). Gender in communication: Women's contributions. In P. Riaño (Ed.), *Women in grassroots communication: Furthering social change* (pp. 30–44). SAGE Publications.

Tabing, L. (2002). *How to do community radio*. UNESCO. https://unesdoc.unesco.org/ark:/48223/pf0000134208

Section II

In Their Own Moving Image: Community Video Practices

Chapter 5

Collaborative Animation
Challenges of Participatory Film-making with the Bhil Community

Nina Sabnani

INTRODUCTION

This chapter discusses a collaborative project, *Telling it Together*,[1] that brought us as designers–film-makers together with artists from the Bhil community in Madhya Pradesh, in an effort to create awareness about the place of painting and visual narratives among the Bhil community. It was an attempt to explore digital media as a means for taking stories from the margins to a wider audience and thus making stories and the storytellers visible through collaboration. Digital media is seen as a powerful tool for empowerment and for information creation and dissemination; its reach is unmatched and unprecedented. However, it is not always as widely accessible as we would like it to be. The means of production, it is often argued, are controlled by a few. It comes with its own burden of social, economic and cultural capital. And in a society

[1] This project has been funded and facilitated by Tata Centre for Technology and Design, Indian Institute of Technology (IIT), Bombay. The author is also grateful to Sher Singh Bhil and Subhash Bhil for their active participation and collaboration in this project.

that is fissured by several intersecting hierarchies and power dynamics, the lack of access to technological tools can add to pre-existing inequalities. This forms the ground for investigating digital media as a platform and vehicle for marginalized stories and voices.

In this chapter, we attempt to problematize the idea of collaboration itself. What does it mean to collaborate when participants and forms of expression come together from across social, cultural and technological boundaries—where some members and forms of expression represent the centre and others represent the periphery? It is a challenging terrain to traverse, because it does throw up ethical issues of what prompts us as outsiders to do this; is it an appropriation of sorts? Who do the stories belong to? Who should be involved in the conservation, preservation and dissemination of their stories? Is the community interested in sharing them and reaching out to a larger world? Are we de-contextualizing or 'museumizing' their art from their life by placing it in a different frame? Is it something they want or is it our desire to find an indigenous art form with which to make animated films? What will the making of a film, or for that matter the creation of any media content, bring to the life of the community? Should it be the community itself or others who see some value in it, or should it be a collaborative exercise? Is this an exercise in conserving an intangible heritage?

INTANGIBLE HERITAGE

Preservation of the tangible arts and artefacts has been a cultural responsibility, as it ensures that diversity is appreciated and respected, which has given birth to museums and other repositories. However, objects do not tell stories themselves, and many efforts have been made to preserve memories of what they mean to the communities through documentation, interpretation and conservation. Storytelling is one form of intangible heritage that has been preserved and conserved in multiple ways. For long, the concerns of preservation were centred on the tangible; the focus on intangible heritage came much later. Intangible culture has been described as traditional, contemporary and living at the same time. The 2003 United Nations Educational, Scientific and Cultural Organization (UNESCO) Convention for the Safeguarding of the Intangible Cultural Heritage defines it as the practices, representations, expressions, knowledge and skills—as well as the instruments, objects, artefacts and cultural spaces associated therewith—that communities, groups and, in some cases, individuals recognize as part of their cultural heritage. This intangible cultural heritage, transmitted from generation to generation, is constantly recreated by communities and groups in response to their environment, their interaction with nature and their history, and it provides them with a sense of identity and continuity, thus promoting respect for cultural diversity and human creativity.[2]

The convention's definition suggests that intangible inheritance can be kept alive only if it has relevance for its community and is continuously recreated and shared across generations, and if the efforts towards conservation are inclusive and community-based. Designers have been concerned with museum design, where they have also included the intangible by way of written narratives or short documentaries alongside the objects and photographs of communities. More often than not, the 'first voice' (Galla, 2008) is barely heard. Film and animation are newer forms of storytelling which allow for inclusion of the 'first voice' that includes the visual language of the indigenous community.

Our prior experience of working with artists' communities from Kutch and Rajasthan had made us acutely aware of the presence of the 'first voice' in films, where it is possible to hear 'first-hand' accounts through voice and imagery created by the community. Our collaboration with the communities was with mutual consent, and our effort was to make the activity as equal as possible, though one cannot claim that it was always so. Familiarity with technology and animation skills tilted the scales in our direction with the responsibility of seeing the work completed and negotiating with publishers and other agencies to disseminate the content. The need to reach a wider audience was voiced by the artists, as they felt their work was not valued as art but rather was seen as a hereditary craft, where individual contribution went unrecognized.

---

[2] The report of the convention states that 'For the purposes of this Convention, consideration will be given solely to such intangible cultural heritage as is compatible with existing international human rights instruments, as well as with the requirements of mutual respect among communities, groups and individuals, and of sustainable development' (UNESCO, 2003, p. 5).

THE DYNAMISM OF THE 'TRADITIONAL'

The process of working together led to a greater understanding and appreciation of their art and ways of living. The immersive process enabled us to experience for ourselves the dynamic nature of the community's culture. Any living culture is dynamic and prone to change, either from within or due to external influences. In our experience of working with the Kutch artists, we had observed that the idea of making narrative tapestries came to them from the outside, after the earthquake of 2001, and yet, if we were to examine their art, the language of the stitches was something they had learnt over generations. This experience also made us look at animation as a way of representing ethnography, as a way to understand a community through a process of working together on making the film, of amplifying voice. It was this approach that we adopted again while working with the Bhil community. Among the factors that motivated us to work with the Bhil community was that many of their oral narratives were about water, its importance and its preservation. As the Bhils' ways of life had changed from nomadic to agrarian, their concerns too had changed. This concern for water turned out to be the cornerstone of their very reason to paint.

THE BACKGROUND: BHILS OF MADHYA PRADESH

The Bhils are among the largest indigenous communities in India, found mainly in the central region of the country. Our focus was on the Bhils of Madhya Pradesh. where their population according to census data is over 4.6 million (Census of India, 2001). The Bhils are not Hindus, and they have their own deities—for instance, Baba Dev, who is the chief deity who grants all wishes, and Titki Mata, a deity who lives by the river and is always surrounded by greenery. Ancestors play a very large role in their lives. The Bhils believe their ancestors include Valmiki and Eklavya, and the community is also mentioned in the Hindu epics Ramayana and Mahabharata. The word Bhil means 'bow'. The term refers to the history of the Bhils as hunters and archers. They used to live in the thick jungles of Madhya Pradesh but have taken to agriculture after they were driven out of their forests. Farming involves growing corn. Shortage of water is a common problem, and often water has to be fetched from far-off places. While large numbers are landless, some live on their small farms. Those who cannot live off the land have migrated to large cities in search of work in masonry, road making and other manual labour.

Theirs is also a history of social, cultural and political oppression, as well as resistance. Since the time of British colonization, the Bhils, like many nomadic and forest-dwelling communities, have been seen as the trouble-making other. It was the imperial government that first labelled them a criminal tribe—a label that has been since replaced with the more innocuous but nevertheless othering 'denotified tribe'.[3] Mahasweta Devi and before her Verrier Elwin have passionately fought for the rights of the adivasis and other indigenous people. Ganesh Devy, inspired by Mahasweta Devi, has been involved in the fight for recognizing the languages of the adivasis through his Bhasha Research and Publication Centre.

BHIL ART AND EARLY INTERVENTIONS

The Bhils have their own unique fairs and festivals where they dance and play music, and their art reflects their lives. Every festival is celebrated through paintings on the walls. Corn is not just food for sustenance, but it has also inspired the painting style of dots in Bhil art. The Bhil community has a rich resource of oral narratives which remains untapped, unappreciated and unknown. The knowledge and wisdom

---

[3] The Bhils were labelled as a Criminal Tribe by the imperial (British) government under the Criminal Tribes Act of 1871. The act 'recognized' certain indigenous groups—incidentally, many of them nomadic or semi-nomadic pastoralists, hunters and gatherers—as having 'criminal tendencies', 'addicted to the systematic commission of non-bailable offences'. This form of discrimination changed legal language with the replacement of the Criminal Tribes Act with the Habitual Offenders Act of 1952 by Government of India, which reclassified them as 'Denotified Tribes' but continued the legacy of considering them 'habitual offenders', asking the police to investigate a 'suspect's' 'criminal tendencies' and whether their occupation was 'conducive to settled way of life' if they were from a denotified tribe. It was only in 2007, on the directive of the United Nations' (UN) Committee on the Elimination of Racial Discrimination, that the government repealed the Habitual Offenders Act of 1952. For more, see https://en.wikipedia.org/wiki/Denotified_Tribes. Accessed: June 2019.

stored in stories are shared orally between members of the community, and this too is progressively getting infrequent, as they get caught up in making a living and have fewer opportunities of sharing and being together. Life and art are still interrelated, but this might not last long, and the younger generations might be estranged from their own stories.

Traditionally, their art was not available commercially; it used to be painted on the walls, which is pertinent to the story we are telling. They began to paint on paper and canvas when the celebrated artist J. Swaminathan came in contact with them in the 1980s and set up the Museum of Man and intervened on their behalf:

> That such communities should be left alone to themselves doesn't seem to be a viable proposition either. Their jungles no more belong to them, they can no more practice their traditional mode of cultivation in the name of conservation of forests (which are anyway being systematically destroyed for catering to 'urban and development needs') they cannot seek and hunt game any more and the inroads of the money economy are seemingly irreversible. (Swaminathan, 1987)

Swaminathan argued that there was a need for intervention, because the resources of the forest the Bhils were used to were no longer available to them. He encouraged them to paint on paper and introduced the work of several tribes through the museum in Bhopal, through fairs and exhibitions. This gave them a means of livelihood. It gave them an opportunity to travel outside their region, engage with other forms of art and expression and have their art seen by others. Today, Bhil paintings are sold at craft fairs and in museums across India. It was at one of these fairs in Orissa that we came in contact with the artist Sher Singh and explored the idea of working together. In a world of mobile connectivity, we were able to stay in touch and meet again a few months later.

COLLABORATIVE WORK

In one of our earliest conversations, Sher Singh told us how painting is considered a sacred activity, as it is through painting that the gods shower rains upon them. To illustrate this point, he told us an origin myth of how the Bhils began to paint. In a time of drought, the Bhils approached their priest Badwa, who suggested they paint trees on their walls. And when they did, it began to rain.

The story held in it a kernel of universal wisdom and portrayed the beliefs and ways of life of the Bhils. We invited Sher Singh and his colleague Subhash Bhil to work with us on elaborating the story, so that we could make a short animation film based on it. Through workshops, conversations and discussions, the story grew. Details and new ideas emerged, and the story started to take on a life of its own.

However, we felt that we did not know enough about their environment—the context from which this story had arisen. So we travelled with Sher Singh to his village and met everyone he felt important for us to meet. He also took us to their place of worship where the local alcohol, *Mahua*, is offered with a sacrificed rooster or a goat. It is a relatively closed community. For outsiders to be included in their rituals is rare. We were fortunate to be allowed in to witness their everyday lives, as well as rituals. Following this brief immersion into the lives of the community, we met other artists at Sher Singh's workplace at the Museum of Man, or the Manav Sangrahalaya (Indira Gandhi Rashtriya Manav Sangrahalaya [IGRMS]), in Bhopal.

Later, Sher Singh visited us again in Mumbai to work on an illustrated book that was published by Tulika Books, Chennai. The book also generated income for Sher Singh in the form of royalty, which he shared with the author. He expressed his confusion at being paid when his paintings had not been bought and physically taken possession of by the 'buyer', and this became one step for him to understand his rights as a collaborator. The illustrated book, *A Bhil Story*, was translated into nine languages, including Gujarati, the language the Bhils speak. This was important, because the artists felt that through these books their children would also remember the stories that they had heard from their elders. In fact, this was one reason the artists had been happy to participate in the project.

The origin myth also became the theme of our animated film where recounted stories were woven into lyrics by professional scriptwriters. Sher Singh painted the key images for the film (Figure 5.1),

Figure 5.1 *Art by Sher Singh*

which were then animated by trained animators. This generated a lot of interest among the community of artists, and we would often receive phone calls from other artists who wanted to work with us. This led to the creation of a website for the artists we had met, so that they may have direct contact with the larger world. In the website, www.bhilart.com, each artist has a page of their own with their paintings and contact details. The artists were keen to learn the technology, so that they could update the website. A workshop was conducted for the artists at IGRMS, Bhopal, where they were introduced to the use of smartphones and social media. Each artist also agreed to teach one, so that we could reach many more. The fact that they could have presence on such a scale motivated the young and the old to come forward and demand more workshops.

EMERGENT ISSUES: STORYTELLING, VISIBILITY AND COLLABORATION

The issues and questions that emerged from our engagement and collaboration were questions about storytelling, memory, visibility and collaboration.

Let us look at the issues of storytelling and memory. Stories construct identities; they make the invisible visible. Stories and their telling construct the identity of individuals and communities. In the case of the Bhils, where their culture and identity have been repeatedly trivialized by the formal education system and the popular-culture industry in general, stories can play a crucial role in the reconstruction of identities. Recounting stories and conserving them can become a way to conserve the community's culture and reconstruct their sense of self. Sharing stories across generations is perhaps the most basic of ways through which culture is created, transmitted and kept alive. The Bhil community has a rich resource of oral narratives which remains unrecognized, unknown and unappreciated. The knowledge and wisdom stored in stories is shared orally between members of the community. In the present condition of the Bhils, with rising economic pressures and migration to cities, this sharing is becoming progressively infrequent. In such a scenario, print and digital media can contribute towards the conservation of these stories and their being shared among the community. As mentioned earlier, the possibility that younger generations of the Bhils would be able to access their stories through the outcomes of our project was one of the reasons for the Bhil artists to participate in it. Digital communication technology can act as a medium *within* the community, for them to tell each other their stories, to strengthen their sense of identity as a community with a rich and complex culture.

The telling of stories can help the community come to terms with the upheavals that they have experienced over the last two centuries, where their way of life, their forests and their belief systems have been progressively decimated by interventions directed at subjugating them and exploiting their natural resources for commercial gain (Baviskar, 2001). Novelist Mia Couto, speaking about the role of stories in post-war Mozambique, has said, 'Storytelling…can help us accept, without fear, the full complexity of a world that is simultaneously based in laws and chaos, compliance and disobedience'. (Esposito, 2013) The origin stories of the Bhils, like the one that our film is based on, are situated in a space that is both real and mythic. It speaks about the very real problem of water scarcity, and about the magical power of trees and painting to bring relief to people. Perhaps it is through this quality of stories, of being neither fact nor fiction, that they help us make sense of the chaos and complexity of the world. The recounting of stories as shared memories becomes a way to bridge a troubled past and an uncertain present.

Stories make visible entire worlds and ways of seeing. The story that Sher Singh told us, on which our film is based, speaks about the relationship between people and the natural environment, and in particular about the importance of water. The story is also indicative of many other cultural beliefs, ideas and ways of being that are part of Bhil life: their rituals and deities and the struggles, tactics and strategies of everyday life. This story, and its illustrated telling, provides an opportunity to listen to what the Bhil storytellers and artists want to share about their community and culture. In making this story widely available through the film and illustrated books, we attempted to open up this opportunity to a much wider audience. The visual nature of these mediums and the use of Bhil art for illustrations had another positive outcome. The audience got a chance to recognize the particularity of Bhil art, which is otherwise often mistaken for Gond art, which has become more popular.

One of the questions that this text had started out with was about the role of digital media in disseminating stories from the margins to a wider set of audiences. We have argued here that the combination of stories and digital communication technologies can make a community 'visible' to outsiders. Yet, we must ask ourselves, what does it mean to be visible, and how does the community benefit from it? Do they even want to be so? The answers to these questions can only be explored with respect to the specific sociocultural and historical contexts of each community. In the case of the Bhils, what does it mean to be visible? The population of the Bhil community in Madhya Pradesh alone runs in the millions, and yet they are barely recognized, acknowledged or valued. Since the time of the British imperialists, they have been labelled 'thuggies', 'DNTs' 'tribals' and so on. Their art has been dismissed as ritualistic, and their stories are even lesser known. Their visibility has been constructed on these negative connotations defined by the oppressive other. The community itself has had little say in its portrayal.

In such a scenario, any project or intervention attempting to make the Bhils visible must be premised on their agency. Such interventions can foreground their ways of seeing and make them the ones who see, and not simply the seen.

Print and digital media, the latter even more so, can be powerful tools of expression, agency and outreach in this regard. Representing the visual and oral culture of the Bhils through these media with their massive reach can ensure that these aspects of Bhil culture and identity are foregrounded. And through the use of digital media and the Internet, members of the community have the power to represent themselves as they wish.

Through their stories and their art, we, the other at the centre, can learn not only about them but also about ourselves. To quote Mia Couto again, 'Storytelling confirm[s] us as relatives and neighbours in our infinite diversity' (Gendy, 2015). Through stories we learn to see our world as a composite of many worlds. And sometimes, the stories told by the other can help us learn something about the world that we share with them. The concern for water reflected in their story today stretches across regions and boundaries. That it is an origin myth of the Bhils emphasizes how fundamental and universal a concern this is. The telling of the story through print and digital media becomes a way for the Bhils to have a voice in the universal discourse on water. That it is their myth told in their visual language to an audience of non-Bhils further subverts the prevailing power dynamic between mainstream and marginalized cultures. The conventional flow of knowledge is reversed. For a non-Bhil audience, this opens up the conversation to points of view and knowledge systems that they may not have considered so far. For the Bhils, this is an assertion of the validity and relevance of their knowledge.

Storytelling belongs to the oral tradition and as a form of intangible heritage has been preserved and conserved in multiple ways. We may argue that the ideal way to preserve the oral would be through the oral, so that its spirit is retained. The oral does not age; it is always relevant, because it is adapted and interpreted by each teller or listener. It is interactive and requires the presence of a performer and an audience. Now, for the retention of the 'oral', we need memory. However, memory has been outsourced time and again since the invention of writing, so the oral has to reside in what Walter Ong (1999) calls secondary orality, which is media. We therefore suggest that animation is a form of storytelling that belongs to Ong's secondary orality, a form that allows for the participants to speak through their own images to a large number of listeners. Further, in the animated-film framework, creative persons from diverse backgrounds can work together and the story can be relevant in more realms than one.

Next, to share our thoughts on what it is exactly to collaborate or have a participatory approach: Is it really possible to be equal in participation, because film-making is remote to the community. Many of the artists have never been to a cinema hall. Some have barely seen the television, so the idea of designing a visual sequence was quite alien to them. Similarly, none in the animation team had ever drawn Bhil art or knew how to make the patterns that are so peculiar to Bhil art. Thus, we had different skills that we brought to the project. We introduced two of the artists to a digital tablet to paint. They were very quick to learn but eventually did not want to use it, because painting is a sacred activity and cannot be virtual. They reflected that they could use it for producing work for sale, but the cost of the tablet was not worth the trouble. Besides its own price tag, it came with other hidden expenses, like electricity, maintenance, etc. The story was discussed and elements added with a larger team of people, including two artists from the community, Sher Singh and Subhash. We together decided it would be from the perspective of the rooster who is usually sacrificed for any ritual performed by the community. In our story he lives to tell the tale and gains respect in the community. This happens if a priest does not sacrifice the rooster but merely plucks a tiny wing off the rooster. Now no one can kill the rooster, because he has been touched and blessed by the priest. Every stage of the film process was shown and discussed with Sher Singh, including the script and storyboard, and he made many valuable suggestions. When it came to recording, he felt most uncomfortable speaking into the microphone and was generally very self-conscious, so we explored the idea of a professional voice. He was relieved and approved of the voice we chose.

Finally, we discussed the title of the film, and this is how our discussion went:

Author: Sher Singh, what could be the title of our film?
Sher Singh: *Ek Mor Ki Kahani* (A Story of a Peacock).
Author: But there is no peacock in our story...
Sher Singh: That's ok, we will paint one and put it in the film.
Author: What happens to the main character in our film, the rooster?
Sher Singh: He will stay as it is. We don't have to change anything.
Author: Why a peacock?
Sher Singh: Because he is beautiful
Author: But that does not make sense. What about *Hum Chitra Banatey Hain*? (We make Images?)
Sher Singh: That's also ok. *Shaandaar hai.* (That's grand)[4]

This exchange reflects the different notions of reality which form Sher Singh's conception of the world, and mine. Norms of cause and effect shape my logic. Sher Singh is not bound by the same norms. It was strange to me that a film could have a name that bore no discernible relationship to its story. Being presented with a contrasting way of seeing forced me to question mine. This interaction reiterates the idea of the collaborative space as one where each participant feels secure enough to have their ways of seeing questioned, and where they may explore other perspectives. Finally, collaboration between partners with different skills can actually be enriching for both. It invokes mutual respect.

CONCLUSION

The larger question that emerged from all these interactions was the role of the designer in such collaborations. In any collaboration the work and credit are shared on equal terms. In a scenario where the partners are

---

[4] For a more detailed description of the process of collaboration and the engagements through which the film took shape, see Nina Sabnani, *Animating Voices*.

not aware of their rights, the issues around possible exploitation need to be examined. How would issues of credit, intellectual property rights and royalty be addressed? Do systems exist or would they need to be created? There is no legislation that informs designers on a code of conduct when it comes to sharing credit or profits with traditional artists; they often operate from their own ethical standpoint. Even the terms such as 'traditional artist', 'artisan' and 'craftsperson' need re-examination and redefinition. For a truly collaborative work to succeed, respect and dignity need to be paramount, along with systems that ensure equality and parity.

REFERENCES

Baviskar, A. (2001). Forest management as political practice. *International Journal of Agricultural Resources, Governance and Ecology, 1*, 243–263. https://www.academia.edu/41666302/Forest_Management_as_Political_Practice

Census of India. (2001). Data Highlights: The Scheduled Tribes. http://censusindia.gov.in/Tables_Published/SCST/dh_st_madhya_pradesh.pdf

Esposito, S. (2013, May 2). We are made of memories: A conversation with Mia Couto. *The Paris Review.* https://www.theparisreview.org/blog/2013/05/02/we-are-made-of-memories-a-conversation-with-mia-couto/

Galla, A. (2008). The first voice in heritage conservation. *International Journal of Intangible Heritage, 3*, 10–25.

Gendy, N. E. (2015, January–February). Interview with Mia Couto: Sexuality, orality and cultural frontiers. *World Literature Today, 89*, 54–56.

Nina Sabnani. Animating voices. In T. Jones & S. Ashwath (Eds.), *History of animation* (Unpublished manuscript).

Ong, W. J. (1999). Orality, literacy, and modern media. In D. Crowley & P. Heyer, (Eds.), *Communication in history: Technology culture, society* (3rd ed., pp. 60–67). Longman.

Swaminathan, J. (1987). *Perceiving fingers.* Bharat Bhawan. http://ignca.gov.in/divisionss/janapada-sampada/tribal-art-culture/adivasi-art-culture/

UNESCO. (2003). *Convention for safeguarding intangible cultural heritage* (p. 5). https://ich.unesco.org/doc/src/15164-EN.pdf

Chapter 6

'Sangam Shot'
Community Video as Assemblage

Madhavi Manchi

Government regulation and censorship of different media and communication technologies is not new—either in India or around the world. One significant example from Indian history is the censorship of the press during the national Emergency declared in 1975 (Krishna Ananth, 2020). Similar examples from recent times include the shutting down of phone and Internet services at the sites of protest against the Citizenship Amendment Act (CAA) (Gettleman et al., 2019; Krishnani, 2019; Nazim, 2019) and the (ongoing) blackout of Internet services in Kashmir in 2019 (Schultz & Yasir, 2020; Zargar, 2020). Such regulation and censorship of media is an important reminder for why people's media and community media are vital tools in democracies. As pirate and community media initiatives (e.g., Radio Alice in Italy, Radio Hauraki in New Zealand) around the world have demonstrated, the very acts of using, creating and sharing media become significant forms of dissent in such contexts. They can capacitate us to question, shape and reconfigure relations of power.

Retaining the examples above as a 'background score', this chapter presents a 'non-media centric' or 'rhizomatic' approach to understanding community media (Carpentier, 2016; Santana & Carpentier, 2010).

Illustrated with an ethnographic account of a community video (CV) project in South India, the chapter, following Carpentier (2016, p. 5), describes how '...community media are part of fluid civil society networks, and how they are connected with other (non-media) civil society organisations and social movements'. In this case, the CV project is embedded within a broader biodiversity and gender justice movement.

The chapter starts with a methodological overview of the study, followed by an introduction to Deccan Development Society (DDS)— the organization running the CV project. Included in this section is a discussion of the organization's guiding principles and other outreach programmes. The second half of the chapter discusses the CV project, unpacking its rhizomatic connections and linkages to other actors, such as the state, market and allies interacting with it. It is argued that the CV project, in its interactions with other actors, works to reconfigure power dynamics along gender and caste axes. Further, the community strives to democratize media resources and question dominant and/or official conceptions of development.

METHODOLOGICAL NOTES

In relation to community media, Tacchi et al. (2009, p. 580) emphasize the need to 'pay close attention to local contexts and power dynamics' when introducing media technologies, for '...any introduction of new technologies and media will happen in richly layered social and political contexts, with or without intermediaries' (Tacchi et al., 2009, p. 580). Peeling these rich layers, as I have argued elsewhere (Manchi, 2014, 2015, 2020), requires a shift in emphasis from media content to media practices—its creation and consumption. Further, it requires us to approach media in a relational manner, mapping its linkages with other actors within an ecology. Santana and Carpentier's (2010) conception of 'media as rhizome' aids in such a mapping of linkages. It allows us to tease apart how media technologies, broadly, and CV, specifically, have the 'power to affect and be affected' (Spinoza cited in Massumi & McKim, 2009, p. 1).

Santana and Carpentier's conception of 'media as rhizome' is founded in philosophical works of Deleuze and Guattari, particularly

A Thousand Plateaus (2008). A rhizome is '...non-linear, anarchic and nomadic' (Santana & Carpentier, 2010, p. 164), and it '...connects any point to another point' (Deleuze & Guattari, 2008, p. 21). Santana and Carpentier (2010) also highlight three aspects of community media as a rhizome. These are: their '...role as at the crossroads of civil society, their elusiveness, and their interconnections and linkages with market and state'. (Santana & Carpentier, 2010, p. 164). Working at the 'crossroads of civil society', emphasize Santana and Carpentier (2010, p. 164), positions community media in catalytic roles, bringing together people from different movements and networks to collaborate, and potentially amplify their capacities (Ash, 2012). Further, community media share an ambiguous, grey relationship with both the market and the state. Their form and content often fit neither those of the state nor those of commercial media. Yet, their ability to forge connections across a fluid civil society gives them their elusive character (Santana & Carpentier, 2010, p. 164). Working in the margins allows community media to both critique and collaborate with state and market actors. This allows for community media to participate in 'cultures of insubordination' (Sundaram, 2007, p. 56) or be 'trans-hegemonic' (Santana & Carpentier, 2010, p. 165). This potential to be trans-hegemonic, as is argued in later sections, is vital to the mobilization of political affectivities within a social justice movement. This chapter draws on ethnographic data collected for my PhD fieldwork conducted in 2011–2012. These consist of interviews with key stakeholders of the Community Media Trust (CMT) and DDS, notes from participant observations and ethnographic field notes. These data are updated with the inclusion of latest literature and annual reports from the DDS website, an analysis of some documentary films created by the CV team and press coverage on the community media team. The next section provides a brief overview of DDS, the non-governmental organization (NGO) that helps run the community media projects illustrated here.

DECCAN DEVELOPMENT SOCIETY

DDS was started in 1983 as an NGO and is based in Medak district, Telangana. It working at grassroots level, the organization's efforts are guided by the three principles: 'gender justice, environmental soundness, and people's knowledge' (Deccan Development Society, 2020a). It works predominantly with female Dalit agriculturalists through a network of women's microcredit groups, locally called *sangams*,[1] spread over 75 villages. The community of women have been advocating the cause of agro-biodiversity through the cultivation of traditional crops of the region. Through the movement, the community works to achieve autonomies over five factors that they have determined as important to their community: food production, seeds, natural resources, market and media (Deccan Development Society, 2020f). Some of the programmes and schemes initiated to this end include: a community grain fund, community seed banks, a Krishi Vigyan Kendra (Farmers' Science Centre), *balwadies* (early childcare centres) and a *pachasaale* (Green School), village medicinal commons, an annual Mobile Biodiversity Festival (MBF), a cafe in Zaheerabad, which serves a millet-based cuisine, and CMT.

The community have built a strong critique of the dominant or official conception of 'development' (*vikas* in Hindi and *abhivrudhi* in Telugu) and taken a strong stance against such 'developmental' policies and practices, including the Indian Green Revolution, commercial monocropping and genetically modified organisms, among others. Further, the community is critical of using 'literacy' as one of prime indices to measure 'development'. As DDS director P. V. Satheesh (1999, p. 9) has remarked:

> Development groups working in rural areas suffer from a feeling of inadequacy if they are not pursuing literacy programmes. They [might] be doing excellent work [by] harnessing people's knowledge in the fields of forestry, fisheries, natural farming, land development, natural resource management whatever.... The irony is that in most of these

---

[1] The word *sangam* carries two meaning in this context. The first refers to the name given to village-level party units by the Community Party of India across the Nizam state of Hyderabad in the 1940s and 1950s. The second meaning of the word draws on the Dalit Bahujan movement's connection to the Buddhist movement of the 5th century BCE. This connotation, as Mookerjea (2010, 111) suggests, refers to the concept of an '...egalitarian and cooperative political community that was formed by the movement in the fifth century BCE'.

activities, literacy has very little to offer.... Time has come to question this exaggerated importance given to literacy in development. I would not like to be misunderstood as an anti-literacy person. I value literacy very much. What I am pointing to is [that] in valuing literacy we should not devalue other capabilities and skills present in non-literate people.

This idea lies at the heart of the community media projects of DDS. CV and community radio (CR) at DDS were set up in 1998 with help from the DDS board of directors and staff members. CR was set up through a United Nations Educational, Scientific and Cultural Organization (UNESCO)-supported programme called *Women Speak to Women* (Pavarala & Malik, 2007). They initially narrowcasted content, moving over to broadcasting in 2008. The DDS community inaugurated a Community Media Centre on 15 October 2001, which included facilities and equipment, such as dubbing booths, editing suits, rehearsal spaces, etc. On the same day, the radio and video team were merged into a single entity named CMT. The merger also bought the ownership of media facilities and the centre under the purview of CMT (Pavarala & Malik, 2007). A detailed overview of the CV at DDS is provided in the sections that follow.

COMMUNITY VIDEO AT DECCAN DEVELOPMENT SOCIETY

The CV team at DDS started with about 13 women, most of them non-literate. The DDS community views CVs as platforms of expression for people who lack representation in and access to mainstream media. CV helps transform people and communities into producers of media that focuses on their interests, rather than remaining consumers of elitist media that makes them invisible. Explaining why and how the initiative came about in an interview, a CMT member said:

> We had an important meeting that needed be to be recorded on video at the time. But the people who were supposed to come and shoot did not turn up that day. Then the DDS *karyakartas* (members) and senior staff opined that if our own people could shoot, they would not have to face a situation like this again. So, they decided that they would

hand-pick a team to train. This is more advantageous as it is our own people and within our reach and we are not dependent on others. (Interview with Manjula, November 2011)

In a CMT-produced film, *Sangam Shot* (Community Media Trust, 1999), the community discusses this further. One member describes literacy as an impediment to expression in media, such as newspapers. On the other land, creating videos is helpful, as one need not know how to write. Another person highlights the advantage of a video team comprising locals. Outsiders, unlike locals, are unable to build trust or rapport, especially with women in the community. Locals make it easier to create spaces for people to speak up freely. In the same vein, the CMT member observes that local video makers would not miss cultural nuances (e.g., word connotations lost in language translation), unlike outsiders. This insider 'know-how' would provide a more 'authentic' portrayal of an issue, in her opinion (Community Media Trust, 1999). An account of their lives and problems in images provides more validation and veracity as opposed to the written word.

In the same film (Community Media Trust, 1999), another *sangam* member speaks of the potential CV had in increasing community solidarity, providing awareness of *sangam* programmes and increasing *sangam* membership. Their videos have often informed viewers on how DDS *sangams* can work as support systems through challenging times, becoming tools for membership recruitment and enhancing camaraderie with non-members undergoing similar trials (Community Media Trust, 1999; Interview with Manjula, November 2011).

The films produced by the community also serve as an archive, preserving traditional knowledge in the forms of oral histories and folklore. The team has recorded many events held in the community, including weddings, meetings and festivals (Manchi, 2015). They have also documented speeches and visits of government officials and other significant guests, which have fed significantly into the community's larger biodiversity movement. (Community Media Trust, 1999; Interview with Manjula, November 2011). The team's path to gaining the skills and competency around making videos, however, was not an easy one. As stated earlier, introduction of media technologies into any context comes fraught with power relations, shifting existing ones and potentially introducing new ones. It was no different for the DDS's CV.

LEARNING TO WIELD THE CAMERA

The CV team were trained in video skills by the director of DDS and another male CMT personnel who had recently trained in video editing at the time (Manchi, 2015; Interview with Manjula, November 2011). The team would alternate between 4 days of training and practising their video skills through the remainder of the month. Some of the specific skills the team learnt included camcorder operation, framing of a shot for filming, camera angles and movements, basic sound recording skills and editing on a Video Home System (Deccan Development Society, 2020b). Familiarizing oneself with new technology was a challenge. When asked how she felt about seeing the film recorder for the first time, a CV team member, Manjula, remarks:

> We had never seen a camera before in our village. The first time I saw it was here, when I joined this DDS team. It is rare for us because we are people who work in the field, who do manual labour. We also never had cameras then. It was difficult getting even our photographs at that time. There used to be one person who would go around taking photos in those days. People would go to him to get their photos taken. As kids we would follow him around the village. (Interview with Manjula, November 2011)

She also recollects her first experience of shooting with the camera:

> It was around the time of the MBF that year. We had just finished our training and Sir [DDS director] asked us whether we wanted to make a film on it. We all got into an argument with each other over who would shoot first- because it was all so new and all so exciting. So, we made a film on the Biodiversity festival. It came out well in the end and we felt really happy. This is a hard task for people who are educated itself, so for us who aren't very highly educated, it was an achievement, and we were so happy about it. (Interview with Manjula, November 2011)

The team were taught the basics of film-making using methods and language known to them. In an almost Freirean sense (Downing, 2001, pp. 45–46), they renamed different camera shots using words from their local dialect and personal experiences (Deccan Development Society, 2020b). In his work *Pedagogy of the Oppressed* (1970), Freire rejected what he termed the *banking model* of education. In the banking model, learners were akin to empty bank accounts, who were then filled with knowledge by teachers. Instead, he emphasized that learners be taught using their own, everyday language and reject '…pre-packaged language and images pulled from the scholar's authoritative shelf' (cited in Downing, 2001, p. 45).

The above ethos is reflected in how the CV team learned camera techniques. For instance, the team used the term '*patel* shot' to describe the camera on a tripod, focused on a plane below eye level. To them it resembled the nearly daily (casteist) practice of a *patel* (or landlord) sitting on his seat, looking down upon a labourer (Community Media Trust, 1999; Manchi, 2015). Similarly, the shot taken with the camera placed below eye level, looking upward was called a '*gaidolla* shot', or slave shot. This name captured the angle's resemblance to a labourer sitting on the ground and looking up at the landlord (Community Media Trust, 1999; Manchi, 2015). A camera angle held at eye level was named a '*sangam* shot'. Team members viewed sangams as spaces of equality, with everyone placed at the same level, and hence the name '*sangam* shot' was chosen (Community Media Trust, 1999; Manchi, 2015).

The above nomenclature for camera angles underscores the deep-rooted caste dynamics of the community. The use of such a film grammar influences the way a shot is framed, in turn swaying and shifting a viewer's attention and perspective. Hence, using a *gaidolla* or 'slave' shot would draw the viewer's eye or attention from the ground level looking upwards. The viewer's perspective is superimposed atop the point of view of a Dalit labourer, opening up a window into their worldview. Similarly, a '*sangam* shot' draws the viewer's perspective to one's eye level, forcing them to look someone or something 'straight in the eye', and could potentially infuse a sense of equality or justice (Manchi, 2015).

It took the CV team a little under a year to complete their training (Interview with Manjula, November 2011). Today, they travel to countries around the world as resource persons, to share their film-making experiences, as well as train others in the skill. They have built connections and networks with organizations doing similar work around the world. Manjula sums this up:

> We've gone to many countries like South Africa, Indonesia, Australia, Denmark, Sri Lanka, Peru, London etc.... Peru is similar to us. They practise hill-side agriculture. They still do things by hand, like planting rice etc. The markets there are nice. In Peru we trained thirteen people in film making with the help of a PR person. We did the training by screening and using our film 'Sangam Shot' for reference. It was a nice. They made a short film in turn and sent it to us. (Interview with Manjula, November 2011)

The team's films have been featured at national and international film festivals and won awards (e.g., the 18th UGC-CEC award for Best Educational Video Film). In 2017, CMT conceived and hosted the Jai Chandiram Memorial Community Media Film Festival (CMFF). The festival showcased 22 CVs and films created by disadvantaged communities from across India (Deccan Development Society, 2017).

The CV team has made over 100 films to date, covering several issues important to their community. The content of DDS's CV films is drawn from their life experiences and includes topics related to biodiversity and development, such as: food sovereignty; genetic engineering in agriculture; control over natural resources; and gender and agriculture. For each film created, community members are invited to share their experiences and stories. The stories arise from the community for production and go back to it for consumption:

> We basically focus on the farmers of our region. We keep track of what farmers are doing each season, what are the challenges they are facing. These come from stories in our own villages and some stories in the newspapers. Out team sits down, discusses and decides what issues we want to make into a film. For example, we've made a film on how Bt cotton has had adverse effects on farmers. This way we've made films on various issues. We recently finished a film comparing the crops grown in our villages by sangam members and non-sangam member. (Interview with Manjula, November 2011)

Another CV film, *Community Conquers Hunger* (2011), looks at the efforts of Dalit Bahujan farmers to reduce hunger and achieve food security for villages through *sangam* participation and traditional sub-sistence agriculture. *People's Agenda for Biodiversity* (2005) is a coverage of the DDS Mobile Biodiversity Festival, describing the genesis and growth of the festival spanning a decade.

Inspired by the work of the CV team, young people in the community have also taken to film-making. For example, Mayuri, the niece of a CMT member, was 11 years old when she started dabbling with video, learning to use both the camcorder and still camera (Manchi, 2015). In one short film, *Naa Chenu Naa Chaduvu* (My Farm, My Studies) (2010), Mayuri profiles some traditional agricultural practices and crops when visiting her grandparents' farm. Such knowledge she says is not taught as part of mainstream school education. In a second film, *Dhanwarlo O'Avva* (A Grandmother in Dhanwar) (2010), Mayuri documents the traditional crops and farming techniques of an 80-year-old woman in Dhanwar, Medak, who uses subsistence farming, with little dependence on the market for food. Mayuri concludes that if everyone was to adopt similar agricultural practices, it would increase food security and sovereignty. Mayuri's films have been well appreciated around the world and continue to be screened at various film festivals (Manchi, 2015; NDTV, 2012).

In summary, the CV team at DDS has grown from strength to strength—from learning to operate the camera to curating a national film festival. This positions them as a crucial node within the larger biodiversity movement the community advocates for, creating local and international linkages and playing a 'catalytic role' (Santana & Carpentier, 2010, p. 164) within the movement. These arguments are elaborated in the next sections.

NODES AS THE CROSSROADS

Picking up on the features of rhizomatic media outlined by Santana and Carpentier (2010), in this section, I outline how CV works to questions and reconfigure power relations at local and trans-local levels. At the local level, consider, for example, the caste and gender relations in the community. The biodiversity movement of the DDS *sangams*, as mentioned at the beginning, is also an anti-caste, gender justice movement. *Sangam* members are predominantly women from the Dalit Bahujan communities across Medak district. Many DDS initiatives have been designed to redress caste and gender justice, including community media. DDS members have expressed how participating in DDS programmes have helped question and shift unequal caste dynamics.[2] In an interview with the Delhi Newsline, Laxmamma, a CV member, says:

> We were earlier made to wait outside the house of the *patel* (landlord), but now he even asks me to come inside his puja [prayer] room for filming the rituals.... (Srivastava, 2005)

For Dalits, especially women, who are to date beaten and publicly humiliated for entering Hindu temples,[3] to be 'allowed' to enter an 'upper'-caste person's prayer room is a significant step in reconfiguring local caste and gender hierarchies. This does not mean that caste has been eradicated from the community overnight. However, Laxmamma's example speaks to the affect participating in initiatives like CV can have on personal agency and capacities, and in turn on social change (see Singh et al., 2017).

Another example of how CV builds local connections and political mobility is through the DDS Mobile Biodiversity Festival. The festival falls on the same day as Sankranti, a Hindu harvest festival. Starting on Sankranti day, a colourful *jatra*, or caravan of bullock carts, decorated with traditional seeds crops, travels to each of the 75 villages of the DDS community. Each village organizes public meetings, symposia, food festivals and screenings of CVs when the *jatra* visits. Such public film screenings of CV are potentially centrifugal, evoking collective

---

[2] An example of this are the village seed banks started by Deccan Development Society (DDS) *sangams*. Traditionally, it was the upper-caste *patels* or landlords who would collect seeds from each harvest. Villagers would need to approach them for seeds each season. The DDS seed banks were started to revive endangered traditional crops, especially millets. Today, it is Dalit women who run the seed banks, with many upper-caste farmers approaching them for seeds (see also Manchi, 2015).

[3] See, for example, this news article from *The Wire* (Shantha, 2019).

memories, provoking conversation and rallying members around the justice movement advocated by the community.[4]

In characterizing alternative or, in this case, community media as working at the crossroads, Santana and Carpentier (2010, p. 164) remark that efforts like CV can '…remain grounded in local communities and become simultaneously engaged in translocal networks'. I would argue that much of how DDS's CV works is rhizomatic in this sense. A good illustration is DDS's campaign and films opposing the cultivation of Bt cotton[5] in India. The *sangam* network under the DDS banner has mounted a severe critique of Bt cotton since its introduction in the region in 2002. In particular, the films the CV team produced on the topic, in collaboration with other international organizations opposing Bt cotton, are noteworthy here.

The DDS CV team produced three films following the stories of how Bt cotton cultivation has adversely impacted farmers in Telangana and around the world.[6] The first film, *Why are Warangal Farmers Angry with Bt Cotton* (2003), was released in 2003. The film is described as presenting the '…story of four farmers and the roller coaster experiences of others like them…' (Deccan Development Society, 2020c), including the losses they suffered when they cultivated Bt cotton. The CV team writes of their experience shooting the film:

> …[they] returned tenaciously to Warangal…sought out their focus farmers, cajoled them to share their information and opinion to be able to, come up with an absorbing film. (Deccan Development Society, 2020c)

---

[4] For an historical overview of the close links between documentary films and social justice movements in India, see Jayasankar and Monteiro (2016, pp. 17–68).

[5] Bt cotton is a transgenic or genetically modified variety of cotton, claimed to be more pest-resistant. It was introduced in southern India states, including Telangana and Andhra Pradesh, in 2002. The cotton variety was sold largely through a partnership between state governments and the Monsanto Company. Monsanto was acquired by Bayer AG in 2018.

[6] At the time of producing the films on Bt cotton, Telangana was still a part of the state of Andhra Pradesh. The two states were officially bifurcated in 2014 with the passing of the Andhra Pradesh Reorganisation Act 2014.

The second film, *Bt Cotton in Andhra Pradesh: A Three-Year Fraud* (2005), works as a compliment to a research report produced by DDS in collaboration with Andhra Pradesh Coalition in Defence of Diversity (Deccan Development Society, 2020d). The film continues to document the devastating losses incurred by Bt cotton farmers. The third film, *Disaster in Search of Success: Bt Cotton in Global South* (2006), completes the trilogy on Bt cotton. For this film, the CV team travelled to and documented stories of the degradation brought on through Bt cotton cultivation across the world. They spoke to farmers in the countries like South Africa, Thailand, Indonesia, Mali and India (Deccan Development Society, 2020e).

The films on Bt cotton present poignant narratives on the plight of cotton farmers in India and around the world. However, for the purposes of this chapter, I want to unpack how these stories travel across DDS networks and potentially mobilize political affectivities. The use of 'affect' or 'affectivities' in these instances is informed by the oeuvre of Deleuze and Guattari (2008). Ash's (2010, p. 657) succinct definition of 'affect' is useful here. He describes 'affect' as '…an outcome of an encounter between two or more bodies (which can be human or non-human, organic or inorganic), which either increases or decreases a body's capacity for action'.

Speaking of the films in a press interview, Manjula remarks:

We screened our film about Bt Cotton at a public meeting, it helped us make our point much more strongly. Otherwise we would talk about our experiences and it would not make such an impact, but this way we had documented it and even the Government had to listen. (*The Hindu*, 2005)

The film screening provoked conversation in public spaces and with government actors. Further, both *Why are Warangal Farmers Angry with Bt Cotton* (2003) and *Bt Cotton in Andhra Pradesh: A Three-Year Fraud* (2005) have been translated into various languages, including '…English, French, Spanish, Swahili, Thai and Bahasa Indonesia' (Deccan Development Society, 2020e: no pagination). The CV team claim that the films, in their translated versions, are '…being used by environmental groups all over the world' (Deccan Development Society, 2020e) to further their respective causes.

These stories, which might have been lost in the white noise of the mainstream mediascape, have travelled via public screenings, translation and collaborations with environmental organizations, amplifying the message *and* the cause of the community. This speaks of the affective dimensions (Ash, 2010; Deleuze & Guattari, 2008) of the film screenings and how they could capacitate action. In viewing DDS's CV as rhizomatic, we can map how stories and political affectivities traverse boundaries. They become, as Carpentier (2016, p. 5) states, '…part of fluid civil society networks…' and are '…connected with other (non-media) civil society organisations and social movements'.

TRANS-HEGEMONIC TENDENCIES

Rhizomatic media are also characterized as being 'trans-hegemonic' (Santana & Carpentier, 2010, p. 164) or participating in 'cultures of insubordination' (Sundaram, 2007). Community media can build relationships and links with some part of the state and the market '…without losing their proper identity and becoming incorporated and/or assimilated. These more complex and contingent positions bring them sometimes to violently critique hegemony and in other cases to playfully use and abuse the dominant order' (Santana & Carpentier, 2010, p. 165). Several community media organizations around the world tend to share such an uneasy relationship with the state and the market and thus operate in the margins. This means that, on the one hand, community media can create content that is firmly rooted in community and serves its community consumers. At DDS, the films such as *Community Conquers Hunger* (2011) and *Naa Chenu Naa Chaduvu* (2010, My Farm, My Studies) described in earlier sections, are good illustrations.

On the other hand, rhizomatic media collaborate with state and market actors to produce and/or distribute content. This is true of DDS's CMT as well. For instance, DDS's CV team has tied up with Doordarshan (India's state-sponsored television channel) and Eenadu Television, a commercial Telugu-language channel. Such collaborations allow periodic broadcasting of the DDS CV films and have allowed the CV team to access a broader audience base. However, these are neither easy nor straightforward relationships, especially when community media hold critical views of their collaborators. For example, on one occasion, CMT at DDS refused to share its archives of folk songs recorded for its CR content. Eenadu Television had requested DDS' Sangam Radio to share folk songs from their archives. This request was vehemently protested by the community. The television channel wanted to use the archival material as content for a series that would showcase folk songs and artists. The community was steadfast in its protest, disallowing the co-opting of cultural and traditional knowledge and artefacts that had taken years to build (Interview with Algole Narsamma, September 2012).

These tenuous linkages between DDS's CV, the state and the market are not, as Santana and Carpentier (2010, p. 165) argue, 'counter-hegemonic' but are 'trans-hegemonic' (Santana & Carpentier, 2020, p. 165). That is, relationships between community media, the state and the market cannot be categorized as purely oppositional or counter-poised. As Santana and Carpentier (2010, p. 165) point out, they '…do not operate completely outside the market and/or state, thus softening the antagonistic relationship (as being an alternative to the mainstream) toward the market and state'. These are, rather, 'trans-hegemonic', because community media '…establish different types of relationships with the market and/or state, often for reasons of survival…'. In fact, it gives community media a de-territorializing tendency, breaking open '…rigidities and certainties of public and market media organisa-tions' (Santana & Carpentier, 2010, p. 165). The amorphous nature of community media allows for firmly established norms and practices of mainstream or state-sponsored media—sedimented over time—to be loosened and reconfigured in their interactions.

These trans-hegemonic tendencies can also be called 'cultures of insubordination' (Sundaram, 2007). Ito (2007, p. 105) remarks that such practices:

> …produce alternative cultural forms that are disseminated through
> everyday peer-to-peer exchanges below the radar of commodity

capitalism; they are a mode of cultural production that does not over-throw capitalism but operates in its shadow...that both rely on and disrupt the dominant mode.

These 'cultures of insubordination' (Ito, 2007; Sundaram, 2007) then do not always overtly work to dismantle dominant systems. Instead, they work to gradually and silently chip away at the borders and peripheries of commercially structured parts of industries, like agriculture and media. Working in the margins, and through myriad links, CV can help imagine and possibly actuate alternatives to dominant narratives and systems—a much-needed impulse for the current times in our democracy.

CONCLUSION

This chapter extends Santana and Carpentier's (2010) conception of alternative media as a rhizome to the case of CV. This view of CV as a rhizome facilitates a cartography of connections, highlighting linkages between CV, civil society, the market and the state. Importantly, this rhizomatic quality helps forge connections and collaborations where there might be weak ones or none at all. It helps mobilize political affectivities within social movements. At DDS, the CV initiative is integral to, and draws on, the biodiversity movement, the lives of its 'ProdUsers' (Jayasankar & Monteiro, 2015, p. 226) and the collective memories of the community. CV content is often based on these various facets of a community's life. Similarly, the folklore, songs and stories populate the community's film content and archives. As demonstrated in the chapter, the films produced through CV inform and initiate debates on current concerns, and they also provide engagement with the community's traditional folklore and songs in a continuous manner. As Larkin (2007, p. 78) points out, '...such [rhizomatic] media technologies and other infrastructures (re)organise our sensory perception, create and sustain conditions of everyday living, as well as give rise to new forms of affectivities and leisure'.

Such rhizomes are often viewed, as Goddard writes (2013, p. 50), as 'a cause for the panic on part of the order of social forces', because they can mobilize a 'massive and unpredictable political affectivity and subjectivity' (Goddard, 2013, p. 50). Such mobilizations can become a contagion. In a milieu where spaces of civic and public engagement and dissent are increasingly being controlled (as in the crackdown against anti-CAA protests), shut down or hollowed out (as in the case of Kashmir's Internet blackout), such contagion is an urgent requirement. We are already seeing parts of this in India, where poems recited at anti-CAA protests go viral and later are picked up by popular news outlets and broadcast.[7] In these times, we need, like the CV at DDS, rhizomes that capacitate subversions, interventions and, most importantly, hope!

REFERENCES

Ash, J. (2010). Architectures of affect: Anticipating and manipulating the event in processes of videogame design and testing. *Environment and Planning D: Society and Space, 28*, 653–671.

Ash, J. (2012). Attention, videogames, and the retentional economies of affective amplification. *Theory, Culture, and Society, 29*(6), 3–26. http://tcs.sagepub.com/content/29/6/3

Aziz, A. (2020). *Sab yaad rakha jaayega*. https://www.youtube.com/watch?v=PHk_5gEXDY0

Carpentier, N. (2016). Community media as rhizome: Expanding the research agenda. *Journal of Alternative and Community Media, 1*, 4–6.

Community Media Trust. (1999). *Sangam shot* (DVD). Deccan Development Society.

Community Media Trust. (2003). *Why are Warangal farmers angry with Bt cotton?* (DVD). Deccan Development Society.

Community Media Trust. (2005). *Bt Cotton in Andhra Pradesh: A three-year fraud* (DVD). Deccan Development Society.

Community Media Trust. (2005). *A disaster in search of success* (DVD). Deccan Development Society.

Community Media Trust. (2010). *Dhanwarlo O'Avva* (DVD). Deccan Development Society.

---

[7] An example of this is how the poem *Sab yaad rakha jaayega* (Everything will be remembered) by Amir Aziz (2020) has become viral in the context of the anti-CAA protests. Penned as a commentary on the violence unleashed against anti-CAA protestors, different versions of the poem were picked up and circulated by popular news media such as *The Quint* (2020a) and Kundu (2020). An English translation of the poem gained new relevance when Roger Waters, the lead singer of the band Pink Floyd, recited it at a separate protest in London (*The Quint*, 2020b).

Community Media Trust. (2010). *Naa Chenu Naa Chaduvu* (DVD). Deccan Development Society.

Community Media Trust. (2011). *Community conquers hunger* (DVD). Deccan Development Society.

Deccan Development Society. (2017). *Community media trust-film festival brochure.* http://www.ddsindia.com/www/pdf/CMT%20FF%20Brochure%202017.pdf

Deccan Development Society. (2020a). *DDS team.* http://www.ddsindia.com/www/ddsteam.htm

Deccan Development Society. (2020b). *An alternative to literacy.* http://www.ddsindia.com/www/video.htm

Deccan Development Society. (2020c). *Why are Warangal farmers angry with Bt Cotton?* http://www.ddsindia.com/www/Why%20are%20Warangal%20Farmers%20Angry%20with%20Bt%20Cotton.htm

Deccan Development Society. (2020d). *Bt Cotton in Andhra Pradesh: A three-year fraud.* http://www.ddsindia.com/www/three%20year%20fraud.html

Deccan Development Society. (2020e). *Activities: Women's media.* http://www.ddsindia.com/www/CMTawards07.htm

Deccan Development Society. (2020f). *About us.* http://www.ddsindia.com/www/aboutus.htm

Deleuze, G., & Guattari, F. (2008). *A thousand plateaus capitalism and schizophrenia* (trans. Massumi B). Continuum.

Downing, J. D. (2000). *Radical media: Rebellious communication and social movements.* SAGE Publications.

Gettleman, J., Goel, V., & Abi-Habib, M. (2019, December 17). India adopts the tactic of authoritarians: Shutting down the internet. *The New York Times.* https://www.nytimes.com/2019/12/17/world/asia/india-internet-modi-protests.html

Goddard, M. (2013). Felix and Alice in Wonderland: The encounter between Guattari and Berardi and the Post-Media Era. In C. Apprich (Eds.), *Provocative alloys: A Post-Media anthology* (pp. 44–61). Mute Books.

Ito, M. (2007). Technologies of the childhood imagination: Yu-Gi-Oh! media mixes, and everyday cultural production. In J. Karaganis (Ed.), *Structures of participation in digital cultures* (pp. 88–110). Social Science Research Council.

Jayasankar, K. P., & Monteiro, A. (2015). *A fly in the curry: Independent documentary film in India.* SAGE Publications.

Krishna Ananth, V. (2020, June 25). India's free press is still tormented by the laws brought by the emergency. *The Wire.* https://thewire.in/history/emergency-free-press

Krishnani, R. (2019, December 14). India: The world leader in internet shutdowns. *CNN.* https://edition.cnn.com/2019/12/14/opinions/india-world-leader-in-internet-shutdowns/index.html

Kundu, S. (2020, March 9). Who is 'Sab Yaad Rakha Jaayega' poet Aamir Aziz? *Deccan Herald.* https://www.deccanherald.com/national/who-is-sab-yaad-rakha-jayega-poet-aamir-aziz-812043.html

Larkin, B. (2007). Pirate infrastructures. In J. Karaganis (Ed.), *Structures of participation in digital cultures* (pp. 74–84). Social Science Research Council.

Manchi, M. (2014). Community radio and collective memory: A mapping of material media practices at a Community Radio Station in Telangana. *SubVersions: A Journal of Emerging Research in Media and Cultural Studies, 2*(2), 53–100. http://subversions.tiss.edu/wp-content/uploads/2018/03/SubVersions-Vol2-Issue2-Madhavi.pdf

Manchi, M. (2015). *Memory, media and biodiversity: A non-representational approach* (Doctoral Dissertation, Unpublished). Tata Institute of Social Sciences.

Manchi, M. (2020). Mapping material media practices: Sangam radio at DDS. In K. Malik & V. Pavarala (Eds.), *Community radio in South Asia* (pp. 232–252). Routledge.

Massumi, B., & McKim, J. (2009). Of microperception and micropolitics: An interview with Brian Massumi. *Inflexions: A Journal for Research-Creation, 3*, 1–20.

Mookerjea, S. (2010). The Sangam strategy: Lessons for a cooperative mode of production. *Affinities: A Journal of Radical Theory, Culture and Action, 4*(1), 110–132.

Nazim, S. (2019, December 19). Why India shuts down the internet more than any other democracy. *BBC News.* https://www.bbc.com/news/world-asia-india-50819905

NDTV. (2012, October 10). *11-year-old girl from poor Dalit family gains international acclaim as filmmaker.* http://www.ndtv.com/video/player/news/11-year-old-girl-from-poor-dalit-family-gains-international-acclaim-as-filmmaker/250335

Pavarala, V., & Malik, K. K. (2007). *Other voices.* SAGE Publications.

Community Media Trust. (2005). *People's agenda for biodiversity* (DVD). Deccan Development Society.

Santana, M., & Carpentier, N. (2010). Mapping the rhizome. Organizational and informational networks of two Brussels alternative radio stations. *Telematics and Informatics, 27*(2), 162–176.

Satheesh, P. V. (1999). An alternative to literacy? *Forests, Trees and People Newsletter, 40*(41), 9–13.

Schultz, K., & Yasir, S. (2020, January 26). India restores some internet access in Kashmir after long shutdown. *The New York Times.* https://www.nytimes.com/2020/01/26/world/asia/kashmir-internet-shutdown-india.html

Shantha, S. (2019, June 19). Wardha: Caste Hindu strips Dalit boy, forces him to sit on hot tiles for entering temple. *The Wire.* https://thewire.in/caste/wardha-caste-hindu-dalit-boy-strip-entering-temple

Singh, N., High, C., Lane, A., Oreszczyn, S. (2017). Building agency through participatory video: Insights from the experiences of young women participants in India. *Gender, Technology and Development, 21*(3), 173–188.

Srivastava, P. (2005, March 9). Camera breaks caste barrier. *Delhi Newsline.* http://www.ddsindia.com/www/IAWRT.htm

Sundaram, R. (2007). Other networks: Media urbanism and the culture of the copy in South Asia. In J. Karaganis (Ed.), *Structures of participation in digital cultures* (pp. 48–72). Social Science Research Council.

Tacchi, J., Watkins, J., & Keerthirathne, K. (2009). Participatory content creation: Voice, communication, and development. *Development in Practice, 19*(4–5), 573–584. http://dx.doi.org/10.1080/09614520902866389

The Hindu. (2005, March 9). *Real women using the power of reel.* http://www.ddsindia.com/www/IAWRT.htm

The Quint. (2020a, February 19). *Dear oppressors, Sab Yaad Rakha Jayega. Sab Kuch Yaad Rakha Jayega.* https://www.youtube.com/watch?v=Qw9DRguBqRs

The Quint. (2020b, February 27). *Pink Floyd's Roger waters recites Aziz's 'Sab Yaad Rakha Jayega'.* https://www.thequint.com/entertainment/celebrities/roger-waters-recites-aamir-aziz-hum-sab-yaad-rakha-jayega-at-london-protest-march

Zargar, A. R. (2020, January 15). The longest internet blackout ever imposed in a democratic nation is easing, slowly. *CBS News.* https://www.cbsnews.com/news/india-kashmir-longest-internet-blackout-ever-democratic-nation-eases-slowly-but-not-over-today-2020-01-15/

Chapter 7

The Disability and Film-making Community in Film Practice-As-Research
The Case of *We Make Film*

Shweta Ghosh

Art has always been a universal necessity. What it has not been is an option for all, under equal conditions.

—Julio Garcia Espinosa, *For an Imperfect Cinema* (1979)

WE MAKE FILM: A BRIEF INTRODUCTION

In an era of burgeoning digital video and Internet access, anyone who wants to make a film should be able to make one. However, the nature of access and creative expression can be severely restricted, particularly for historically marginalized communities, such as people with disabilities (PwDs). In the Indian context, much is left to be done to ensure the complete participation of PwDs as creative contributors to the ever-growing media and film industry, given the barriers such as negative cultural attitudes, inaccessible spaces, education and technology.

The fact that a person with disability (PwD) has the same right as a non-disabled person to aspire for creative opportunities and expression through film may seem like a rather basic assertion. However, it is an important one that needs to be made, given the current context of regressive terminology[1] and a culturally widespread approach in the country of treating PwDs as 'different' or 'abnormal'. PwDs are still seen as the 'other'—pitiable or heroic—but rarely as complex people with dreams, aspirations or emotions. In the case of on-screen representation, these stereotypical narratives continue to exist, albeit reinvented today with more polished production values. The 'ordinary lives' of PwDs rarely find space in news media, online content, television or commercial cinema.

My PhD practice-as-research project *We Make Film* explores the interaction of disability, film-making and creative expression, to understand and support the work of film-makers and video makers with disabilities (FwDs) in contemporary urban India. It aims to develop a space for dialogue among creative film practitioners across abilities but focuses particularly on the narratives of d/Deaf[2] and disabled[3] film-makers as they share their creative journeys, barriers to creative expression and their negotiation with these barriers. The research also

---

[1] The problematic term *divyang* (*divya* + *ang*, meaning 'divine body') was introduced by Narendra Modi, Prime Minister of India (2014–present), in his radio show *Mann ki Baat* in 2015 (https://www.youtube.com/watch?v=M0yTlInxoNw) as a new way to address people with disabilities. This nomenclature was adopted without consulting with the wider disability community (and to this date, it is rejected for its connotation of disabled people as 'superhuman'). Yet, it was adopted as the official nomenclature by several government bodies.

[2] 'Deaf': a person who identifies with Deaf culture, values and identity and sign language; 'deaf': a person who does not hear as a result of hearing impairment and may prefer to use spoken language.

[3] There is much debate about whether it is more appropriate to use person-first language (persons/people with disabilities) or 'Deaf' and 'disabled' (which draws from the social model that states that it is society that disables and not merely impairments that do so). While I primarily use the official terminology used in the United Nations Convention on the Rights of Persons with Disabilities and the Rights of Persons with Disabilities Act, 2016 (i.e., people with disabilities [PwDs]), there are places where I use the terms 'Deaf' and 'disabled', particularly for film-makers and film-making communities that identify as being part of Deaf culture.

aims to connect practising FwDs with aspiring FwDs, as well as non-disabled film-makers in the future, to create a pool of academics and practitioners committed to disability diversity within film-making. In the process, the project also encourages non-disabled/hearing film-makers to engage with d/Deaf and disabled film-makers, reflect on their able-bodied privilege and access and develop thoughtful allyship and collaboration across the film-making community.

A research that focuses so heavily on themes of identity and 'community' is bound to bring up thorny problems with defining the same. How does a community define itself, given the multifaceted nature of identity? How does one understand barriers and negotiations that are specific to the d/Deaf or disability community within the film-making community? And does everyone *want* to be a part of the wider film-making community in the same way?

In this piece, I discuss the above questions and themes, through my reflections on the *We Make Film* research and film process. I explore how the intersectional approach (Crenshaw, 1989) can help understand disability and d/Deaf identity and community in deeper ways and how this can then help identify barriers facing FwDs which are specific to the d/Deaf and disability community. I also explore how an engagement with multiple identities (by the film-maker participants, researcher and crew) can provide common starting points of access 'into' each other's communities and build solidarity across film-making approaches and practices.

DEVELOPING A METHODOLOGY BASED ON PARTICIPANT AGENCY AND COLLABORATION

To build the methodology of this research, I drew from methods in film studies (i.e., film close analysis), visual ethnography (i.e., visual elicitation and creative interviewing) and reflexive documentary practice. I initiated four creative workshops with d/Deaf and blind film-maker participants between March and May 2018, to work on a short film script that reflects their own experience of film-making, creative expression and disability or d/Deaf identity. The research adopted a case study approach, and I worked with those who were available and willing to participate, given the constraints of time and budget; film-maker participants comprised three individuals (AS, DG and MJ) and one group of film-maker participants (RH Films) across four cities in India, whose details are as below:

- AS from Virar, Maharashtra (reported to be Maharashtra's first blind woman trained in mass communications and journalism);
- RH Films from Dombivli, Maharashtra (a Deaf theatre and film group[4]);
- DG from Kolkata, West Bengal (a deaf animator from National Institute of Design, currently an Animation Specialist at Tata Consultancy Services [TCS]); and
- MJ from Irinjalakuda, Kerala (a self-taught Deaf film-maker who has won several awards at the India International Deaf Film Festival).

Individual workshops lasted 5 days and group workshops lasted 2 days, and they included visual elicitation based on film-maker participants' previous films, unstructured in-depth interviews and a short-film scriptwriting exercise. The film-maker participants' short film scripts were expected to develop based on discussions on their aesthetic approach and content-related choices and reflect experiences of being d/Deaf or disabled film-makers. Unstructured creative interviews were interspersed through the 5-day period, to understand film-maker participants' social, economic and educational contexts, film-making aspirations, formal film training and access to opportunities and technology. The script workshops with each of the film-maker participants were filmed to build the content for my own thesis film *We Make Film*, a reflexive, participatory documentary. A brief breakdown of the workshop format is as follows.

- *Days 1–2—Visual elicitation*[5]: Clips from films previously made by film-maker participants, as well as some clips from renowned films

---

[4] Inspired by the work of another Mumbai-based Deaf film-making company: Deaf Entertainment.

[5] This method made space for the participant to decide their own course of action or explanation and discuss a familiar product and/or process in detail. It also

on Deaf/disability issues, were selected for viewing and discussion on days 1 and 2 to address specific questions regarding film form and content, to know in-depth about the film-making experience and choices behind the sequence/s and to understand the film-maker participants' views on on-screen representations of disability. The film-maker participants were also encouraged to share films they found relevant, and extra-textual elements, such as shooting scripts, intentions and research notes to explain their process.

- *Days 2–4—Film-making exercise*[6]: This included the writing of an audiovisual treatment note and development of a shooting script and/or storyboard for a 5-minute audiovisual project: a documentary, fiction (or both), animation or any other creative audiovisual project, based on the participant's expertise or interest. The film-maker participants' film projects were not necessarily expected to be autobiographical or even relating directly to disability (this is discussed in detail in Section IV) but rather ways to bring out experiences important to them with respect to creative expression and film-making. The film projects could also be a way to explore unique visual and/or sound choices and narrative structures, or discuss broader issues important to the film-maker participants.
- *Day 5—Wrapping up, feedback and future planning*: On the last day of the workshop, the film-maker participants were invited to narrate their script and audiovisual treatment on camera, shown relevant parts of the footage taken over the week and invited to provide feedback.

The title of the research and film project 'We Make Film' refers to both the collaborative methodology, where the researcher and the film-maker participants *make* a film or script, and a larger assertion by film-makers with disabilities—that they *can and do* make films. The focus on reflexivity in the methodology recognizes that both the

---

encouraged the film-maker participants to reflect on their aesthetic choices and politics, so that this could inform the film-making exercise undertaken during days 2–4.

[6] This step was also intended to add positively to the film-makers' body of work and career; the idea, script and/or storyboard developed could be used in the future as a starting point to pitch or make a new short film.

'researcher' and the 'researched' are thinking individuals, negotiating constantly with their identities and contexts. The collaborative workshops thus draw upon participatory ethnographic methods, to allow engagement with film-maker participants as 'active agents of knowledge building' rather than passive 'objects of inquiry' (Pauwels, 2013). Each person within the research scenario has juggled roles as film-maker/researcher, crew member/research associate and subject/film-maker participant. It is a research about film-makers, by film-makers, which draws upon the technical expertise and creativity of both. It is therefore crucial to identify the collaborative relationships that were at work during the research and filming process, to understand in depth how the idea of community was understood and consolidated further.

The first level of collaboration and participation was with the film-maker participants during the workshop and for my thesis documentary. While the larger workshop flow was designed by me, it was adapted and shaped to a very large extent by the film-maker participants themselves, in a way that represented their specific contexts. The film-maker participants brought their own ideas and topics to discuss throughout the workshop, and the aim was to establish as equal an exchange as possible through the workshop, where the researcher–film-maker and the crew members were also asked questions about their practice, creative journeys and intentions for this project.

The second level of collaboration was within the filming process, with two crew members and two interpreters (one each for RH Films in Mumbai and MJ in Kerala). Among the core crew were Priyanka Pal (assistant director and additional sound), a disabled female film-maker, and Sumit Singh (sound recordist and additional cameraperson), a non-disabled male film-maker. Both crew members brought in their own expertise and insights on documentary and accessible film-making, participatory and community-based research and their field-based experience with disability and Deaf culture. The engagement of this mixed crew with the film-maker participants made for very rich interactions, and a self-reflexive approach proved significant in fostering relationships and exchanges between the film-maker participants, the crew and myself during the process.

DISABILITY WORLDS[7]

My sister and I grew up with conversations around disability at home. Not only is my father a person with a physical disability, but my parents also brought in conversations on disability rights via their social development work throughout our childhood. My knowledge of disability and the rights-based approach came from these conversations and the experience of living with my father, but I truly began to think of the intersections of disability and film-making practice during the making of my debut film, *Accsex*.

In 2013, when looking for crew members for my film on gender, disability and sexuality, I had consciously looked to build an all-woman crew. We were to discuss sensitive and private issues of gender and sexual expression and sexuality, and I wanted my film subjects to be as comfortable as possible. It wasn't until I worked with my friend Natasha (a deaf illustrator who was also featured in the film) for some illustrated sequences that it struck me that I had not looked for Deaf and disabled women film-makers for my crew. My family experience of disability had given me access to some aspects of disability, thereby making me part of the extended community, but mine neither was actual lived experience nor covered the vast range of disability experiences; there was still a long way to go to recognize my own able-bodied privilege and access.

It is not uncommon for able-bodied kin of disabled family members to be actively involved in disability rights advocacy (Ginsburg & Rapp, 2001), but there is always the danger that they end up speaking on behalf of (or sometimes over) their own family members or other disabled people, explaining their own lived experiences to them. Even those of us who have been largely understanding or 'well-read' allies to our disabled friends and family members can often fail to recognize and support their rights, and this can, of course, also hold true for non-disabled people who work 'to champion' the rights of disabled people. My own experience of disability at home, professional interest

---

[7] This title is borrowed from an article of the same name authored by Rapp and Ginsburg (2013).

in disability and experience as a film-maker were good starting points for conversation. Participants also understood my motivations for this research more clearly when they learned that my father is a person with disability and that my family and I had assisted him at several points to make the images he wanted to make (although this did not always come up in conversation with each participant). My levels of access to the community therefore were determined primarily by the level of my involvement in and knowledge of disability experiences.

It was therefore crucial that the slogan 'nothing about us, without us'[8] informed my approach while working with the Deaf and disability community. For *We Make Film*, the idea was to focus on disabled and d/Deaf film-maker participants' stories within the workshop process and make space for reflection by non-disabled film-makers vis-à-vis FwDs' experiences (as opposed to the other way round). And it was assistant director Priyanka Pal's collaboration on this research as a crew member that became crucial in building trust between the non-disabled and disabled participants and crew members. Pal's experience of disability and creative film and design practice, as well as her previous work experience with some Deaf communities in India, helped consolidate our own understanding of the practical challenges and benefits of working together as a mixed (disabled/non-disabled) crew. In some ways, it also had an impact on film-maker participants' perception of my intentions as a researcher: Some film-maker participants shared at the end of their workshop that my choice to have Pal on board for this project reflected the genuineness of my motives to 'walk the talk' and support the careers of FwDs. They also felt encouraged to open up and share their stories when Pal cited personal examples from her experience as a disabled film-maker. Where there were gaps in my knowledge, the methodology helped build a collaborative atmosphere where film-maker participants (and Pal, as a crew member) asked me questions or 'called me in' (Ross, 2019) to build my understanding of experiences of d/Deaf and disabled people.

At the same time, it is important to note that membership of the disability/Deaf community by virtue of lived experience may not

---

[8] This slogan became significant in the disability rights movement in the 1990s (Masutha, Rowland, Charlton, and others).

guarantee a parallel political understanding of the community's rights and experiences. PwDs can portray other PwDs just as problematically and can function creatively in both positions in mainstream media—'as contributors to and creators of equally problematic disabled imagery/ stories, or as "cultural revisionists" offering new media perspectives on disability' (Ellis, 2016, p. 113). There are also hierarchies built within the disability community based on other identities and privileges, and members may view someone with another disability as the 'other', take up too much space and refuse to 'pass on the mic'.[9]

An intersectional approach helps understand the various layers of oppression and privilege within the disability and Deaf community and how they may enhance or reduce access to the film-making community. For example, a cis upper-caste, upper-class male film-maker who has a leg amputation and uses a prosthetic leg would face some mobility challenges, but this may be mediated by his ability to afford car travel. It is also possible that the privileges granted by his presentation as a cis man allow him to navigate barriers within the film-making field more easily than a Deaf non-binary film-maker who prefers to use sign language and may not face physical mobility issues but may be subjected to double marginalization owing to their identification with a gender and linguistic minority.

To give an example from one of the workshops from the *We Make Film* research process, MJ and I exchanged roles as film-maker/subject, and he led the film-making process for a day. Among other exercises, we undertook a feedback session by MJ, the crew members and myself, and it was up to MJ to frame each crew member's feedback. MJ decided to compose a frame where Pal had her crutches placed deliberately on top of her, while ordinarily she kept them beside her. This focus on her disability also mirrored some of his patronizing behaviours towards her in earlier interactions. While Pal expressed that she was comfortable discussing her disability and making it visible, she was uncomfortable about this one-dimensional representation and gave this feedback to MJ, resulting in his revising his approach. *We Make Film* therefore engages with the idea that PwDs' participation in film-making is not

---

[9] Quoted from a tweet by Khabeer (2017).

without its complexities. The off-screen participation and engagement of d/Deaf and disabled film-makers is absolutely crucial if we are to question and change problematic on-screen representations. However, this conversation needs to happen within, as well as outside, the disability and Deaf communities and also acknowledge the fact that people have multiple identities and are members of more than one community. This would then extend membership of the disability and Deaf communities, making space for non-disabled and hearing allyship. It would also help understand how d/Deaf and disabled people experience privilege and oppression within the wider film-making community, and it would point towards specific barriers and forms of the nature of access to film-making.

FILM-MAKING WORLDS

Given the diverse membership of the film-making community in terms of identity and creative practice, a challenge within this research was therefore to define, to the maximum extent possible, a 'film-maker'. While it would have been ideal for this research to reduce the scope of this definition to understand film-maker participants' practice and contexts in greater depth, the limited number of willing and available film-makers meant that this definition was kept broader. Therefore, for the purpose of the *We Make Film* research, an FwD refers to any person who is currently making or aspires to make films of any kind—animation, documentary or fiction, including a mix of any of these forms. The film-makers could have received formal training at media or film schools or have been self-taught. The scope of this definition also included those who may be 'amateur film-makers' (Espinosa, 1979), which helped broaden the very definition of what constitutes 'cinema' or 'good film-making' and deserves space, to ensure taking into consideration the diverse levels of access to resources and accessibility. The film-making community in this research is therefore a broad umbrella term for all those involved in or interested in creative film practice, within and outside of traditional film and media industries.

The intersection of the Deaf or disability identity with class, caste, gender, race, religion and/or language may mean that some FwDs identify as 'disabled artists', connecting content and/or aesthetic expression to corporeal and cultural experiences of disability. Many others may not associate their work with disability at all and may identify as artists and film-makers who happen to have disabilities. In a preliminary interview, film-maker participant DG mentioned that she chose to express her experiences as a woman and as a lip-reading deaf person in her animation videos. Some of her work features her unique experience of sound via cochlear implants, the straddling of deaf and hearing worlds via lip-reading and so on. At the same time, there are film-makers, such as Subhash Kapoor (a feature film director of commercial Hindi films, such as the *Jolly LLB* films) who, despite a visibly amputated forearm, mentions in published news interviews that he has 'never thought of not having a hand as a handicap' (*Open Magazine*, 2013) or faced any particular challenges, and indeed he does not articulate this experience via his film-making.

The confluence of identity and aesthetic expression does not, in any case, need to focus on our primary identities. If we all have multicultural identities, then our experiences do and must reflect our composite realities. Disabled people do not *have to* (and do not, indeed) make films focusing on their experience of disability only. An excellent example would be the work of Deaf film-makers (from the works of RH Films and Deaf Entertainment to many other film-makers' works at the India International Deaf Film Festival) who have made a range of films in terms of style and content: While some have made short comedies on demonetization and dramas, others have focused on making horror films or animated comedies. While their work is not related to disability or deafness in the strict sense, these films do the very important job of making visible on screen Deaf culture, multiple concerns and ways of being and dialogues in sign language. They inherently address issues of accessibility as well, given the prevalence of spoken-language dialogues in hearing directors' film (which are subtitled later, if at all). The films of RH Films, Deaf Entertainment and the Deaf film-makers such as MJ lend visibility to the everyday stories and interests of the Deaf community beyond mainstream films that focus on the d/Deaf experience as an 'issue', and in a way that is readily accessible to the Indian sign language (ISL) community.

While it is important to connect d/Deaf film-makers with 'mainstream' film industries and practices and ensure better access to these opportunities, it is equally important to support the existing community of d/Deaf film-makers and nurture more specific film (sub-)cultures. Deaf film and the theatre organizations such as RH Films (and Deaf Entertainment, which inspired RH Films) often set up screenings for their films by renting out large halls to project their films. This garners tremendous interest from the Deaf community and creates space for enjoyment, interaction and exchange at the 'cinema', an experience only partly accessible for the Deaf community within current mainstream cinemas in India. The crew and I documented one such curated screening by RH Films in Mumbai and noted how this was a space for enthusiastic discussion between the film-makers and the audience about the films, the expression and celebration of Deaf culture and, most importantly, enjoyment and engagement at the cinema. For any person with no or limited knowledge of ISL, the Deaf cinema experience would need to be mediated by interpreters or supportive d/Deaf friends (which is usually the reverse case for d/Deaf people at mainstream cinemas with non-subtitled screenings). This is also the case of the India International Deaf Film Festival, which provides an opportunity for d/Deaf film-makers to exhibit their work within the Deaf community (where film-makers like MJ have won multiple awards). While we did work with MJ to develop common vocabularies and practices across cross-ability film-making contexts (which became their point of access into the 'mainstream'), the Deaf community–specific cinema experience proved equally important, as it was a platform to nurture and grow film cultures and spaces specific to disability, linguistic and cultural expression. There were benefits to embracing the 'label' of disability, as well as of identifying with the wider film-making community.

This is exactly what *We Make Film* seeks to uphold and develop further: More d/Deaf and disabled film-makers do indeed need to enter the industry and make films, and accessibility and disability representation must not be an afterthought but part of well-rounded storytelling. At the same time, the research also seeks to understand and support the need for expression and stories that are embedded within a specific disability or Deaf community's context—something that adds value and expresses solidarity among those who identify with that particular community. An intersectional approach to understanding identity and oppression can help build solidarities across diverse sets of film-makers and creative practices.

CONCLUSION

The aim of the *We Make Film* research project is to recognize and amplify disability-specific conversations within the urgent conversation on the need for more caste, class, gender, regional and linguistic diversity in film-making. As part of its outcomes (the documentary and published work), it identifies three key areas for further analysis: accessible technology, inclusive education and accessible production contexts. Initiatives need to encourage film-making by PwDs through going beyond sporadic, one-off competitions and projects, opening up the world of audiovisual storytelling in a way that recognizes disability as a valid life experience and identity and making the disability-specific accommodations that are needed to make the process, technology and training accessible.

With its intersectional approach to disability and creative expression, the project also seeks to expand our understanding of Deaf and disability communities within community media initiatives and practice. While some initiatives do actively focus on facilitating the participation of specific minority groups, disabled and d/Deaf people (within these groups and the wider community) still remain mostly sidelined. The needs and experiences of disability groups tend to be subsumed into those of the wider 'community', and the resulting representations of disability (if any) in the stories that emerge are often ableist and/or inaccessible. It is vital that community media initiatives recognize the agency of d/Deaf and disabled members, identify disability-specific and intersectional barriers and offer the accommodations and assistance necessary to facilitate accessibility to ensure true, equitable participation by all. The creative material emerging out of this enhanced participation of minority groups must also support themes that are of interest and significance to the group, rather than encouraging only 'issue-based' or educational stories and perspectives.

FwDs need to make films not just because we need more stories of disability across our multiple and diverse communities but also because in their most basic sense, films and video strive to tell stories that are multi-layered, well-rounded and fresh on perspective, to be interesting, engaging and enjoyable. The assertion that PwDs have complex experiences 'just like anyone else' must form the basis of supporting their creative presence in mainstream and independent film-making, as well as community media initiatives. This does not mean making disability and Deaf culture invisible, or flattening out stories to fit the existing mould, but means taking a multi-layered approach to foster the sustainable growth and participation of Deaf and disabled people in film-making and video making.

REFERENCES

Crenshaw, K. (1989). Demarginalizing the intersection of race and sex: A black feminist critique of antidiscrimination doctrine, feminist theory and antiracist politics. *University of Chicago Legal Forum, 1989*(1), Article 8.

Ellis, K. (2016). *Disability media work: Opportunities and obstacles*. Palgrave Macmillan.

Espinosa, J. C. (1979). For an imperfect cinema, translated by Julianne Burton (2005), copyright *Jump Cut: A Review of Contemporary Media, 20*, 24–26.

Ginsburg, F., & Rapp, R. (2001). Enabling disability: Rewriting Kinship, reimagining citizenship. *Public Culture, 13*(3), 533–556.

Khabeer, S. A. (2017, February 12). *You don't need to be a voice for the voiceless. Just pass the mic*. https://twitter.com/drsuad/status/830838928403988480?lang=en

Ross, L. (2019). I'm a black feminist. I think call-out culture is toxic. *New York Times*. https://www.nytimes.com/2019/08/17/opinion/sunday/cancel-culture-call-out.html

Open Magazine. (2013). *The satire of Subhash Kapoor*. https://openthemagazine.com/cinema/the-satire-of-subhash-kapoor/

Pauwels, L. (2013). Participatory visual research revisited: A critical-constructive assessment of epistemological, methodological and social activist tenets. *Ethnography, 16*(1), 95–117.

Chapter 8

Dalit Camera
Resisting Caste Atrocities Through Video

Raees Mohammed[1]

'Capturing stories that other[s] choose to hide' reads the banner on the home page of the Dalit Camera YouTube channel. Scroll below, and one of its latest uploads is on COVID-19 and Islamophobia, followed by playlists titled *Chalo HCU—Justice for Rohith Vemula*, *Dalit Women* and *Dalit Songs*, among others.

Established in 2011, Dalit Camera is a YouTube channel that covers issues of Dalits, adivasis and minorities in India through songs, lectures, recordings of public meetings and raw footage of crucial events and incidents. The channel was founded by Raees Mohammed, who before his recent conversion to Islam was known as Ravichandran Bathran. Run largely by student volunteers in Hyderabad, Mumbai and Calcutta, Dalit Camera through its reportage on Dalit news, movements and thinkers offers an alternative to how caste is covered in mainstream India—'through un-touchable eyes', as the tagline of the website and the YouTube channel proclaims.

---

[1] Mr Muhammed was interviewed for this essay. Ms Maanvi and Mr Nikhil Ambekar provided editorial assistance.

According to Mohammed, 'Dalit Camera does the work of a chronicler, and that of a postman'. He argues that Dalit Camera represents an 'ideology which has been neglected by the so-called mainstream media and academicians'. This is the ideology espoused by Dr. B.R. Ambedkar which advocates for 'getting rid of caste, which is a part and parcel of Hinduism'.

Mohammed says,

> So many news channels have emerged, and a number of online portals too. Most importantly, many people now have access to smartphones as well. But atrocities on Dalits still go on unabated. These platforms still echo the mainstream narrative. These platforms are yet to discuss atrocities. I believe the simple reason behind the present situation is that caste has been normalised.

Community media projects in India, especially those driven by development sector organizations or priorities of funding agencies, are often structured in ways that do little to mitigate skewed power relations—an important factor when it comes to questions of representation. Dalit Camera's premise, as a chronicler, is that it is shaped by the aspirations, protests, knowledge resources and demands of the Dalit communities. For example, Dalit Camera's series of videos on protests against the death of Rohith Vemula show an engaged insider's point of view in the movement—not that of a dispassionate outsider looking into the movement. This continual engagement with the community, while simultaneously offering to shape the Dalit discourses in India, is probably one of the reasons why the YouTube channel is one of the popular anti-caste collectives online.

But how did Dalit Camera start? Whose stories does it endeavour to tell? And what are the challenges it faces in a crowded media landscape in India?

THE ORIGINS

In 2011, a female Dalit panchayat president, Krishnaveni, in Tamil Nadu was stabbed by four people who were reported to be caste

Hindus.[2] She belonged to the Arunthathiyar caste, a Scheduled Caste (SC) community. It was the fourth such incident in the region where a Dalit panchayat president had been attacked. Covering the protests that came up in the aftermath of the incident was the beginning of Dalit Camera. 'The entire Arunthathiyar community was protesting. I also wanted to contribute to the protest, so I made a documentary. That was the beginning of what is now known as Dalit Camera', says Mohammed. The 23-minute documentary was the first of many such videos posted by Dalit Camera, covering incidents of atrocities against Dalits.

This happened at a time when mainstream media would ignore Dalit issues, or give it limited space. According to journalist Sudipto Mondal (2017), now a reporter with Dalit Camera, as recently as 10 years ago, the 'English newspaper editors were still telling reporters that there was no readership for stories of atrocities on Dalits, Adivasis and Muslims'. According to 'Who Tells Our Stories Matters' (2019), a report by Oxfam and Newslaundry, an overwhelming majority of editorial leadership positions in the news organizations studied were occupied by journalists from the upper castes. On news television networks, three out of four anchors of flagship shows were from the upper castes and none from SC, Scheduled Tribe (ST) or Other Backward Class (OBC) communities. Among the English and Hindi newspapers surveyed, no more than 10 per cent were written by Dalits and adivasis. In online new media, 72 per cent of the articles with a byline were written by people from the upper castes.

While little seems to have changed in the make-up of most mainstream legacy and online news media ecosystems, according to Mondal (2017), 'they are paying airfares and booking taxis for reporters willing to travel to remote villages and report the latest atrocity down to its last emotional detail'. Mondal attributes this new-found interest, or 'course correction', to the increasingly large number of audiences attracted by several online outlets run by editors from the historically marginalized sections of society. He adds, 'Thanks to force-multipliers like Facebook

---

[2] See https://archive.indiaspend.com/cover-story/krishnavenis-story-and-the-era-of-women-panchayat-presidents-98310

and Twitter, websites that would earlier get dismissed as fringe are now in the middle of the wolfpack that's chasing breaking news', and he credits Dalit Camera prominently, along with other forums like 'Round Table India, Velivada, Adivasi Resurgence, Sahil Online, *Milli Gazette*, Kashmir Reader, Raiot and Thumb Print'.

The motivation behind establishing Dalit Camera was also to mobilize and spark debate in the Dalit community. Mohammed adds,

> After 15 years of activism, I have realised that what Ambedkar said is the solution to caste [relations of power]. Every year, new leaders are emerging among Dalits, but the status of Dalits is the same. The Dalit community also does not recognise the contribution made by these leaders for them. So, I believe that the Dalit movement needs people who can record their voices and make it available to masses.

Thus, Dalit Camera's YouTube channel emerged not just as a chronicler but also as a teacher—popularizing arguments made by Dalit thinkers and activists. For Mohammed, the question was simple. 'Why are the views and histories of great people not recorded during their lifetime, but so vociferously remembered only when they are dead? I thought it is important to record such people's views; like the biography of Prof. Kancha Ilaiah was one such initiative'.

In 2012, Ambedkar statues were desecrated in Andhra Pradesh.[3] At the time, Dalit leaders were giving press statements, which according to Mohammed were being ignored by mainstream media. Dalit Camera stepped in to 'record entire press conferences and upload them, to make up for the casteist myopia' surrounding the reportage on most Dalit events, says Mohammed. In many ways, the incident set the foundation for how Dalit Camera established itself in a cluttered media space as a channel exclusively focused on mainstreaming Dalit narratives—as shaped by the community.

The channel has also been instrumental in changing the discourse on news cycles about Dalit communities—like the issue of the

---

[3] See https://www.outlookindia.com/newswire/story/andhra-tension-after-desecration-of-ambedkar-statues/748769

controversial Ambedkar cartoon in May 2012.[4] Controversy broke out around a cartoon published in a National Council of Educational Research and Training (NCERT) textbook by well-known cartoonist K. Shankar Pillai. The cartoon showed former Prime Minister (PM) Jawaharlal Nehru holding a whip, who along with Dr B. R. Ambedkar was driving a snail representing the Indian Constitution. The cartoon was eventually removed from the NCERT textbook, but not before it snowballed into a political controversy, causing adjournment of proceedings in both the Rajya Sabha and the Lok Sabha.

While mainstream media coverage on the issue was ongoing, Dalit Camera's coverage brought nuance to the issue. As Mohammed says, 'while the entire left-liberal intelligentsia was snapping at the heels of the Dalit movement, I took a video of Dr. Satyanarayana on the Ambedkar Cartoon which really contributed and changed the angle and presuppositions of the discussion'. Again, during the Lakshmipeta massacre in 2012,[5] Dalit Camera got in touch with activists working on the ground and was able to take interviews and post videos from the village—making itself a source of authentic and accurate information. Apart from disseminating accurate information, Dalit Camera also has taken on the role of breaking down complex caste-related laws. As Mohammed says,

> When the Special Component Plan debate was going on in Andhra Pradesh[6], many Dalits were not aware of it, including me. So, I decided to make videos explaining what the SCP is. Similarly, I have made videos illuminating other topics also, such as the SC/ST Atrocity Act,[7] etc.

---

[4] See https://www.indiatoday.in/india/north/story/intolerance-ncert-books-cartoons-br-ambedkar-115745-2012-09-11
[5] See https://www.thehindu.com/news/national/andhra-pradesh/four-dalits-done-to-death-in-srikakulam-village/article3520527.ece
[6] See https://www.news18.com/news/india/ap-assembly-to-discuss-scst-special-component-plans-524217.html
[7] See https://www.ndtv.com/india-news/supreme-court-recalls-2018-order-that-was-seen-to-dilute-provisions-of-a-law-protecting-scheduled-ca-2110071

HOW DOES DALIT CAMERA WORK?

As of May 2020, Dalit Camera has 60,700 subscribers, but according to Mohammed, the YouTube channel on its own hardly generates revenue. It has also not been easy sailing for the channel, with it being briefly suspended in January 2017. According to the online video sharing giant, the suspension was due to an infringement of copyright. However, since the termination came after news reports of the Hyderabad police allegedly profiling Mohammed, it caused an uproar. In an email interview, years after the incident, Mohammed clarified that since the channel had received three strikes—allegedly due to the background music used in some videos being under copyright—the channel had been suspended. Describing the incident, Mohammed explains,

> YouTube has weird rules. For example, if you tag a video of Dalit women speaking on violence as 'Dalit women violence', it will be scrutinised by YouTube. I would get a notice that it is not suitable for audiences. Even after appeals to cross-check the contents of the video, YouTube has not changed its stand. Similarly, YouTube has problems with videos which discuss social issues. The other issue is that sometimes, there will be a good video which would be useful for the larger public, but it would not be made available to the larger public.

According to YouTube's guidelines available online, once a channel is suspended, the owner receives an email explaining the reason for the same. According to the guidelines, a YouTube channel can be suspended due to repeated violations of community guidelines, a single case of 'severe abuse', a policy violation and copyright infringement claims.

With YouTube seemingly being an unfriendly place for Dalit Camera, why does the channel choose to emphasize video? The reason, according to Mohammed, is that video is a powerful tool. He says, 'Visual media is easy to convey and a powerful tool to reach the larger public. The Indian audience is largely focused on video'.

In many ways, Dalit Camera's independence can be traced to how it uses technology, specifically YouTube. In another era, videos shot and edited by student volunteers associated with Dalit Camera would need the platform of conventional media to be noticed—newspapers, magazines and television. On YouTube, the cost of publishing content, distributing and steadily building an audience is relatively low. The videos published by Dalit Camera are often shot on smartphones, with minimal equipment, which further ensures that the space created by the channel can be relatively free of external interference. This intersection of technology and caste politics is what establishes Dalit Camera as an innovative community media project in India.

The mobilization of Dalits online has also led to a situation where at least on social networking sites with active Dalit presence the direction of a news cycle on Dalit issues is largely determined by the Dalit community. As Arvind Kumar Thakur (2019) argues in an essay titled 'New Media and the Dalit Counter-public Sphere',

> Online networking has brought social and cultural capital for the Dalit community, enabling millennial Dalits to employ social media for political purposes. Common online users in the Dalit community are becoming primary interpreters and agenda builders for the political claims on social networking sites, no longer depending heavily on non-Dalit leaders and the intelligentsia to represent claims to justice and equality.

However, this does not mean that YouTube—and by extension the Internet—is a utopian platform that has democratized self-expression. While Dalit digital activism on Twitter and Facebook, and the emergence of the platforms like Roundtable India and Dalit Camera, has raised Dalit consciousness, the Internet is not free of caste realities either. As argued by Pardeep Attri, the founder–editor of Velivada, a Dalit news organization, and quoted in Livemint,

> Social media, I always say, is not social at all. It is not democratic, no matter what the social media companies claim. Different communities are sitting in their bunkers and firing at each other, and even here dominant castes set the narrative and supress dissenting voices. (Harad, 2018)

Furthermore, the online world does not exist in isolation from the offline world. As Tejas Harad (2018) writes in Livemint, 'There is danger in conflating a movement with the tools it uses. As various technology sociologists have argued, the binary of online and offline is false. Online is not a different world that we separately inhabit' (Harad, 2018).

As for Dalit Camera's online reach, Mohammed is not happy with the number of subscribers the channel has amassed till now and its consequent reach. He says, 'Virtual spaces, even if we have to discuss a Dalit audience which the channel has reached, I would say it has reached nothing'. A comparison with mainstream news publishers on YouTube and their reach may put this statement in context. *Aaj Tak*, one of the biggest Hindi news channels in India, has 36.8 million subscribers. Digital-only publishers, like *Scroll*, have 284,000 subscribers. However, the comparison is an unfair one, since unlike that of most newsrooms Dalit Camera's organizational structure is entirely volunteer-driven.

According to Mohammed, '99.9% of the videos uploaded on the channel are done by student volunteers' who are studying in universities across India. For longer documentaries, Mohammed mobilizes money, which he then uses to cover the production expenses and run the channel. He says, 'Certainly, Dalit Camera cannot sustain with this model. Student politics in universities are changing with the current regime. Dalit Camera will need volunteers who are political and can contribute their time to record others' voices'.

'Dalit Camera does not run a political platform, but an ideological movement', says Mohammed, making it clear that allying with political parties is not an objective of the channel. However, he is unsure about the contribution of Dalit Camera to the larger Dalit movement in the country. 'Dalit Camera cannot speak about its contribution in the movement. For me, confidently embracing Islam and having the courage to bury my Hindu identity is the biggest achievement of Dalit Camera'.

KEY CHALLENGES

At a time when mainstream media is increasingly toeing the line of the government, where does Dalit Camera stand in the larger media landscape in India? According to Mohammed,

The mainstream media popularises online spaces of only those who maintain the status quo of Indian society. If one discusses Ambedkar leaving Hinduism, no one shares our videos. This is the reason our channel never gets attention. Sadly until this date, Dalit Camera has not got any mainstream coverage.

However, importantly, Mohammed is not even sure whether Dalit Camera—with its eponymous website and YouTube channel—can be called 'media' in the conventional sense of the word. 'It's a space of its own', he asserts, where a nascent community is taking shape through critical internal exchanges and public debates outside.

Another challenge that faces Dalit Camera is the articulation of Ambedkar's vision of complete eradication of caste, even within the Dalit community in India.

Most movements, particularly those not in Maharashtra, do not seem to take Ambedkar's contribution in eradicating caste seriously. Similar to the Left and Periyarists, Dalits too, hide their caste by saying they are atheists. It has been a challenge to articulate this not only through Dalit Camera but also in my everyday life.

Challenges also crop up when Dalit Camera allies with movements. Mohammed says,

the Dalit Camera travelled covering protests of dalit movements particularly in Telangana and Andhra Pradesh. During these travels, we saw the movements keep protesting, and their only agenda is to implement the constitutional law. Though the fight against caste is an ideology, the anti-caste movement's solution is to implement the constitution without changing the social structure. It is this, the only protesting mode, I call very masculine in nature.

WHAT IS THE FUTURE?

For Dalit Camera, the bigger challenge is the one facing most media organizations in India in the post-COVID-19 world—that of survival. Citing the example of 'Dalit Murasu', a Dalit magazine published in

Tamil Nadu, Mohammed pointed out how the magazine is under financial duress. In such a scenario, Mohammed wants Dalit Camera to be independent and yet expand its impact. He says, 'I believe we can be independent of big companies and political parties. We can never be fully independent; our audiences are the larger public who came to us because of our work and we are dependent on this audience'.

It is also this audience that he wishes to have an impact on. As Mohammed says, 'I want to see Dalit Camera as a media outlet that will have a far-reaching audience. Whenever a video is uploaded, it should have an impact on the lives of those who give us voices'.

REFERENCES

Harad, T. (2018). *Towards an internet of equals.* https://www.livemint.com/Leisure/c7XqIj7NcWEhmcV3Wdeaul/Towards-an-internet-of-equals.html

Mondal, S. (2017). *Indian media wants Dalit news but not Dalit reporters.* https://www.aljazeera.com/indepth/opinion/2017/05/indian-media-dalit-news-dalit-reporters-170523194045529.html

Oxfam India and Newslaundry. (2019). *Who tells our stories matters: Representation of marginalised caste groups in Indian newsrooms.* Oxfam India and Newslaundry. https://www.oxfamindia.org/sites/default/files/2019-08/Oxfam%20NewsLaundry%20Report_For%20Media%20use.pdf

Thakur, A. K. (2019). New media and the Dalit counter-public sphere. *Television and New Media, 21*, 1–16.

Section III

Durable Margins: Asserting Citizenship

Chapter 9

Community Media and Potential for Responsive Listenership on Campus[1]

Nikhil Thomas Titus

Community media is hailed for its empowering potential in regions with sparse media presence, meeting specialized or local information needs of low-income and marginalized publics, and even in crises and disaster relief efforts. Within such a framework that positions community media as a low-cost placeholder in *markets* that cannot afford to and are not serviced by mainstream networks, is there a case to be made for investment in participatory communication infrastructure in dense urban environments like Mumbai? Cityscapes come with constraints on space that marginalized populations can access and a proliferation of cost-effective mobile technologies that intersect class, caste and religious stratifications. While physical space within the city is at a premium, all manner of texts and devices that enable access to representations of life within such concentrated environments are available at reasonable costs. Unauthorized and indigenous distribution networks are stigmatized due to their 'illegality' in relation to copyright infringement and the

[1] I express my gratitude to the students of the Post Graduate Diploma in Community Media (PGDCM) and my colleagues at the School of Media and Cultural Studies, Tata Institute of Social Sciences, Mumbai (2012–2016).

uncritical association of such economies inspiring criminals in lower-class audiences and felonious tendencies within the city at large. Mobile phones with high-end cameras, media players, frequency modulation (FM) receivers and a host of additional transfer, storage and projection gadgetry constitute a vital node that connects ecologies of industry, labour and leisure in such informal and unorganized sectors. In 'The Other Cinemas' (Titus, 2020), I have referenced the phenomenon of micro media centres and contraband traders proliferating across various localities in Mumbai which facilitate media distribution through downloading content from file sharing networks and transferring them onto phones and memory cards. These brisk and lean traders ensure access in communities that might not be able to connect with mainstream platforms because of affordability or lack of technical knowledge. Given the commonly illicit nature of such transactions, there is a concerted effort to clamp down on avenues of leisure and entertainment for the working classes, which include single-screen theatres and video parlours where factions of society encounter each other and a range of messaging and media.

While such piecemeal purchase and consumption of media are affordable and ensure a reliable stream of mass-market information and content, the overall percentage of costs are significantly higher than most legitimate, subscription-based models. Access and pricing are only some of the significant concerns; the content produced also reflects gender, class and caste biases that constitute media industries and the general nature of all economic activity and ownership in the country. Exercising weak ownership and agency in determining media representations and

> denying rights of existence to such institutions is not just an expression of anxiety over cultural forms and aesthetics, but also the manifestation of a strong bio-political sentiment against the enculturation of certain bodies within certain boundaries—based on consumerist notions of rights and privileges of citizens. (Titus, 2020, p. 175)

An analysis of the Indian media industry by Oxfam India (2019, p. 6) indicates the glaring absence of Dalits and adivasis in leadership roles in major media houses. Among its highlights, the report states,

Of the 121 newsroom leadership positions editor-in-chief, managing editor, executive editor, bureau chief, input/output editor—across the newspapers, TV news channels, news websites, and magazines under study, 106 are occupied by journalists from the upper castes, and none by those belonging to the Scheduled Castes and the Scheduled Tribes.

A popularly cited study, *Caste and Entrepreneurship in India* (Iyer et al., 2013, p. 53), observes,

> As late as 2005, Scheduled Castes and Scheduled Tribes were significantly under-represented in the ownership of private enterprises, and the employment generated by private enterprises. Such underrepresentation in the entrepreneurial sphere was widespread across all the large states of India, and was present in both rural and urban settings. Moreover, despite more than a decade of rapid nationwide economic growth, the share of SCs and STs in firm ownership and employment generation over the period 1990–2005 increased only very modestly.

Participatory and community media networks, which serve as an alternative to for-profit media structures that generate revenue through advertisement and consumption data, seem imminent yet perpetually furloughed. While the need for such media is obvious, there is a paucity of critical discussion around the plural narratives, publics and objectives that such networks can generate and pursue, usurped by a directness of address of 'under-represented' issues.

When mainstream media tend to take up issues around underserved publics, they garner larger viewership, exhaust generic talking points around the event and, occasionally, urge civic and administrative action and bring about incremental wavering in public opinion. The success of the Aamir Khan-hosted television (TV) series *Satyamev Jayate* (2012) that dealt with issues ranging from caste discrimination and female infanticide to the water crises in India, the critical and box-office success of Marathi film *Sairat* (2016) and the Bollywood art house productions like *Masaan* (2015) focusing on inter-caste relationships, migrant- and agriculture-focused journalism database PARI (People's Archive of Rural India) by P. Sainath, the widening funding opportunities for independent films and the increasingly savvy global and critical audiences with diverse means of access to the documentaries like *Jai Bhim*

Comrade (2011) and *Gulabi Gang* (2012) are only some of the sensitized initiatives that appear to take up the mandate of guiding public thought on critical issues. While such traditional mass media tools have produced engagement with a range of socially relevant topics, these instances lack community participation at levels of content, finance and ownership and act more as aberrations to hegemonic purchasing rhythms in society. Mainstream media programming is now being supplemented by staggering amounts of content sourced through various grey and legitimate means from platforms like YouTube and social media sites such as Facebook, WhatsApp, Instagram and the more recent entrant TikTok. Lately, much of the hard-hitting and unscripted coverage of issues, such as the violence against cattle traders by vigilante *gau rakshak* (cow protection) groups, visuals of protests against the CAA–NRC, 2019 (Citizenship [Amendment] Act–National Registry of Citizens), the attack on students inside Jamia Millia Islamia and Jawaharlal Nehru University in Delhi, and a host of other lighter content, like the discovery and serendipitous minor stardoms of singers, poets, activists and artists from underprivileged communities, has been made possible by the union of user-generated content and news-producing and -curating social media accounts. One can imagine how this viewership is profitable to mass-market corporate platforms; however, even as the number of independent creators grow, the value to users appears to remain restricted to a few bloggers and traditional content creators with new-media wings, where information on revenue sharing is privately regulated and advertisement-driven. If large-scale corporate media diversifying based on language and other considered interests are fulfilling such local and nuanced imperatives, what role does community media justify within such environments?

Community media practitioners point out the lack of representation and long-term perspectives by and for low-income and minority communities within media reportage. This dearth of agency is compounded by issues of gatekeepers and pillaging of opinion by media that are largely conceived and produced with no input from marginalized groups other than visual and sound bites on immediate impacts. While percentages of coverage are difficult to establish, resourceless publics attract media glare for extreme or unique situations, leaving everyday struggles for basic amenities, identity and recognition to be dealt with through alternative platforms that range from forceful protests and political sympathy to resource-and reach-deficient productions. Depending on relative size, such groupings also constitute valuable vote banks that can be repetitively fashioned into exploitative alliances in order to have those basic requirements fulfilled. A media apparatus focused on timelines, sales and non-participatory processes can result in a phenomenon of turning people into whom we need them to be (Low et al., 2016, p. 18), where a lack of control and knowledge over media processes can make publics more prone to random determinations and breaches of trust by authorities. In agreeing with claims of media ownership and content development which community media can challenge, I pose opportunities of employing university groupings to follow through on imagining, interpreting and perpetuating a loosely bound and creative archive of a vast number of media productions and an even larger number of prospective motions spread across organizations and communities. Acting as a body of learners, interpreters, reviewers and critics, student communities create space for much-needed dialogue in the public sphere around issues of marginalized persons and alternative media, pushing them beyond frames that offer merely production quality and legal and moral counterpoints. A striking instance in the Indian mediascape has been the organization and coverage of a range of protest rallies, speeches and events around issues of grave national concern. The protests against the Citizenship Amendment Act (CAA), the increasing scrutiny of student politics in Delhi and at other university sites, the exodus of migrant workers from cities to escape starvation and the coronavirus pandemic are events with inevitable national and global repercussions which have been documented, in good measure, by distressed individuals and their allies, with support from conventional media platforms. One of the functions of these media artefacts is to serve as documents of proof about what was said, heard and acted out during these grand upheavals with innumerable fleeting demonstrations. In their quivering dynamism, these media often lack in quality, and patriotic, communal, nationalist, contestable, fictional and factual 'things' within make the productions appealing to various social participants. It is the absence of canonical compositions and authenticity, a conceptual fogginess and dispersal of grain, that adds attractive value to the works and draws in a reader, listener, amateur critic, layperson or citizen to contribute more than opinion and feel invested in the display. Such events are significant in precipitating social change, but reliance on movements of this scale to generate manoeuvrability is akin to the situation that poor communities experience in any case where tragedies have brought media and political attention and temporary relief. I suggest that harnessing the 'drawing in' and 'investments' of audiences within such media, alongside but not exclusively related to their proof function and outcome orientation, is one mode of conceptualizing community media production and dissemination.

A few years ago, I presented a paper about migrant populations and informal housing in Mumbai, referencing the extreme disparity in the city when it came to accessing media or even the basic amenities like water and electricity. An audience member commented that the presentation put on display a 'disreputable picture of Mumbai'. In a globalized and privatized landscape, the issues of basic amenities and violation of rights of fellow citizens often take a back seat to the reputation of the city. Conceptions of standards and quality of life based on revenue and branded valuations of space provoke questions about whether it is the actual dearth of information, historical documents or conventional archives that is the reason for the lack of empathy towards a majority of deprived citizens or immigrants in policymaking in Mumbai. 'Stickiness' manifests, a term utilized by Sara Ahmed (2015, p. 90) to describe the structuring of power through which objects attain their disgustingness, contingent 'on histories of contact that have already impressed upon the surface of the object', affixing causation of economic, financial and social deterioration to marginalized and unregulated lifestyles. In an environment where operational technics enable interpretation of only a selection of coordinates as reliable sets of opinion, data and histories, alternate deployment of media seeks to produce reliable and authoritative provenance and proof of existence and engenders recognition of counter-narratives and systemic injustice that fixes the viewer to the filmed subject. Or is this an apparatus masquerading as a producer of coevalness, promising a counter-history while serving as a handmaiden for hegemonic mobilizations? Can participatory media practices by migrants, low-caste communities, minorities and those without an illustrious heritage that is in tandem with the hegemonic cultural perceptions of the time break the association of coordinates of congestion and freeloading on taxpayer money and instantiate archives as legitimate citizens? How does one relate to this production of a reliable and authoritative voice of history for those left out of mainstream representations? *Other Voices* (Pavarala & Malik, 2007) is one of the first and only comprehensive academic publications on the state of community media in India, focusing largely on grassroots organizations in rural and semi-urban locations in the country. Further, Pavarala (2015) has elaborated on questions of 'voice poverty' in the Indian community media sphere through a series of publications, focusing on the initiation, growth and concentration of regulation and control of alternative media platforms, pointing out that in the less cost-intensive and less production-intensive field of community radio, many applicants and practitioners are elite educational institutions. Communities outside such institutional binds lack the know-how to navigate a complex licensing system or may not be in 'good standing' with governments that issue these permits. A report published by UNESCO (United Nations Educational, Scientific and Cultural Organization) (2007) suggests that the Indian government had plans to promote 4,000 community radio stations in various underserved regions of the country (UNESCO, 2007); of these, Pavarala claims that barely 200 have come to fruition, and, given the change in governments since 2014, the numbers do not show much scope for growth even in 2020. The inquiries into voice are compounded by a series of publications, such as 'Community media interventions and the politics of listening' (Dreher, 2009), *Community-based Media Pedagogies* (Low et al., 2016), *Community Media: International Perspectives* (Fuller, 2007) and 'Being Heard' (Bailey et al., 2014), that probe issues of corresponding listenership. How and where does a diverse, productive and responsible listenership arise and, alongside activist and immediate survival goals, how can the objectives of this sensitized audience include long-term historical and archival considerations of community media practice?

Moved by the volume *Mining the Home Movie* (Ishizuka & Zimmermann, 2008) and the radical potential attributed to the form, I attempt to posit a bourgeois pursuit like home movies against a more grassroots approach to video through community media initiatives. If the personal narrative of a home video can intersect and participate in national and large-scale historical accounts, then what place do communally produced media hold in relation to personal, corporate and national trajectories? The chapter looks at select video production exercises as part of the Community Media Programme at the Tata Institute of Social Sciences (TISS) during 2012–2016 in collaboration with various non-governmental organizations (NGOs) and community-based organizations (CBOs) in Mumbai, India. The objective of the exercise was to enable the community to initiate the production of a reliable, communally produced record of conditions that they perceive as significant to their existence and, possibly, even enable the pursuit of favourable policy change through advocacy. Most of the productions are not publicly searchable for reasons ranging from permissions for public distribution from participating organizations to fears of interpretation of such an archive as a convenient assembly of hate receptors within the city, producing identifying coordinates for those who are already vulnerable. The contestation against the home movie apparatus is that it is an integral part of the over-determined field of media technology and production that is unable to disassociate from the colonial extractive ideology of the filmic apparatus. Through an interrogation of the documents produced with these community media initiatives, the chapter seeks to put forth the potential for trans-institutional and communal collaboration and examine what incremental development, if any, may be contained within such practices. I combine a narrative of the video camera to convey my personal viewpoints and enable residual access to communities who were gracious in sharing their time, effort and lived experiences for the attempt at producing community media.

The International Association of Media and Communication Research (IAMCR) defines community media as 'a field of media communication that exists outside of the state and the market (often non-government and non-profit), yet which may interact with both (Rennie, 2006, p. 4)'. Extremely visible and, often, beyond the sensibility of the bourgeois and political elite, alternative perspectives are diverse in their formal and structural construction from that of mainstream media in the city. Communities share traditional networking and communication strategies, but shifts in mediascapes and technologies over the past two to three decades have altered the pace and scale of messaging, alongside the boundaries of such groupings. The spread of digital technologies in the early 2000s enabled a stream of NGOs and community organizations to initiate audio and video projects that paralleled community media objectives outside direct state and market influence. However, within a few years, most of these initiatives ceased because of obvious logistical and resource constraints in producing, storing, disseminating and purposefully archiving such content. Alongside an explosion of news and entertainment programming, the enormous amount of mobile and user-generated content has hinted at potential threats to and opportunities for the field of participatory communication. Through concepts of open and free access for all, there is a popular discourse around the supposed non-thing and non-place of the digital, with presumptions of *clouds* and *streams* that can, without bias, store and instantly dispense these bits of information. The belief is that these pulses within the archive are incapable of deterioration, weightless, timeless and potentially infinitely replicable packets, able to constitute any permutation and combination of programme—all reflected onto our mobile and light devices that can inspire alternative media—fantastical and idyllic spaces constructed in response to the shock of disparity through thick and unsustainable urban modernity (Singer, 2001). Film shares a keen historical and affective association with overbearing aural and visual experiences of the city, and the increasingly opaque technologies of digital devices have enabled a sense of democratization or at least a spread of such forms that combine shades of literature, art, music and theatre forms across social strata that congeal through moving image and audio formats. Analog media have demanded huge investments of capital, which even in their most radical applications were restrictive in participatory applications and dissemination; on the other hand, mobile and digital technologies, like video, defy normative prerequisites and entry barriers, and there is no doubt of the potential of such apparatuses in the production of a more reliable mapping of populations and territories, of the generation of reams of data inconceivable just a few years ago—a form of history that is not possible to achieve through just writing or the adoption of classical mediums but a simultaneity of geographical and temporal coordinates and views that stretch in directions of both a hegemonic social structure and more subversive implications. This fundamental 'lightness' of video and versatility of mobile technologies can be experienced in an environment with alternative, low-budget, participatory media, opposed to the 'heaviness' of film apparatuses.[2] But how are these devices being used in the production of media content, and how are they conceived, circulated, archived and made available for review and interpretation to a larger network of publics who may not be directly impacted by issues but can be considered accountable stakeholders? The process of integrating such loose and unpredictable, non-state-, non-market-generated content and channelling it into meaningful discourse requires the active participation of a wide range of social investors—universities, community groups, NGOs, media practitioners and theorists, and even sensitized governmental institutions. Goddard is alleged to have said that he was not able to produce a new type of TV in Mozambique because the land was occupied by the government, and 'within government, creativity is not possible' (Ekotto & Koh, 2009, p. 118). The disenfranchised often struggle not to dismantle the government but to be rightfully accounted within it, to be registered, to be notarized and identified and, hence, to receive entitlements of a citizen.

Community media is a site of struggle, a creative exercise trying to incorporate those lost to heritage and history and merely existing or unaccounted within the state. The (re)creation of such radical narratives and their acceptance and application within communal and political folklore demand continuous dialogue, involvement and evolution of methodologies of access and study that can be provided through university systems and like-minded institutions. Archives have traditionally been spaces intended to restrict access; evidently, the realm of the digital has brought about changes in the nature and extent of time and labour in producing meaning and theory. The challenge is to get the media to parley with the chaos of fieldwork experiences and correspond with the scatterings of, often mundane, experiences and fragmented, amateurish sketches that a collection of community viewpoints precipitate. Responsible and dynamic listening of community narratives can work to empower administrative and social empathy through its demystification and deployment of critique and commitment to

---

[2] See: Post-cinema (2016).

favourable sites between communities and institutions, people and their governments. Without such extensive input and circulation of contributors alongside imaginings of community, the field is bound to fall short of a critical intellectual mass that can engage with and redefine innovative directions for the sector.

In 2012, I began participating in a community media diploma programme initiated through TISS, Mumbai. We took the conventional idea that community media serves as a voice for the marginalized to be our focus in the programming, while always reiterating that development programming and communities sidelined within mainstream discourses were not the only ones such initiatives were intended to serve. An initial surge in the number of community media forums had by 2012–2013 transformed into a slow trickle of productions from a meagre number of organizations in Mumbai. In an urban location where the operational participatory media set-ups are restricted to a few middle-class residential enterprises and universities, the toughest task was to find a suitable model around which programming could take shape. MUST Radio at Mumbai University was one of the only community/campus media establishments that had an operating schedule to match professional media enterprises and remained open to coordinating with student learning initiatives.[3] Even without the risk of radio towers or TV stations, slum communities and other marginalized groups that most need access to information and communication networks are conceived as threats and undesirables within the city. The imagination is sustained by media coverage of crime and deprivation at such locations and an overt political and commercial will to sustain angst about employment, hygiene and security against migrant and poor populations in the city. Community media seemed to be somewhere out there in the interiors of the country and for everyone except those in the city. Through an *in-house* collaboration with the M-ward Project (TISS, 2016) at TISS that had a registered network of NGOs and CBOs, it

---

[3] Begun in 2008, Mumbai University Student Transmission is run from the Mumbai University campus in Kalina, Mumbai. Students and community members constitute the staff of the station. The organizations such as Partners for Urban Knowledge, Access and research (PUKAR), Akshara, Video Volunteers and Yuva also have a community media presence in Mumbai.

was not difficult to find issues and short-term projects that are ideal for student projects based on academic-semester time frames. Several organizations were willing to dedicate resources and labour to allow students to train community members and local staff in basic media production operations.

Initial negotiations with NGO field coordinators morphed into group discussions with eager, or drafted, members of the community. Within a couple of days, given resource and time constraints on the part of both students and participating residents, consultations around crucial topics and simultaneous training modules were designed with available mobile phone and video cameras provided through the NGO and student groups. A series of videos, across communities, organizations and semesters, on water problems in the city of Mumbai describe invariable situations where entire communities are denied regular supply due to the lack of property documents. Pushed to the very edge of the city and their humanity, they reside over swamps, filled in by the refuse of the city. An issue several decades old, video evidence is now a mere reiteration, another addition to dispersed repositories of persons in critically depressed and mildly catastrophic conditions in the city. One of the major deliberations is how to put on display the dignity with which people go about their lives. Given the gendered nature of the issue, most participants are women from the community, since they dedicate significant labour to ensure adequate supply of water for the household. One video begins with an NGO worker introducing the location, which is situated right next to Asia's largest, and colonial-era, dump yard in Deonar, Mumbai. Then it cuts to local women who describe the erratic supply of water and the persistent daily scramble. After these roles are played a few times, resident after resident recaps a situation that seems unbelievable when captured on video—houses constructed on soft land that bubbles during the monsoon and sinks in the summer heat, cast with tarpaulin, metal and concrete scraped together from the garbage of the city and insufficient savings. The threat of eviction by municipal corporations and the wait for the next load of recyclable materials mean that people and construction appear in states of perpetual stress and flux. Houses channelling makeshift drains, clothes lines, cracked pieces of stone, red bricks, cement sacks and prized storage drums dot the neighbourhood. People, stuff and stray animals are everywhere, and yet what is starkest is the lack of structure, order or even a suggestion of convenience and meaning. But the troubled exterior of waste has been turned around, to attempt a creative space, sewn together from metal fragments, wooden pieces, bits of cloth, plastic parts and indifferent energies from a city oblivious to these derivations. Cameras controlled by residents and the student coordinators swoop in and out of storage tanks and trail snaking green plastic pipelines that spew out brackish water for a few minutes every day. If it is evidence being pursued, a root cause and source of dysfunction, then one need not look any further than the sickness and morbidity in the community apparent in the vibrant shades of toxic water flowing into receptacles and expressly impacting bodies. In one shot, a camera zooms into a stainless-steel tumbler, and as the lens closes in, the water turns a frightful and gut-wrenching yellow with things tingling inside. In retrospect, every other shot, and the personalities within them, is given a very resilient but uneasy tone.

The region has one of the lowest Human Development Index ranks in Mumbai, and the visuals justly and objectively represent the power inequalities that shape the lives of the community.[4] The NGO's area coordinator requests interviewees to elaborate on their answers for the camera; a woman states that it costs ₹7 to purchase a canister of water from the tanker mafias, and another person adds that they are not able to boil these quantities of water because of fuel costs and time constraints. A man carrying two massive canisters of water on either side of his bicycle is stopped—the cycle is rented on

---

[4] See TISS (2016).

The M-East ward, one of the twenty four administrative divisions of Mumbai and home to over 8,07,720 (Census, 2011) residents, is also one of the poorest areas in the city. Its human development index is the lowest in the city representing an infant mortality rate of around 66.47 per thousand live births, out-of-school children between the ages of 6 to 14 years is 1,490, more or less equally divided between boys and girls, and more than 50 percent children are malnourished (HDR, 2009). The child malnutrition levels in the area, have been equated to Sub-Saharan Africa and a life that is full of poverty, insecurity and everyday violence.

an hourly basis. The camera is waiting to focus and produce a varia-tion of frames; the man is asked to move from one end of the frame to the other. Residents contrast the supply of electricity and regular collection of tariffs by a private corporation against the irregular supply of the far-less-profitable and publicly owned water connec-tions. The conversation gravitates towards the lack of responsiveness from political leaders and the admission of the strategic vote banks that precarious communities constitute, even when, election after election, promises are not fulfilled. Temporary relief and perennial stress and sickness ensure stable voting models and, not to mention, prescribed and infinitely replicable narratives that perform cathartic functions with an audience. In the sweltering summer heat, with the pressure of producing a narrative arc, eventually, the community coordinator suggests that they form a group that can meet once a week and figure out ways to appeal to the administration for support. This production has provoked some discussion among the groups; how far it can lead them to produce results is not easy to determine. The productions reference a basic need and its vastly complicated entanglements that can be altered to suit a series of topics and peoples—health, educa-tion, occupation, connectivity, freedom—slight modifications on the surface that conflate questions of attendance with proactive listening, through representation.

We assume that these productions are meant to inform and educate those outside the communities, effect action by administrators, but they also build listenership within the community—triggering pent-up emotions and authority and collective engagement on issues within and outside the scope of intended texts. Often, subjects who were cooper-ating just before the camera began to capture, change their mind, are too shy, scared, untrusting or uncertain, turn around and walk away and do not express any reason for doing so. Hastily organized and shot, camera shakes, unintended conversations, blurred subjects and overwhelming details within each frame create apparent gaps through which a hidden archive of emotions, sentiments and politics bares itself in these moments of alterity. The lack of continuity, resources and time to dwell on images—problems that plague the subjects and, in general, also influence the media produced around them—expresses a directness and melodramatic quality, a longing for dialogue that keeps the document from becoming what Robert Dawidoff (Ishizuka & Zimmermann, 2008, p. 69) has described as the 'merely historical'. Even in its apparent conclusion and textual resolution, the situation and concerns of the community remain festering and unpleasant in its coarse collective execution. In 2016, the Deonar dumping ground caught fire and smoke began to billow towards the city. This medium of fire and dust, displaced from the heaps of garbage back into the high-priced living quarters of the city, brought together the waste-gathering communities around the dump yard and middle-class residents. In its gloom and suspicious origins and discourse, the collective force of particulate pollutants appeared to bridge, momentarily at least, generational caste, class and religious divides. Without inciting further distress, the hope is to produce empathetic responses to conditions of survival of those at the edges of society. In our student-oriented community engagements, a substantial hurdle to overcome was ensuring continuous processes and mentorship over semesters. Each year brought with it a new batch of students, modified assignments and different organizations working alongside new communities. The output and level of training that could be managed in a couple of weeks was impressive, and several organizations were excited to support the media workshops as an ongoing feature. While resources are a key aspect of continuity in any programme, the process of questioning and meaning making are just as central to understanding the social creativity on display in resolving housing, occupational, financial and cultural issues in everyday life. This task is aided by a push for praxis, not exclusivity of publications, production or institutions but a perpetual conversation that classrooms ferment, provoking active audiences who further the combination of lived experience, technical support and critical presence to move it beyond the stage of project participation and precipitate formations of more robust groupings and insights of community.

My first encounter with a home video camera was in the late 1990s. I had seen family videos, mostly weddings, sometimes baptisms, shot by professional videographers, but the thrill of the home video camera was just something else—on birthdays, weekends, every day—a very different degree of investment in producing and viewing the footage, and attempts to fabricate an estrangement with one's environment, eliciting performances of and from the familiar, producing 'non-commissioned' moments for an archive. Siegfried Kracauer (Ginzburg, 2012, p. 184), in his essay on photography, refers to 'the stranger who does not belong to the house, the photographer who is called to take a photograph', as someone who through the alienation is able to delve into the depths of a prevailing condition, disinvestments producing the possibility of a radically altered view—fledgling archivists, with an endless array of commands and postures for their subjects, flitting through gatherings, building representational coordinates in their attempts to abandon fears of an inevitable and irreconcilable absence. If the home movie is an acknowledgment of death, the community vision is for the apparatus to be inverted and empower the likelihood of living for the marginalized and disadvantaged to whom notions of loss are unfairly proximate and persistent. Teltumbde (2010, p. 9) notes, 'Writing in 1853, the year the railways were introduced in India, Karl Marx prophesied that the new mechanized transportation system would catalyse the collapse of caste'—the hope that modernity, itself a product of the enumeration project of colonialists, would act as a sieve that fashioned a more equitable heritage for all countrymen. But this example also demonstrates how the object of common heritage can be upset. In 2013, the Indian Parliament passed the 'Prohibition of Employment as Manual Scavengers and their Rehabilitation Act'; its implementation remains incomplete, in large part because the Indian Railways is the largest employer of manual scavengers in the world.[5] Not only did new technology not fulfil its promise of alleviating disparity, but it was also that very technology that furthered communities from their assimilation into society, a dilation from realms of the supremacist to the neo-liberal.

---

[5] The United Nations India report on the issue states:

> Manual scavenging refers to the practice of manually cleaning, carrying, disposing or handling in any manner, human excreta from dry latrines and sewers. It often involves using the most basic of tools such as buckets, brooms and baskets. The practice of manual scavenging is linked to India's caste system where so-called lower castes were expected to perform this job. Manual scavengers are amongst the poorest and most disadvantaged community in India. (UN India, 2020, also see Moyna, 2015)

Perhaps, film could have played an integral role in this production of counter-archives of history, in resisting tyranny, as Frick (2011, p. 8) points towards in Roger Smither's edited work *This Film is Dangerous: A Celebration of Nitrate Film*:

> The belligerent tribes of the Khyber Pass area of India and also those of the Khurdish region of Iran and Iraq…used to raid the local cinemas periodically and cart off all the (nitrate) movie film on hand, which they would later shred for gunpowder. It worked fine, and put British patrols in the tragic-comic predicament of being decimated by an early edition of Beau Geste or The Great Train Robbery.

The 'thing-ness' of film produces smoke, fire, haziness, respiratory issues, smog, dangerous and toxic stuff and unique modes of audio and visuals interacting with the real beyond representations, not inherently associated with technological progress for social development. Digital media formats, with their 'lightness' and 'cloud' potentials, assuming the form of analogue media narratives, imitating with the hope of improved and affordable technologies filling in qualitative, financial and social gaps, is a flawed expectation and treatment of apparatuses— a reference to its watered-down revolutionary potential, the turn of the possibility of a wildfire into mere spectacle. This new potential of technology to be omnipresent is absorbing, and it seems we have no choice but to participate and involve others but with shared blueprints of what its outcomes should not replicate. The move to considering film and media production to be simultaneously texts, representations and contexts through which a history of subjects and acts of legitimizing life can take place is as much activism, technical skill and politicking as it is an act of theorizing, silently, reclusively, inclusively, a different world view and asking of society a different set of questions through its projections.

Accompanying democratization of production and dissemination practices, and a seeming universality of media, must be the distancing of image and signification, of intentionally leaving traces in history, producing innovative perspectives on life in a city with extremities of means. Without a process of participatory, productive listening and spectatorship, we feel obliged to polish, correct and rationalize texts and subjects, to pass judgement and right the wrongs we have been subjected to by these media. We must be vigilant in not assuming that engaging with the media is bridging social, economic and knowledge schisms that constitute our mandate. Under unreasonable pressure to manifest change and results, both producers and audiences can find themselves in the position of forcing action based on *evidence*, of deprivation, flouting of rights and dysfunctional administration, but without critical dialoguing and concerted review. As Thomas Gisborne (in Steedman, 2002, pp. 44–45) cautions about the 'domiciliation of authority' and 'gathering with other justices in petty sessions',

> the principal share of his business is transacted in his own house, before few spectators, and those in general indigent and illiterate. Hence he [the magistrate] is liable to become dictatorial, brow-beating, consequential, and ill-humoured, domineering in his inclinations, dogmatical in his opinions and arbitrary in his decisions.

Social, cultural and educational stratifications can ensure access to media texts while denying admission to affected publics; correspondingly, these texts can substitute participation with grasping storylines and social lamentation. Out of sight from those who provide the necessary stamps that certify citizenship and existence, small-scale, participatory media within the city strive to produce resilient objects from the frayed, partial and lethal elements that constitute existence. As Steedman (2002, p. 81) theorizes, a fundamental engagement with these archives, documents, texts and productions reveals circumstances where one 'cannot help what is not really there' and can only make a series of substitutes in lieu of sources and origins. Perhaps the task is not to record but to narrate radically, to make possible the fissures, respites and spaces that can then be inhabited by memories, and this making sensible should not be entirely dependent on community film-makers and historians. Engaging the use and dissemination of texts through inconsistently imagined communal histories, non-history or counter-history, with visions of a more egalitarian epoch, is to affirmatively follow the community expression of constructing creative markers and refuge from minor, sidelined and rejected produce.

REFERENCES

Ahmed, S. (2015). *The cultural politics of emotion* (2nd ed.). Routledge.

Bailey, A., Farquharson, K., Marjoribanks, T., & Nolan, D. (2014). Being heard: Mentoring as part of a community media intervention. *Communication, Politics & Culture, 47*(2), 1–16.

Dreher, T. (2010). Speaking up or being heard? Community media interventions and the politics of listening. *Media, Culture & Society 32*(1), 85–103.

Ekotto, F., & Koh, A. (Eds.). (2009). *Rethinking third cinema: The role of anti-colonial media and aesthetics in postmodernity.* Lit; Distributed in North America by Transaction Publishers.

Frick, C. (2011). *Saving cinema: The politics of preservation.* Oxford University Press.

Fuller, L. K. (2007). *Community media: International perspectives.* Palgrave Macmillan. http://site.ebrary.com/lib/alltitles/docDetail.action?docID=10194091

Ginzburg, C. (2012). *Threads and traces: True, false, fictive.* University of California Press.

Ishizuka, K. L., & Zimmermann, P. R. (Eds.). (2008). *Mining the home movie: Excavations in histories and memories.* University of California Press.

Iyer, L., Khanna, T., & Varshney, A. (2013). Caste and entrepreneurship in India. *Economic and Political Weekly, 48*(6), 52–60.

Low, B., Salvio, P. M., & Rose, C. B. (2016). *Community-based media pedagogies: Relational practices of listening in the commons.* Taylor & Francis Group. http://ebookcentral.proquest.com/lib/pitt-ebooks/detail.action?docID=4710852

Moyna, M. (2015). Railways pulled up over scavengers. *Down to Earth*, July 4, 2015. https://www.downtoearth.org.in/news/railways-pulled-up-over-scavengers-39328.

Oxfam India. (2019, September 2). *Who tells our stories matters: Representation of marginalised caste groups in Indian newsrooms.* Oxfamindia.Org. /workingpaper/who-tells-our-stories-matters-representation-marginalised-caste-groups-indian-newsrooms.

Pavarala, V. (2015, December). Community radio 'Under progress': Resuming a paused revolution. *Economic & Political Weekly.* https://bi-gale-com.pitt.idm.oclc.org/global/article/GALE|A438302103?u=upitt_main&sid=summon

Pavarala, V., & Malik, K. K. (2007). *Other voices: The struggle for community radio in India.* SAGE Publications.

Post-Cinema. (2016, April 11). *3.4 Splitting the atom: Post-cinematic articulations of sound and vision.* http://reframe.sussex.ac.uk/post-cinema/3-4-shaviro/

Rennie, E. (2006). *Community media: A global introduction. Critical media studies.* Rowman & Littlefield.

Singer, B. (2001). *Melodrama and modernity: Early sensational cinema and its contexts. Film and Culture.* Columbia University Press.

Steedman, C. (2002). *Dust: The archive and cultural history. Encounters.* Rutgers University Press.

TISS. (2016). *Transforming M Ward—Field action project*. https://www.tiss.edu/view/11/projects/transforming-m-ward/

Titus, N. T. (2020). The other cinemas: Recycled content, vulnerable bodies, and the gradual dismantling of publicness. In A. Monteiro, K. P. Jayasankar, & Amit Rai (Eds.), *Diginaka: Where the digital meets the local in India* (pp. 168–193). Orient Blackswan.

Teltumbde, A. (2010). *The persistence of caste: The Khairlanji murders and India's hidden apartheid*. Zed Books.

UN India. (2020). *Breaking free: Rehabilitating manual scavengers*. https://webcache.googleusercontent.com/search?q=cache:l1q78m8Z62wJ:https://in.one.un.org/page/breaking-free-rehabilitating-manual-scavengers/+&cd=1&hl=en&ct=clnk&gl=us

United Nations Development Programme. (2009). *Overcoming barriers: Human mobility and development*. Human Development Report. http://hdr.undp.org/en/content/human-development-report-2009

United Nations Educational, Scientific and Cultural Organization. (UNESCO). (2007). *India to establish 4000 community radio stations under new community radio policy*. http://www.unesco.org/new/en/communication-and-information/resources/news-and-in-focus-articles/all-news/news/india_to_establish_4000_community_radio_stations_under_new_c/

Chapter 10

Muslim Community Media and the Public Sphere
The Contribution of *The Milli Gazette* and *TwoCircles.net*

Mahtab Alam

The importance of media as avenues for self-representation, debate, mobilization and outreach can hardly be emphasized enough. This rings true for the Muslims of India as well, who had recognized their significance early on while dealing with adverse situations. This awareness reflects remarkably well in the following verse of the 19th-century Urdu poet and civil servant Akbar Allahabadi:

> *Kheencho na kamaano ko na talvaar nikaalo*
> *Jab top muqaabil ho to akhbaar nikaalo*
>
> Do not string your bow or take out the sabre
> When faced with cannon fire, publish a newspaper[1]

In fact, the use of newspapers and periodicals by Muslim leaders and community organizations to voice their concerns, opinions and grievances had begun much before Allahabadi wrote the couplet cited above. There were many newspapers and journals that were being

---

[1] Author's translation.

published and edited by Muslims, much like the other communities of the country. Apart from Urdu, which then enjoyed the status of lingua franca, there were publications in English and other languages, such as Bengali and Malayalam, as well.

In this article, I seek to examine the evolution and development of Muslim community media in independent India. In doing so, I focus on two prominent English-language publications, namely *The Milli Gazette* (MG) and *TwoCircles.net* (TCN). Based on secondary sources and my own experience of working with these two projects, directly and indirectly, I seek to explore the extent to which these two initiatives have been able to change the larger narrative around Muslims in India. Moreover, I try to explain the challenges that they face. I also present some prescriptive arguments over what could be done to resolve the challenges faced by the Muslim community media organizations in India. I further explore possible ways to make them more inclusive, accessible, culturally vibrant, financially viable and user-friendly.

According to Siddharth Varadarajan (2009),

> in the early 19th century, one finds the emergence of newspapers essentially as a vehicle for the articulation of community-centric griev-ances or concerns, sometimes in a benign way—centred on religious reform, for example—but often in a manner that posited communities as antithetical, opposed to each other. (Varadarajan, 2009, p. 101)

However, he further notes, 'there were moments when the Indian print media tried to transcend the religious divide and strive for the elabora-tion of an Indian identity. One such moment in the history of Indian journalism arguably occurred in 1857, when Delhi had a very active Urdu press' (Varadarajan, 2009, p. 101). In this regard, Varadarajan cites the example of two Urdu publications, namely *Sayyed-ul Akhbar* and *Delhi Urdu Akhbar*, which played a prominent role in the First Indian War of Independence of 1857. It can be noted that *Delhi Urdu Akhbar* was published and edited by Maulvi Muhammad Baqar, who was eventually shot dead by British military officer William Stephen Raikes Hodson, after the recapture of Delhi. Many believe that he was the first journalist to sacrifice his life for the freedom of India and that he 'was perhaps the first editor who paid with his life for advocating a vision of an India that was based on the unity of people, not simply on the elaboration of sectarian interests' (Varadarajan, 2009, p. 101). During the freedom struggle, Muslim community media outlets played a very important role in amplifying the anti-colonial movement, apart from raising their own concerns and grievances.

MASS MEDIA AND MUSLIMS IN INDEPENDENT INDIA

However, with the partition of India and the subsequent decline of Urdu, the issues, voices and concerns of Muslims, particularly of North India, found marginalized representation in the media, especially main-stream media. What was also unfortunate was the fact that independent India projected only the Urdu-speaking population of Muslims of northern India, mainly Uttar Pradesh and erstwhile Bihar, which included Jharkhand, as comprising the 'real' or 'mainstream' Muslims—this, despite the fact that a large number of Indian Muslims resided in non-Urdu-speaking states, such as Assam, West Bengal and Kerala. Since the Muslims of these regions did not speak or write Urdu, their voices were further marginalized. At the same time, mainstream media organizations left no stone unturned to present Muslims 'as "fanatical" and "fundamentalists", and the acts of a few individuals belonging to the community were perceived as being approved by the (entire) community' (Engineer, 1999, p. 2132). It has also been observed that not only communally blatant or well-known right-wing media outlets, but also a few liberal outlets and a large section of mainstream organizations, have been doing this in the name of maintaining balance or giving opportunity to 'all sides'.

Moreover, as Avinash K. Mishra has rightly pointed out, mainstream media have 'paid little attention to the history and contemporary social and economic conditions of "ordinary" Indian Muslims.... Whenever there is a communal conflict, all Muslims are seen by the media as not only supporters of Pakistan but also loyal to it' (Mishra, 2010, pp. 20–21). According to Hasan Kamal, a noted Urdu writer, lyricist and columnist, this has led to a situation wherein Muslims of India have been deprived of credible and empowered sociopolitical leadership, and 'thus the socio-economic condition of the Muslims never gained

192 | Mahtab Alam

attention in Independent India' (Mishra, 2010, p. 21). Mainstream media is divided into two contradictory groups as far as the projection of the image of Muslims is concerned, a point noted by late journalist Dileep Padgaonkar. While one stereotypes them as fanatical and fundamentalist, the other fails to understand how a community projected as above 'always does exceptionally well in music, sports, entertainment and in education too, like the former Indian President Dr. Kalam' (Padgaonkar cited in Kumar, 2011, p. 60).

This dominant narrative painted by mainstream media gave one an impression that nothing else was happening with Muslim communities across India. It was in order to fill this gap and to put forward an alternative and comprehensive narrative about Indian Muslims that two English-language Muslim media organizations were started in the first decade of this century. The two platforms that have done a considerable amount of work in this time period are MG (only its website is now functional, while the print version is defunct) and TCN (digital platform). These two publications are important, because over the years, they have been able to amplify the issues and concerns of the community. And in several cases, reportage by these publications has led to wider coverage of such issues in mainstream media. These platforms have also worked as forums to discuss a range of sociopolitical, cultural, educational and religious issues, including intra-community debates. Moreover, they have also served as launch pads for several budding journalists from the community, as well as having helped hone their talents.

The phrase often used by Muslims to describe Muslim community media organizations or platforms is 'Milli Media'. The term *milli* has Arabic origins and is used to describe both the 'nation' and the 'community'. These organizations might not strictly subscribe to the definition of community media; however, they come across as one in their essence, functioning and objectives. '*Milli* media', like other community media, are used as a 'tool of communication' which allows the community 'to create their own means of cultural expression, news, information and dialogue' (Bellardi, 2016). Similarly, these projects are run on a not-for-profit purpose. MG, for example, was published by Pharos Media & Publishing Pvt. Ltd, but it did not ever aim to earn profits like any other private limited company. On the other hand, TCN is registered as a non-profit organization in Massachusetts, United States, which is governed by a board of directors and accepts donations to carry out its activities.

Before we proceed further, it is imperative to state that these were not the only attempts in this direction. Towards the end of the 1980s, the Muslim elites in Delhi, led by noted Islamic scholar Sayyid Abulhasan Ali Nadwi, former civil servant and educationist Syed Hamid, the owner of Hamdard Laboratories (India), Hakim Abdul Hamid, and some other businessmen, made a failed attempt to launch a daily newspaper in English. Subsequently, in October 1989, a tabloid, *One Nation Chronicle*, was launched under the editorship of Syed Hamid from Delhi, but this too failed to make a mark and was made a fortnightly under a new name, *Nation and the World*. Similarly, during this period, another English-language magazine, called *Meantime*, was launched from Bangalore. Also, in 1983, diplomat-turned-community-leader Syed Shahabuddin launched the monthly *Muslim India*. And in 1988, a news wire service, *Feature and News Alliance* (FANA), was launched from New Delhi under the leadership of journalist Maqbool Ahmad Siraj, better known as M. A. Siraj.

MG was started in the year 2000 as a 32-page fortnightly newspaper by Dr Zafarul Islam Khan, a Manchester University (United Kingdom)-educated, bilingual—Arabic and English—journalist and writer. The web portal TCN was started in 2006 by Massachusetts (United States)-based Kashif-ul-Huda, a person of Indian origin.

THE STORY OF *THE MILLI GAZETTE*

At the beginning of the millennium in 2000, the fortnightly MG was launched by a small team of journalists, writers and translators, headed by its founder and editor-in-chief, Dr Zafarul Islam Khan. According to Khan, the main reason for bringing out MG was:

> that most of the news regarding the Muslim community was ignored by the mainstream media and only Urdu newspapers published them. You don't find any in the English-language newspapers. I have always said that

whenever you pick up an English-language Indian newspaper, it seems
as if the 200-million-strong community of Muslims did not exist at all.
Had they been sleeping the whole previous day and did nothing at all?
This can't be possible. Many must have done things worth mentioning.
Someone might have written a book or done something which should
be acknowledged. Someone might have won an award in recognition of
his meritorious services. Someone might have founded an educational
institution like a school, college or university. But the national, I mean
non-Urdu, media seems to have no interest in Muslims. But, of course,
if someone has given triple talaq to his wife or some such mischief then
this will be big news for the national media. Having this scenario in our
mind, we decided to bring out a newspaper wherein we could publish
and celebrate the achievements and contributions of the Indian Muslim
community. (Bastawi, 2017)

Hence, it was not surprising to see that every issue had regular columns and dedicated pages, such as news from the states, particularly
Jammu and Kashmir, Gujarat and Kerala. It also had sections such
as 'Community News' and 'News Makers', apart from columns on
foreign affairs and human rights and cartoons. One important facet of
MG was that it bridged the communication gap that existed between
Urdu-reading Muslims and those who could not or did not read Urdu
but were interested in knowing about the community if information
was made available in English—these included both Muslims and non-
Muslims. Every issue would carry scores of translated, curated and originally reported pieces about the activities of the community across India.
What made MG distinct from other Muslim publications, like *Radiance
Weekly* and *Islamic Voice*, was that it tried to cover all kinds of news and
views that pertained to Muslims of India. This comes out quite clearly
in the case of the publication of a report (16–31 October 2004) titled
'Model Nikahnama: A Victim to the Ego of Muslim Activists'. The
report was very critical of the practice of triple *talaq*[2] and the stand taken
by the All India Muslim Personal Law Board (AIMPLB). Criticizing
the MG report, Uzma Naheed, a member of AIMPLB, wrote a letter
to the editor saying:

---

[2] See https://blog.ipleaders.in/need-know-model-nikahnama/ for more information on Model Nikahnama and triple *talaq*.

It was really painful to read the report on Nikahnama. I never expected a newspaper that is being edited by you to be carrying such a biased report on a sensitive subject. It's a pity that while working for masses we have to fight with friends and foe alike for any cause; sometimes I feel that we don't deserve any solution and our sufferings are out of our own misdeeds and unnecessary conflicts. (Naheed, 2004)

Responding to Naheed's rejoinder, the editor replied:

From the very first issue, I have tried to keep *Milli Gazette* as an open forum for the *Millat* (Muslim community as a whole). You may not like someone's ideas and that someone may not like yours and mine but he/she has a right to be listened to. Problems in societies and countries start when this right is denied. Freedom of expression and healthy debate are necessary to have a healthy society. (Khan, 2004)

Moreover, MG also published a detailed rejoinder by the AIMPLB member and a reply to the same by the writer of the original story, M. H. Lakdawala (2004).

There are several other important aspects of the newspaper. It did not limit itself to just one dominant voice within the community but ensured that differing voices within the community were also given space. It was fiercely independent in its coverage and rose above the sectarian interests within the community and the intra-community conflicts. Unlike most other Muslim community magazines and journals, it always strove against becoming the mouthpiece of any particular organization or sect. This was possible because MG was not brought out or funded by any one organization or *jamaat*. The newspaper was largely funded by the editor himself, from the money he had earned through doing Arabic-to-English translations, publishing books and running newspaper clipping services. Apart from that, he also received some financial help from like-minded people and advertisements from some business houses, along with subscriptions. Despite the lack of any political or financial backing, MG did not hesitate to take anti-establishment stances, be it against the Indian National Congress (INC), the Bharatiya Janata Party (BJP) or any other political party that was in power. MG was so fiercely independent that it did not think twice before publishing a news item prominently about the editor's father and noted Islamic scholar Maulana Wahiduddin Khan when the latter tacitly supported the BJP ahead of the Lok Sabha elections in 2004 (Imam, 2004).

Owing to its inclination towards upholding a bold stand always, it started facing a lot of pressure from the BJP-led government in recent years, especially after the publication of a report titled "'We Don't Recruit Muslims" : Modi govt's AYUSH Ministry'. The report was based on information obtained through the right to information (RTI) by a senior journalist, Pushp Sharma (2016). The report exposed how the Ministry of Ayurveda, Yoga & Naturopathy, Unani, Siddha and Homoeopathy (AYUSH) exhibited a policy bias of hiring candidates belonging to only certain castes and religions. The story was picked up by mainstream media channels and newspapers and snowballed into a 3-year-long battle between the Delhi Police and the publication. According to a news report (Sarkar, 2019), the battle involved an allegedly forged complaint letter, intimidation techniques, the paradoxical arrest of the reporter and the purposefully delayed proof that was directed to be furnished by higher authorities, all of which culminated in the closure of the print edition of MG at the end of 2016. Calling it an attack on the freedom of the press, the editor of MG wrote on the first page of the July 2016 edition:

> ...this three-pronged attack on *MG* simply shows the desperation of the Modi government to silence this little nagging bird. We are fighting and will continue to fight against this injustice through all legal venues open to us. But should the Modi Govt succeed in silencing this feeble voice, we will call it a day and will leave it to history to remember this as yet another colossal injustice to the freedom of Press the like of which was inflicted by the colonial rulers on Maulana Azad's Al-*Balagh* and Muhammad Ali's *Hamdard* and *Comrade*. (Khan, 2016, p. 1)

Another strong point about the publication was its documentation of the Muslims of India, because of which it has achieved an unparalleled archival value in the country. There was hardly any important aspect of the community which was not documented by the publication in its 16 years of publication, all of which is readily available online, without any cost. Apart from its print edition, the publication has had a very good online presence from the beginning, with strong search engine optimization (SEO). Hence, it was not just limited to those who subscribed to the physical paper or read it in libraries but also accessible to netizens across the world. The newspaper also focused on news related to instances of communal amity in different parts of the country and published them quite prominently and regularly. For example, in 2010, the paper on its front page published a news report, along with pictures, with the title 'Sikhs Rebuild Mosque Demolished in 1947'—of an incident that had taken place in Sarwarpur, 10 km from Samrala town of Punjab. Taking note of the news, famous novelist and writer Khushwant Singh had written in his column:

> On the front page of *The Milli Gazette* there was a news item written by its editor Zafarul ul Islam Khan, which I felt should have made to the headlines of every national daily and TV channels. But I did not see it appear in any other journal and felt saddened that our media had failed to perform its duty. (Singh, 2010)

Like any other scarcely funded and short-staffed publication, MG too had its share of shortcomings. One of the major weaknesses of the newspaper was that it lacked substantial original and ground reporting. A large chunk of the content published in the newspaper was reproduction of what was already available online, translation from Urdu and Hindi sources and re-publication from foreign journals and newspapers. Another shortcoming of it was that it was very text-heavy, and little attention was paid to how the content should be produced and presented. Lack of designing and imaging often made it look monotonous. Moreover, with dwindling postal services, it increasingly became difficult for MG to deliver the paper on time. On the other hand, with the boom of digital news and views platforms, the readers were able to get news and information in real time. By the time copies of MG reached them, they had already accessed large portions of the content published in the newspaper, in one way or the other. It is in this context that the initiation and functioning of the online media platforms like TCN become important. Over the years, TCN has emerged as the best source in English from which to get news and information about Muslims of India.

EMERGENCE OF *TWOCIRCLES.net*

TCN was started to cover issues related to Indian Muslims and to narra-tivize their lifeworld. However, its founder and editor, Kashif-ul-Huda, was quite clear that 'we are not pro-Muslim'. In an interview with *Open Magazine*, he explained to the interviewer that, 'We are Muslim-focused. We are not here to promote anyone's agenda. We are not an Islamic website. We are a Muslim news organization'.

Explaining the rationale behind starting TCN, he added that,

> mainstream media does not devote the time and space needed to show the complete picture. Usually, Muslims tend to hit the headlines in negative contexts—terrorism, *fatwa*, backwardness.... So we said, 'We need to read Muslim stories in a positive context. Not just for the community's sake, but for the nation's sake. (Polanki, 2010)

He rightly claimed that the website was

> often critical of our leaders.... And we want to be more critical of trends in the Muslim community. We are not here to say that there is no terrorism or radicalism. While community media tends to get emotional and sectarian, or uses religious terminology, we avoid that. (Polanki, 2010)

According to the former *Indian Express* journalist Irena Akbar (2011), the most striking thing about TCN is that it is not Islamic and there is no section dedicated to religious discourse, and its readers are not just Muslims. The readers 'include policy planners and politicians as well'. In an op-ed that she wrote for the *Indian Express*, she further states that Syeda Hameed, a member of the Planning Commission, described TCN 'as a portal that reports on the development/discrimination binary' (Akbar, 2011).

However, what made TCN really distinct from MG or other Muslim community media initiatives was not the stance that it took or the diversity of opinions that it published but the space that it gave to ground reports and news as opposed to opinions. It also narrated the stories from a journalistic angle despite wearing the communitarian lens. TCN reporters and contributors were always in search of new stories, and over a period of 5–7 years, TCN managed to break several stories related to Muslims of India. At one point of time, its reporters and contributors were based in different parts of the country—Kerala, Assam, Bengal, Uttar Pradesh, Bihar, Maharashtra, Gujarat, etc.—apart from Delhi, and they reported extensively on issues that were local, as well as of national importance, and related to Muslims of India. One of the biggest journalistic contributions of TCN was the number of special series of ground reports that it carried out over the years. In 2008, after the alleged police 'encounter' in Delhi's Batla House locality,[3] Azamgarh town of Uttar Pradesh was branded as 'Aatankgarh' (den of terrorism) in the mainstream media discourse. Two of the Muslim boys killed and a few others arrested in cases related to the September 2008 serial blasts in Delhi happened to be from Azamgarh. Instead of just reporting on the police claims, as most of the media organizations were doing at that point of time, TCN sent its reporter to ground zero, which resulted in a series of 10 stories titled 'Azamgarh Speaks'.[4] The series covered the presence of fear in the wake of the encounter and the arrests, the community life of the town, including Hindu–Muslim relations, and issues related to the progress and development of the community, as well as the town. One of the stories from this series (Falahi, 2008) reported how Muslim girls in Azamgarh were giving a tough fight to the boys in the field of higher education. Interestingly, a few years later (June 2010), the BJP used a picture from this series, of Muslim girls working on computers, in a full-page advertisement published in several dailies of Bihar, projecting that those girls were from Gujarat, with the claim of 'Muslims Shining in Gujarat' (Express News Service, 2010). This happened a day before the then chief minister of Gujarat Narendra Modi arrived in Patna to attend a two-day BJP national executive meeting. The same photo was lifted by the INC government of Rajasthan in March 2012, for the advertisement that it issued to celebrate the 63rd Rajasthan Diwas, which was published in several newspapers, including some national English dailies like the *Hindu* (Falahi, 2012).

---

[3] A detailed account of the alleged encounter and its aftermath can be found at https://revolutionarydemocracy.org/batla/batla.htm
[4] See http://twocircles.net/special_reports/azamgarh_speaks.html

Another important series commissioned and published by TCN was about the Nellie massacre[5] of 1983 in Assam[6] (2009). On 18 February 1983, over 1,000 Muslims were massacred in Nellie region of Assam in less than 24 hours. According to official reports, the massacre left 1,819 people dead and several other thousands injured. However, unofficial sources and the people of Nellie believe that the death toll could actually be around 5,000. In the Nellie massacre series, six stories were published which covered different aspects of the violence that had taken place, such as the names of those killed, testimonies of the family members of the deceased, as well as the injured, the genesis of the 'anti-foreigners' movement of Assam, which led to the massacre, and the current status of the cases. This was perhaps the first such extensive coverage of the issue in any English-language media outlet. Similarly, TCN ran a series titled 'Terror Tales'[7] under which more than 50 stories, mainly ground reports, were published between 2009 and 2014. These stories were about the Muslim youth who had been wrongly implicated in terrorism cases all across India. In most of the cases, TCN was the first to bring out the stories of those who found themselves on the wrong side of justice, which were later picked up by mainstream media. These and other stories of TCN were also lifted by the Urdu media and other community media platforms in different languages. Moreover, going beyond the anti-Muslim violence of 2002 in Gujarat, TCN ran a series of seven stories covering the Muslim history of the state, the marginalization of Muslims and the lives and struggles of different Muslim communities in the state. Furthermore, it ran a series on the situation of Muslims 5 years after the publication of the Sachar Committee Report.[8] The focus of the series was to find out who benefitted most out of the report—the politicians or the common Muslim on the street—the extent to which it benefitted them and what measures had been adopted as far as the committee's recommenda-tions were concerned. In addition to all these, TCN also regularly

---

[5] Please see https://www.thequint.com/explainers/nellie-massacre-explained

[6] See http://twocircles.net/special_reports/nellie_1983.html

[7] See http://twocircles.net/Special_Reports/terror_tales.html

[8] See http://twocircles.net/2011nov19/tcn_series_situation_muslims_after_5_years_sachar_report.html

published report cards of Muslim leaders elected to the Parliament of India. It is pertinent to note that the stories commissioned and published by TCN were not always about gloom and doom. TCN regularly gave space to uplifting stories about the community under the section 'TCN Positive'.[9]

One of the most innovative projects taken up by TCN was its Ramadan Photo Series (Borpujari, 2018) from the year 2012. In this series, it published one picture every day depicting different aspects of the month and how it is observed. According to the editor, the idea was to show Ramzan beyond food pictures—after all, it was a month of fasting and seeking purification. 'It was again a way to drop all the stereotypes and have a fresh look at the community'. The project was led by a young female Muslim documentary photographer, Natisha Mallick. It began in Delhi but was later taken to different cities with the help of other photographers. Over the years, TCN emerged as a model for professionally managed community media organizations. Mohammed Reyaz (2021) rightly notes that TCN's success inspired and led to 'the mushrooming of many such news portals, including *Muslim Mirror, India Tomorrow, Caravan Daily* (renamed as *Clarion India*), TheCognate.com, Indian Muslim Observer, Siyasat.net, etc. often started by former employees or contributors of TCN'. For example, former news editor of TCN Mumtaz Alam Falahi himself helped in running and managing three such portals, namely *Muslim Mirror, India Tomorrow* and *Caravan Daily*, at different points of time after leaving TCN. Moreover, community initiatives, like MG and TCN, also helped in training a new breed of journalists directly and indirectly, 'who feel that unless they sit up and do something, the English media's coverage of geopolitics and terrorism will not improve' (Menon, 2013). Similarly, many people who worked with TCN at some point of time, either as staffers or as regular contributors, eventually joined mainstream English media houses, such as the *Hindu* and the *Indian Express*.

In the last few years, TCN has tried to 'reimagine' itself and become a voice for the marginalized sections of India and not just the Muslims of India. At the ideational level, this was indeed a novel move in the

---

[9] See http://twocircles.net/special_reports/tcnpositive.html

202 | Mahtab Alam

right direction. However, in order to become true to its tagline—'Mainstream of the Marginalised'—a lot of human and financial resources were required. Unfortunately, TCN could not gather or avail of these resources. As a result, as it eased its original focus on Muslims, it was not able to do justice to the issues related to other marginalized communities, such as adivasis and Dalits. Over the years, the focus also seems to have shifted from English to Hindi. However, the lack of able hands and good reporters in Hindi too has left TCN bereft of being able to leave a mark or make its presence felt in the market as it was able to do in the first 10 years of its operation, from 2006 to 2016. As of today, TCN is on the verge of becoming yet another website providing news about Muslims of India. It has lost its uniqueness and speciality in the market of ideas and journalism. This has happened due to various reasons, and there are several commonalities between the experiments of MG and those of TCN.

CONCLUSION

There is no doubt that the community media initiatives like MG and TCN have been able to push the boundaries, break stereotypes about the Muslim community, challenge the dominant narrative and develop a new breed of young dynamic journalists, mostly Muslims, who can write about Muslim issues objectively. However, much of the task set out by these organizations, or what actually needs to be done in order to paint a true picture of the community or provide accurate and timely news about the community, still lies unfinished and unfulfilled. There are four broad reasons for this state of affairs, namely the lack of funds or a business model, the lack of human resources, or the so-called 'brain drain', an individual-centric system, or the lack of an institutional mechanism, and the lack of understanding about the nature and functioning of the media industry. First of all, over the years, both MG and TCN had to scale down their operations due to financial constraints. In private as well as in public conversations, the people behind these initiatives have complained about the lack of funds (Raza, 2018). Due to lack of funds, it also becomes very difficult to hire suitably trained people, as they come with a certain minimum cost or expectation of a basic salary. Moreover, this is also linked to the 'brain drain' problem of community media organizations. Since they are not in a position to pay decent salaries and provide other benefits to their employees, skilled people who often work with these organizations move on to greener pastures for want of better opportunities. This also happens because while working with community media organizations, journalists have to carry the burden of being associated with the tag of 'community media', and they are not taken seriously by their own fellows and friends in the larger journalistic fraternity. Hence, it becomes very difficult to maintain the quality of journalism. The third issue faced by community media organizations is the lack of an institutional mechanism, as most of these organizations, as was also observed in the case of MG and TCN, are one-person-driven or revolve around one person. Hence, as long as the person is able to give their time and undivided attention to the project, they do really well, but once they start focusing on other sources to earn their livelihood and to sustain themselves, the organizations are not left in a position where they can sustain such initiatives in the long run. Furthermore, since most of the people who run these media initiatives do not have enough prior experience of running media houses or have not worked in newsrooms for long, they are often not able to understand the nature, functioning and dynamics of the industry, which in turn becomes a handicap while dealing with the broader ecosystem, often pushing things to the margins.

There is however enough scope for re-imagination as far as Muslim community media platforms (including TCN) are concerned. For example, they are yet to adapt mobile and online new media and make use of multimedia platforms to narrate stories in an engaging and powerful manner—this, despite the fact that there are several freely available ready-to-use apps that present stories in an innovative way. Needless to say, mobile and online new media today are the most powerful media to tell stories and/or build counter-narratives. In this regard, during the protests against the Citizenship (Amendment) Act (CAA), one such experiment (Nair, 2020) was done by Mohammed Tasleem, a student of Jamia Millia Islamia, whose Facebook page 'Jamia World' emerged as a popular platform with more than 100,000 followers. 'My motto is to ensure that the news that most mainstream media outlets do not want to show for whatever reasons reaches the people. This is what I do using social media', he said in an interview with the *Hindu*. According to the newspaper, he uploaded 'close to half-a-dozen videos, popular among which are speeches delivered at the protest site, graphic details of police lathi-charge, live telecast of Delhi Police intrusion into the Jamia library and so on' (Nair, 2020). If this can be done by a single person, it can certainly be done by community media organizations with a little help from seasoned multimedia journalists and producers.

Fortunately, unlike two decades ago, there are several organizations and individuals today who are ready to advise these community media organizations on the effective ways of content production, curation and dissemination. What is also required is to train community journalists and correspondents across languages and regions, so that the content becomes more diverse and inclusive. In this regard, the organizations like Video Volunteers and Ideosync Media Combine can be approached. Apart from these, community platforms also lack perspectives and skills to check the so-called 'fake news', disinformation and harmful propaganda. It would be very useful if community media organizations were to invest in this direction as well, especially because a large chunk of fake news is directed towards Muslims. Similarly, the use of data-driven and infographics-based interactive stories needs to be prioritized as well, so that complicated stories can be explained in accessible and easy-to-understand formats.

In short, there is no denying the fact that in the last two decades, English-medium Muslim community media initiatives have made substantial progress. Thanks to these initiatives, slowly but surely, mainstream media narratives about the community are being challenged. However, much needs to be done in order to make the voices of the community heard and represented properly. This would only be possible through making these platforms independent, financially viable and professionally competent.

REFERENCES

Akbar, I. (2011, March 12). The good word. *The Indian Express*. http://archive.indianexpress.com/news/the-good-word/760752/

Bastawi, A. A. (2017, February 4). *English fortnightly Milli Gazette says goodbye to readers*. Urdu Media Monitor. https://www.urdumediamonitor.com/2017/02/04/english-fortnightly-milli-gazette-says-goodbye-readers/

Bellardi, N. (2016). *What is community media?* http://europeanjournalists.org/mediaagainsthate/what-is-community-media/

Borpujari, P. (2018, June 16). The month of the spirit: The everyday lives of Muslims during Ramzan. *The Hindu.* https://www.thehindu.com/society/the-month-of-the-spirit-the-everyday-lives-of-muslims-during-ramzan/article24171203.ece

Engineer, A. A. (1999). Media and minorities: Exclusions, distortions and stereotypes. *Economic and Political Weekly, 34*(31), 2132–2133.

Express News Service. (2010, June 12). In Modi Government Ad, Azamgarh girls become Gujarat's new Muslim face. *Indian Express.* http://archive.indianexpress.com/news/in-modi-government-ad-azamgarh-girls-become-gujarat-s-new-muslim-face/632927/

Falahi, M. A. (2008, November 24). *Muslim girls in Azamgarh getting higher education, giving tough fight to boys.* TwoCircles.net. http://www.twocircles.net/2008nov23/muslim_girls_azamgarh_getting_higher_education_giving_tough_fight_boys.html

Falahi, M. A. (2012, March 31). *Now Rajasthan Govt. lifts TCN photo of Azamgarh girls.* TwoCircles.net. http://twocircles.net/2012mar31/now_rajasthan_govt_lifts_tcn_photo_azamgarh_girls.html

Imam, M. (2004, April 16–30). Vajpayee Himayat committee. *The Milli Gazette.* http://www.milligazette.com/Archives/2004/16-30Apr04-Print-Edition/1604200418.htm

Khan, Z.-I. (2004, November 16–30). Letters. *The Milli Gazette.* http://www.milligazette.com/Archives/2004/16-30Nov04-Print-Edition/163011200441.htm

Khan, Z.-I. (2016, July 1–15). Modi Govt is after Indian Muslims' Newspaper Milli Gazette. *The Milli Gazette.* http://www.milligazette.com/news/14437-modi-govt-is-after-indian-muslims-milli-gazette

Kumar, A. (2011). Mass media and muslims in India: Representation or subversion. *Journal of Muslim Minority Affairs, 31*(1), 59–77.

Lakdawala, M. H. (2004, October 16–31). 'Model Nikahnama': A victim to the ego of Muslim activists. *The Milli Gazette.* http://www.milligazette.com/Archives/2004/16-31Oct04-Print-Edition/163110200408.htm

Menon, M. (2013, April 26). Media and Muslims: Fact and fiction. *The Hindu.* https://www.thehindu.com/opinion/blogs/blog-free-for-all/article4657442.ece

Mishra, A. K. (2010). Introduction. In Y. S. Sikand & A. K. Mishra (Eds.), *India mass media: Prejudice against Dalits (&) Muslims* (pp. 15–44). Hope India Publications.

Naheed, U. (2004, November 16–30). Nikahnama report is misleading. *The Milli Gazette.* http://www.milligazette.com/Archives/2004/16-30Nov04-Print-Edition/163011200495.htm#reply

Nair, S. K. (2020, January 26). Channelling the citizen: Role of YouTubers, bloggers in anti-CAA protests. *The Hindu.* https://www.thehindu.com/news/cities/Delhi/channelling-the-citizen/article30654995.ece

Polanki, P. (2010, December 15). Do not let others define you. *Open Magazine.* https://openthemagazine.com/features/world/do-not-let-others-define-you/

Raza, D. (2018, May 26). How Muslim voices are breaking stereotypes online. *Hindustan Times.* https://www.hindustantimes.com/india-news/how-muslim-voices-are-breaking-stereotypes-online/story-53VW85LMW7jFuytPD-HyxhP.html

Reyaz, M. (2021). New media, identity and minorities: The role of internet in mainstreaming of Muslims in India. In S. Malhotra, K. Sharma & S. Dogra (Eds.), *Inhabiting Cyberspace in India: Theory, Perspectives, and Challenges* (p. 62). Springer.

Sarkar, G. (2019, February 14). The curious case of '*The Milli Gazette*'. *Newslaundry.* https://www.newslaundry.com/2019/02/14/the-curious-case-of-the-milli-gazette

Sharma, P. (2016, March 11). We don't recruit Muslims. *The Milli Gazette.* http://www.milligazette.com/news/13831-we-dont-recruit-indian-muslims-modi-govts-ayush-ministry

Singh, K. (2010, June 13). Rebuilding secularism, Gandhi style. *Hindustan Times.* https://www.hindustantimes.com/india/rebuilding-secularism-gandhi-style/story-sFLZqPyGeoQqYUl2cU0kuO.html

Varadarajan, S. (2009). Minority images in the Indian Print Media. In A. Farouqui (Ed.), *Muslims and media images: News versus views* (pp. 100–113). Oxford University Press.

Chapter 11

Theatre for Community Education, Capacity Building and Research

Madhura Dutta

INTRODUCTION

The use of theatre beyond entertainment on stage has a long history. Through changing times, it has been used to mobilize social change through community education and empowerment, raise consciousness, voice concerns and take actions towards one's own development. Such theatre, where the issue of social development is given more importance than theatrical aesthetics, is often referred to as social theatre. Social theatre is 'theatre with specific social agendas' and has some unique characteristics: it is performed in different spaces depending on the participant communities and mostly in places which are not usual spaces for theatre. It aims to build self-esteem, confidence and the capacity to manage emotions, and create new approaches to learning. It facilitates participatory community development and creates leaders at the grassroots level to take charge of their own development. It accommodates 'non-performers' from among the audience into performances.

Inspired in large part by Augusto Boal,[1] under whose aegis participatory forms of social theatre emerged as an effective instrument for
social development in the 1970s, social theatre movements have taken
place in India and have been promoted by the intelligentsia, activists, change leaders, civil societies, etc. to bring about social change
and grassroots activism. This chapter discusses methodologies and
case studies relating to a particular civil society organization in West
Bengal, Contact Base, which has uniquely adapted and integrated
existing social theatre models into effective strategies of participatory
development. Theatre for development, as they call it, has additionally
been inspired by the strong culture of theatre in the state, including popular village theatre and city-based urban theatre, as well as theatre with a
social agenda: the 'new' theatre by Indian People's Theatre Association
(IPTA) and Badal Sircar's non-proscenium political theatre.

Contact Base was established in 2000 in West Bengal. It is also
known popularly as 'banglanatak dot com' after its website (www.
banglanatak.com). It uses theatre as a tool for community education,
capacity building of the grassroots service providers such as health
workers, sanitation coordinators, community leaders, panchayats, etc.
and community-based participatory research. The goal is to bring
about social change and empowerment of the marginalized through
community-led action. The organization works on a project basis
supported by various funders. Although Contact Base started its work
in West Bengal, the organization has since worked across India on
various social issues and has successfully established community action
groups and networks that continue their activism for their own social
development.[2]

One important feature of Contact Base's work is its relationship
with the state. Its philosophy is that for long-term sustainable impact
and for bringing about policy change where required, it is essential

[1] Augusto Boal was a Brazilian director and activist known for developing the
'Theatre of the Oppressed', and specifically a participatory theatre form called
Forum Theatre. A description of Forum Theatre is given in the 'Discussion' section.
[2] This chapter is based on the author's work at Contact Base between 2002
and 2012, as well as her work as a PhD scholar at School of Media and Cultural
Studies, Tata Institute of Social Sciences, between 2011 and 2015.

that the local state machinery be involved in the development process in a conscious way. It tries to align its work with existing schemes and programmes wherever relevant, to build awareness and capacities of the government service providers who are mandated to serve the rural communities but are often ill-equipped to do so, and generally to build a positive relationship between these government service providers and the community. It is possible that in places where the local administration is unfriendly and creates hindrances, the community must design their actions in a different way. However, in most cases, it has been found that the local administration has realized with time that this is an advantageous situation for it and that joint action with the community can strengthen all community work programmes.

In the remainder of this chapter, representative case studies are presented, chosen from several areas across India where Contact Base has worked in, illustrating the three major pillars of its social theatre application: community education, capacity building and participatory research. These case studies have been gathered from personal experience, direct field interviews and internal project reports shared by the organization. Potential concerns about external development agendas getting imposed through this model are also discussed, with a focus on how Contact Base has dealt with this concern.

COMMUNITY EDUCATION

The format used by Contact Base for community education is street theatre integrating local folk theatre forms. The objective of this form of theatre includes creating awareness among rural marginalized communities on various social issues and rights, as well as mobilizing them to take action against social vices and problems in an informed way, through involvement, participation and leadership.

The marginalization and deprivation of remote rural communities is aggravated by a lack of effective information and communication about various rights, laws, schemes and programmes supporting their access to an improved quality of life. Theatre creates a physical space for community engagement, which is the first step to community education. Street theatre has the advantage of physically reaching out to communities, localizing content, integrating local culture and breaking cultural barriers, making communication effective. When used for social change, it also establishes a relationship with the viewers which enables participatory communication, discussions and mobilization. Contact Base motivates the engaged audience to voice out their own stories, feelings and grievances after the shows through a platform of audience interaction which creates an enabling environment, mobilizing action by the informed group of viewers. Subsequent to the theatre shows, the more active members are invited to community meetings for discussions to identify ways in which the community can organize to address the issues. For example, to tackle issues of child trafficking and child marriage, Contact Base has formed local community watch groups to keep track of vulnerable children and get in touch with the Childline if the need arises, or report unfamiliar persons in the village to the panchayat. Parallel to creating an informed community, Contact Base also mobilizes multiple stakeholders to work with community groups in a collaborative manner. It takes community feedback to stakeholders in the local administration for appropriate action and, when necessary, proposes new development initiatives. Overall, it takes a constructive approach through using multiple resources and existing systems to support and strengthen community action. Thus, what it practises is not activism against the administration but rather collaborative action through participation of community action groups in planning and actual action.

In order to understand the gaps and vulnerabilities on the ground, Contact Base carries out a needs assessment study before designing the campaign. This not only enables them to ensure effective information dissemination but also helps avoid an externally imposed top-down approach.

The nature of the actual show varies from one place to another, because different local theatre forms are used in different campaigns. Locations and timings of shows are usually predetermined and pre-announced. Typically, before a show starts, the performers play their instruments or use drums to attract and gather the audience. When the audience gathers around them, the theatre show starts. The show always takes place at a location inside the village or the local market and is always a street performance. No stage is made. The audience gathers around the performers in a circle. It is a scripted show with a story that builds up to a conflict and a climax. Social messages are intertwined in the entire story and are embedded in the dialogues of the characters. There is also a protagonist who is usually depicted as the senior person of the village, or a local health worker, or a non-governmental organization (NGO) representative or a panchayat officer, who is in a socially responsible role and is trusted by the villagers. Local entertainment elements, masks, songs and dance are used in the play to engage the audience better. The audience often gets very involved, and when the show ends, they start interacting freely with the actors. This interaction is coordinated by a field coordinator. As Contact Base works with local stakeholders and service providers, wherever relevant and feasible, it requests local stakeholders, such as *anganwadi* workers, the panchayat *pradhan*, doctors, schoolteachers, etc., to be present to address questions and grievances of the viewers. The names, addresses and contacts of the active participants are also noted down for subsequent follow-up on forming action groups.

The local folk theatre groups or community groups go through a training process that consists of two parts. One part of the training, discussed in more detail in the next section, is about knowledge building of the performers on the social issue or problem to be addressed. This is done through participatory workshops where the participants share their own understanding of the problem and the ground realities and exploitations related to the problem. The trainers, who are usually members of the organization, train them on the various dimensions and complexities of the issue at hand, including the social, legal, psychological and physiological implications. The problem then is understood not as something local and personal but as a more widespread societal issue, thus establishing its importance. The participants also learn about specific and relevant rights, laws, helpline numbers, etc., to be able to interact with and mobilize the audience in an informed way. The second part of the training is about developing the actual theatre production, which involves training on acting and communication skills, including creativity, image making, dialogue, etc. Contact Base also trains the theatre groups in a standard format of the theatre shows to make the delivery of information consistent and strong. These shows usually run for 25–30 minutes, followed by community interactions.

The case study of a campaign in rural Malda (2009–2012) on the issues of child marriage and female child education illustrates Contact Base's theatre-based community education methodology. Contact Base used a folk theatre form called 'Domni', an indigenous satirical rustic folk theatre form of Malda which is popular among the local villagers. There are no female artists, and men dress up as women and play the role of female characters when necessary. The script is developed locally by the artists, and songs and dances are important parts of the show. Traditionally, Domni was performed as small skits, mainly on day-to-day social events, but over time the form evolved to become a longer production. It is traditionally performed in the Khotta language (a mixture of Hindi and Bengali), which is the primary language of the villages where it is popular, though it is often translated into Bengali or Bhojpuri when performed outside Malda. In addition to professional Domni groups, a community self-help group (SHG) of tribal women and a group of adolescent girls who came forward to learn and perform street theatre shows were also trained and engaged in the campaign. The process through which the NGO motivated these representatives of potential victim groups to directly participate in the initiative is also interesting in itself and is described in the next section.

An impact assessment study was carried out by the NGO after the intervention, through interviews and group discussions with the project participants. A state consultation was held by the United Nations Children's Fund (UNICEF) and the West Bengal Department of Women & Child Development and Social Welfare with officers and NGOs to discuss actions taken and impact achieved and to draw up a long-term action plan. A state-level festival with adolescents and children from across the state had also presented their manifesto. The data and case studies from the assessment indicate that the campaign has had a considerable impact. There is improved awareness of problems of early marriage, trafficking, rights of the female child and laws for her protection and opportunities for education and skill empowerment. After the campaign and sensitization, villagers have been able to stop early marriage of girls in their village. Village girls, Panchayati Raj

Institutions (PRI) members and SHG members have provided leadership. Members of the adolescent girls' group themselves have served as an inspiration to many other adolescent girls of the villages who have resisted marriage at an early age. Headmasters of local schools started discussions on the ill effects of early child marriage and dowry, laws against domestic violence and child marriage in life skills education classes in schools. In some cases, villagers are taking care to check the credentials of the grooms before marrying off their daughters. Youth clubs and Gram Unnayan Samitis (Village Development Society) in some villages have started mobilizing against early marriage. Two-way communication channels helped in identifying problems and needs at the grassroots level. The villagers have stressed on building a system through which they can seek the support of law enforcement authorities.

In response to this assessment, a police helpline was started in 2012. The district administration also put in systems for convergent action and set up a Social & Behavior Change Communication Cell (https://web.archive.org/web/20190412105311/https://sbccmalda.org/).

Thus, the campaign in Malda did not remain limited to street theatre shows but mobilized community groups in taking action to stop female-child marriages and facilitated creation of a safety net by informed villagers.

CAPACITY BUILDING

Contact Base uses theatre-based methods for training and capacity building of grassroots service providers, such as health workers, teachers, panchayats and the police. Such methods create a non-threatening environment, which in turn makes learning both participatory and easy. Various theatre-based methods, especially games and participatory exercises, are used to build life skills, communication skills, team building and issue-based learning. According to Contact Base, theatre-based workshops encourage self-realization among the participants, helping them recognize their own potential and build their self-esteem and confidence, eventually allowing them to overcome limitations posed by social exclusion, shyness, inhibition, ignorance and illiteracy. Such methods are also useful for improving communication skills, bringing about greater sensitivity to the opinions and needs of others, and improving problem solving, conflict resolution, needs analysis and multitasking abilities. The participants in theatre workshops learn by doing, which allows them to realize that they have the power to transform their own realities. This realization empowers them to start taking ownership of and eventually control and lead their own development. Theatre-based activities as a method create a space for open discussion, which helps identify local myths, misconceptions and other possible barriers. They encourage community participation and, through taking local knowledge into account, evolve solutions and action plans from within the communities instead of imposing them from the outside.

When Contact Base first started its campaign in Malda, it decided to mobilize the vulnerable girls of the villages to integrate their voices into the process. Hence, it carried out a series of sensitization and capacity development workshops to motivate the female children, which led to some of them deciding to run their own campaign and take action against child marriages. These girls were then trained through a series of workshops. A typical workshop included sessions of interesting exercises, games and discussions. It started with an aspiration mapping exercise wherein the female children were asked to close their eyes and build an image of what they aspired for in their lives. When asked what they had imagined, they narrated that they dreamt of becoming doctors, teachers, social workers, engineers, etc. As part of the same exercise, they were again asked to close their eyes and think and build images of the barriers that existed towards their attaining their aspirations. It was found during the sharing session that most of them attributed their disadvantaged situation to lack of awareness of the importance of female children's education and poverty. After this aspiration mapping exercise, a more positive imagination game was played. The girls closed their eyes, and the facilitator tried to transport them to a surreal world and asked them to experience the feeling from what he narrated. Initially, they were asked to imagine the feeling of walking on fire, ice, etc. Then, they were transported to a utopian world through a story as it was being told, where no evil existed and only friendship prevailed. This exercise created an imagined situation of an aspired life for the girls and also established the power of imagination for positive and constructive thoughts, which was the first step they could take to bring changes into their lives. As part of this exercise, through participatory discussions, what was brought to the fore was that only dreaming of a beautiful world would not suffice and that their leadership and conviction was also required to ensure their rights. As a follow-up to the imagination game and as a more analytical exercise, the girls were divided into groups for mapping and discussion on their village situation, health condition of the villagers, safety and security of the adolescents, domestic violence, etc. This initiated an independent thought process and created a platform for the adolescents to voice their feelings and opinions. As they discussed issues, common feelings among the girls were shared, which also created a feeling of team and collective will to do something together. After the sense of a team was initiated, a team building exercise was conducted to instil the idea in the participants that working as a team would bring greater strength and resilience for them to complete difficult and almost unattainable tasks, such as fighting for their own rights. A girl was asked to stand in the corner of the room. The other participants were informed that their friend (the girl standing in the corner) was in grave danger. She needed help to get out of the corner; otherwise, it would prove fatal for her. The girl in the corner was at a loss and could think of no means to come out of it. The task of the friends was to rescue the girl, with the condition that they could not touch the girl in the corner, although she could touch them. However, if she moved from her given position, her feet were not allowed to touch the ground. After a short discussion, her friends resorted to a laudable action. They unhesitatingly lay down on the floor, without thinking of their beautiful dresses getting spoilt. Then they summoned the girl to cross over with the help of the human bridge they made. It is important to note that the participants took the given problem as their own and tried to solve it after deliberation.

Theatre in this case was used to mobilize and orient the adolescent girls with a sense of independent thinking, confidence and team building for creating an environment where these girls could choose to take action if they wished to. This was a situation where these girls started thinking for themselves with the understanding of their rights and linking those to their own dreams and aspirations.

As an outcome of such workshops, some of the girls came forward to express their desire to take action, and that is when Contact Base started working on their theatrical skills to give them the power of expressing their stories and emotions through a non-threatening but educative tool like social theatre.

When interviewed later by the author, the adolescent girls' group narrated that after they volunteered to perform, they also received training on the issue of child marriage, the negative implications of child marriage, the risks involved and the various messages that could be delivered through the shows. They could also describe the messages on child marriage which they delivered through their shows. They also stated that before they had started their theatre shows, child marriages took place more frequently in their village, but since the time they started doing these shows in their village, child marriages had not been happening. They were of the opinion that once the village audience understood the ill effects of child marriage from their shows, they would stop marrying off their female children. They also said that they themselves had gained information and knowledge. They were now better aware of their rights and could take informed decisions in their own lives. They were also able to better articulate these issues to their parents and sisters. They felt that the attitudes of their own parents towards them had changed, and the parents were now more conscious of the equal rights of both boys and girls and that the girls should get education and be treated in the same way as boys. The children themselves also realized how important education is for their own development.

Another interesting case of capacity building is theatre-based training sessions with multiple local stakeholders (*anganwadi* workers, accredited social health activists (ASHAs), NGOs, community-based organizations, etc.) in the areas of behavioural change, communication and life skills development. Contact Base has realized through its work that several factors related to life skills and communication skills, lack of information on issues at hand and lack of motivation reduce efficient functioning of these grassroots service providers. It was also interesting to note that though these stakeholders on the ground level are assigned for specific functions, the state usually invests very little in building their capacities. Contact Base through its fieldwork has identified this gap and, to make the systems work better, has undertaken a strategy to address the stakeholders at either end—the villagers, who in an informed manner not only demand good services but also own the issues and work in collaboration with the service providers, and the service providers, who with better information, capacities and skills have increased motivation to function as desired and are also pressurized by the community-led action groups.

Theatre games can demonstrate how to bring out the joint responsibility of all the stakeholders for improving village life. Udaipur is an interesting case study in this context. Contact Base was working on child trafficking issues in rural villages of Udaipur, where multiple stakeholders were brought together in a workshop. The group constituted *anganwadi* workers, ASHAs, teachers, villagers who are parents of children, panchayat members, etc. In one of the issue-based games played, one of the participants was asked to stand in the middle of a room and the other participants were asked to imagine that this person was a child. Another participant was identified as an outsider who was visiting the village. Then, two of the villagers were told to imagine that they were the parents of the child, and therefore they formed a ring around the child by holding their hands and locking the circle. As they did so, they were asked to prevent the villager role-playing the outsider from touching the child who was standing inside the circle. They failed to do so, and the external person could touch the child. Then, the two health workers were asked to join the parents and make the circle bigger by holding hands. This time, the external person found it more difficult to touch the child. This exercise was followed by panchayat members joining, other villagers imagining themselves in the role of the police joining. As this exercise continued, the circle around the child became bigger and stronger, and they could easily protect the child. It is interesting that though this appears as a simple concept to a formally educated mind, the participants shared with the author that this role-playing made a far greater impact on their mind in terms of their understanding that it takes a village to protect a child and that everyone in their respective roles have a responsibility towards the same. Along with this kind of role-playing, the factors of vulnerability and ways of prevention were also discussed through participatory methods. Contact Base uses such theatre exercises not only to create awareness and build knowledge of the stakeholders but also to train them in basic communication and life skills that enable them to perform their duties better.

COMMUNITY-BASED RESEARCH

Specific theatre forms, such as forum theatre, have also been adapted by Contact Base for use as a participatory research method, for researching prevailing vulnerabilities and community-based case studies on very sensitive and private issues, such as child abuse, child trafficking and human immunodeficiency virus/acquired immunodeficiency syndrome (HIV/AIDS). In rural areas, there is a taboo on speaking about experiences in these areas of threat and vulnerability due to shame and fear. Contact Base designed such participatory research methods in Goa (2005–2006), North Bengal (2005–2006) and Udaipur (2006–2007) to assess the causes and consequences of the vulnerabilities mentioned. The research tool used was interactive street theatre incorporating audience participation and feedback. The primary goal of the project was to understand the problem of growing child abuse, human trafficking or HIV/AIDS from the perspectives of the people at the grassroots, and to identify factors leading to increased vulnerabilities. Once this understanding was achieved, the objectives of the project were to evolve, with community participation, ways of strengthening community structures to tackle these problems, as well as to inform the community about NGOs that work for the protection of women and children, and support services such as the Childline.

The specific type of interactive theatre used included the structural aspects of forum theatre. For example, a mock quarrel between two men, who were actually actors in the play, was used to draw the attention of passers-by. People crowded around the quarrel, which led to the actual theatre. As the audience watched the play, they could identify with the situations being depicted, and this led to their involvement with the issue. In the middle of the play, at a heightened emotional situation, the actors stopped and invited the viewers to come and play the role of a father or a daughter. Some typical themes and storylines would better convey the nature of the shows. One storyline depicts a young girl whose ambition is to become a television star. Her boy-friend, promising to take her to a music contest, lures her to leave her village. The girl is subsequently forced into sex work. Another story shows a boy who is promised a lucrative job by his neighbour but is ulti-mately pushed into the life of a bonded labourer. Another play is about a young girl, Pinky, who lives with her mother. Their family is regularly visited by Chandrakant, who was a friend of her father. One day, Pinky is sleeping and does not get up when her mother calls her. Thinking that she is sick, her mother decides to take her to the doctor. Pinky tries to tell her mother something about Chandrakant uncle, but her mother does not pay any attention. Pinky becomes angry and does not say anything. One day, as Pinky is playing, Chandrakant uncle comes in and tries to embrace her from behind. She tries to escape, but he is persistent. In the meantime, Pinky's mother comes in and sees the whole thing. She screams at Chandrakant and forbids him from ever entering their house again.

The intense emotional and involved contact motivated many of the viewers across various theatre shows to come and play the role of a character in the play. As they did so, they expressed their emotions and fears and sometimes narrated their own life experiences where they had themselves sold off their daughters or had not gone to the police to report missing children's cases. Similarly, in the case of shows on HIV/AIDS, the viewers got so involved with the shows that after the shows, they went and shared cases and vulnerabilities with the actor–doctor, forgetting that the latter was just a play actor. This strategy of using interactive/forum theatre was effective. As the viewers participated, at the end of the shows, others were also motivated to participate in spontaneous public discussions on the issues and also suggest ways of combatting these situations through community-led actions. The actors and field coordinators held group discussions subsequent to the shows to develop community action groups and plans.

In order to support case study–based data, Contact Base interviewed the local police stations, panchayats, etc. Interestingly, it was found that though there were many missing children cases in the villages, few were reported to the police, because villagers neither understood the ramifications of trafficking nor did they know that legal structures exist for rescue. In the weeks following the campaign, there was increased reporting at police stations and the Childline, as well as phone calls received on missing children, suggesting that the shows had indeed created awareness and led to discussion and dialogue.

DISCUSSION

It is important to place Contact Base's approach to social theatre in the wider context of efforts to 'develop' Third World countries. Till the 1970s, such efforts were based on the premise that Western economic and political institutions and values were superior, and emulating the modernization and industrialization of the West constituted the appropriate path to development. This not only led to the transfer of modern Western technology to the Third World for increasing efficiency and per capita output but also sought to influence traditional societies with modern Western values. This modernization theory eventually faced a crisis of uneven development, pressures on natural environments, ethnic violence and conflict and increasing political repression (Banuri, 1987). Beginning in the 1970s, the definition of progress underwent re-evaluation to accommodate the concepts of equitable growth, meeting of basic subsistence needs, education, healthcare and livelihood and protection of physical and cultural environments.

These new alternative concepts of development considered participation of the people crucial for shaping and achieving developmental goals and hoped to improve the living conditions of people through involving them in the process, so that they would take charge of their own development (Prasad, 2009; Wang & Dissanayake, 1984). The new paradigm focused on equitable distribution of information and benefits to the poorest of the poor, designing relevant and meaningful plans of development based on feedback of the beneficiaries, using local skills and resources to strengthen developmental initiatives and make them self-sustained and integrating new ideas with traditional ones

(Melkote & Leslie Steeves, 2001). Pieterse (1998, p. 369) summarizes these approaches by noting that:

> A fundamental change that has taken place in the 'modern history of development' is that agency has become more important. Development is now more anchored in people's subjectivity, rather than in overarching structures and institutions—the state or international bodies such as the IFIs or UN agencies. (...) Participation is increasingly a threshold condition for local development. Democratization is increasingly a condition for national-scale development.

Development communication based on participatory approaches of communication emerged in parallel with these new concepts of development, where empowerment, leadership and decision-making capacities of the grassroots communities were considered critical to bring about social change. According to Prasad (2009, p. 77), the goal of participatory communication is to facilitate 'people's involvement in decision-making about issues impacting their lives by addressing specific needs and priorities relevant to people and empowering communities towards development'. Participatory communication for development also encourages the use of traditional, interpersonal means of communication which enable communities to become conscious of their problems and, through dialogue, come up with solutions of their own within their local cultural contexts, thus leading to empowerment. Empowerment is a crucial component of participatory communication. As Melkote and Leslie Steeves (2001) explain, empowerment is more than just information dissemination and requires giving grassroots marginalized individuals and groups the capacity to organize and undertake social actions for their own development.

In the emerging communication strategies for the revised concepts of social development, cultural media started playing a significant role through imbibing and using local cultural forms and symbols of the grassroots communities. According to Prasad (2009, p. 190),

> The folk media have several advantages over the mass media in traditional societies. They are spontaneous expressions of culture and touch the hearts and minds of the rural masses due to their proximity and

intimate relationship of folk forms. The people are familiar with the form, content and dialect of communication which help in achieving greater clarity in communication. Cross-cultural barriers are almost absent as there is an immediate rapport established between the folk performers and the audience.

As this chapter discusses social theatre and its use in participatory development communication, it may be interesting to lay out the progression of social theatre in phases, as detailed by Schininà (2004). In the 1950s, theatre started being used for political interventions and reiteration of societal rules through performances and for social therapy. The beginnings of this transitional theatre found expression through the works of Julian Beck and Judith Malina, Richard Schechner's *Performance Group*, Luiz Valdez's *Teatro Campesino*, Peter Schumann's *Bread and Puppet Theatre* and the works of Jerzy Grotowski, Peter Brook and Eugenio Barba in Europe, Augusto Boal and Vianna Filho in Brazil and many more groups in South America. In the 1970s, new concepts developed, including 'workshop theatre' and theatre as a strong means of communication for mobilizing social and political participation. Over the second half of the 20th century, the social role of theatre strengthened and led to its applications for therapy as in Boal's *Theatre of the Oppressed* or for enabling social inclusion of marginalized populations, creative self-expression for psychological development and social communication as in 'community-based theatre'. By the 1990s, social theatre evolved into a tool for direct communication of individuals and groups and was 'ready to become an instrument of social action through laboratories, workshops and performances with a goal of healing and of heightening the quality of social interactions' (Schininà, 2004, p. 22).

Augusto Boal and Paulo Freire in particular pioneered new forms of participatory and interactive community education techniques designed to bring about social change and community empowerment. Freire was a Brazilian educationist who is known for his emphasis on 'dialogue' in popular and informal education. Boal was a Brazilian theatre director who was influenced by Freire, and during the 1970s he developed *Theatre of the Oppressed* (Boal, 2000), a participatory theatre that fosters democratic and cooperative forms of interaction among participants and initiates a 'rehearsal of life' through theatre designed for people to collectively evolve ways of fighting back against oppression in their daily lives. Forum theatre is a particular form or branch of *Theatre of the Oppressed* which presents a scene or a play that must necessarily show a situation of oppression that the protagonist does not know how to fight against and fails. The audience is invited to replace this protagonist and act out—on stage and not from the audience area—possible solutions, ideas and strategies. Those who do so then become 'spect-actors' (a term coined by Boal). The other actors improvise the reactions of their characters facing each new intervention, so as to allow a sincere analysis of the real possibilities of using those suggestions in real life. All spect-actors have the same right to intervene and play their ideas. Forum theatre is thus a collective rehearsal for reality.

Kidd has termed social theatre as *popular theatre*, which he defines as 'a means of building up people's confidence, participation, self-expression, and critical awareness and aiding in the development of popular organisations and popular action' (Kidd, 1985, p. 265). According to him, popular theatre is increasingly being used in the Third World for mass education and grassroots communication. Popular theatre addresses people's issues and encourages communities to voice out, organize and challenge situations that oppress them. Because it is performed in the language and idiom of the people and involves the communities at large, it is more acceptable to the community and builds upon the knowledge and strength of the communities. It gives them confidence and awareness, which eventually initiates social action. Kidd (1985, p. 266) explains that

> the process of making a drama or coming together with others to watch, participate in and discuss a drama helps in developing a collective understanding of a particular problem and a group or community identity. This creates a potential for collective action beyond the drama activity.

Kidd has also divided the applications of popular theatre into a number of categories, such as freedom struggles, mass education and rural extension, community-based participatory development and community organization. He substantiates his discussions with illustrations from across the world. As an example of popular theatre for freedom struggle, he cites the example of the nationalist movement in Indonesia, where the nationalists made use of indigenous shadow puppetry (*Wayang*) in popularizing their struggle against the Dutch. In fact, such interventions were so effective that they led to the Dutch rounding up and destroying hundreds of these puppets. Theatre also played an important role from early on in the Indian independence movement, leading to the implementation of the Dramatic Performances Act of 1876 that was subsequently used to suppress seditious nationalistic theatre.

'Mass education and rural extension' includes educating the masses on issues of health, sanitation, literacy, family planning and other social concerns. Such usage of theatre proliferated not only for educating grassroots communities but also for developing a national identity among them and mobilizing their participation in implementing various national policies and programmes. According to Kidd, two of its earliest promoters were Rabindranath Tagore from India and James Yen from China. This form of mass-education theatre accommodates informational or motivational campaigns on a short-term basis to fulfil agendas of national development plans and thus adopts a 'top-down' approach. Kidd criticizes this form of theatre, because it is a message-oriented persuasive form addressing a passive audience who are not involved in developing the content of the communication. In the cases where post-performance discussions are generated, they take the form of a question–answer session that reiterates the messages of the theatre show, rather than an open-ended two-way discussion. Contact Base's theatre for community education largely falls into this category, with a few important modifications.

'Community or participatory development' occurs when theatre stimulates involvement of the community in raising issues, participating in discussions, challenging apathy, critically examining social issues that affect them and motivating collective action. The theatre of Jana Sanskriti, an NGO that has been using forum theatre for over three decades in West Bengal, is similar to this approach. However, though this form of theatre develops bottom-up participatory approaches, Kidd points out its limitations through a critical analysis. According to him, the programmes using this form of theatre are based on the understanding that the target community is homogeneous, thus failing to consider different material interests within a community and its impact on the well-being of the community itself. He explains that 'organizing on a community basis often ignores the different material interests within the community and serves to deepen class oppression, making it possible for the local elites to monopolize development benefits' (Kidd, 1985, p. 273). Other factors also limit the effects of using theatre, such as the lack of an environment conducive to organized action. Even though awareness is created and collective action is mobilized, action beyond the theatre activity does not kick off and sustain unless the right conditions for organized action are present, for example, support from local organizations.

'Conscientization' or popular education involves theatre that represents the 'reality as it is', in order to focus on the issue and generate discussion, and then stimulates analysis of the reality and the concerned issue within the group to explore the 'other reality', the reality which 'could be'. This involves a process of critical learning. Bertolt Brecht was one of the early pioneers of theatre as a consciousness-raising tool. Augusto Boal's *Theatre of the Oppressed* is one of the best examples of this process of challenging reality or reflecting upon it through focusing on 'dramatized images of reality' and then turning back to 'drama-making' for concretizing the analysis of the reality.

To summarize, social theatre takes performance theatre into the 'social field' with the purpose of intervening, participating and collaborating with the people who live in these 'fields'. According to Thompson and Schechner (2004, p. 16), 'by creating a theatre of, by, and with silenced, marginalized, and oppressed peoples, social theatre workers assert that we *all* can experience performance in a broader and deeper way than before.' It is not the mere coming together of theatre and social work but rather the dynamic interaction between the two that can change both disciplines. Contact Base connects theatre and social work and generates this dynamic exchange between the two disciplines, which not only leads to organization of collective action but also enriches the two disciplines further (Dutta, 2015).

There are concerns about application of social theatre too. Kidd (1985, p. 273) says:

> It can be 'liberation-oriented', deepening confidence, building group or organisational unity, and inspiring collective effort. But it can also be used to 'domesticate', that is to coerce people into accepting their situation or adopting practices contrary to their interests. It can also be a form of 'sponge theatre', providing a means of participation through which people can 'let off steam' but failing to channel their grievances into organised action.

Though the risk remains, especially as it works on a project basis with external funding, Contact Base tries to mitigate the risk through carrying out a needs analysis study before a theatre-based communication is designed. This helps align the community education and community organization work with the interests of the people. Contact Base also has a unique approach of involving, engaging, training and mobilizing grassroots service providers to support community action groups so that collective action can be channelized through existing mechanisms and systems. The interesting aspect of engaging stakeholders within these systems is to build their capacities and knowledge to effectively channelize community action. Also, Contact Base points out that while broad areas are determined by the agendas of funding organizations, details of the communication are determined by field studies that incorporate feedback from local stakeholders. In fact, the process through which a communication plan is formulated is perhaps a more interesting aspect of its work, compared to the actual theatre shows that are fairly routine when eventually performed as part of a campaign. The NGO does try to measure the effect of its intervention through systematic baseline and endline studies. While the degree of success varies, there does seem to be measurable short-term effects, and enough information is available that longer-term studies could also be done in principle.

It is difficult, however, to analyse exactly how much social theatre has contributed in bringing about social change, and perhaps this is not a relevant question at all. Social change at the macro level is inevitably brought about by larger socio-economic changes, usually implemented using state machinery through policy actions. The more important observation here is that villagers, after becoming conscious of their vulnerabilities, rights and entitlements and after acquiring the skill to rationally address social issues affecting their lives, have been engaged in fighting for a proper delivery mechanism of services—social, legal and political—as well as for resisting the operation of power relations in their everyday lives. Contact Base thus facilitates access and internalization of intellectual inputs, knowledge and the attitude of questioning one's existing social reality, which leads to internal changes reflected in increased confidence, leadership and capacity to break free from a state of marginalization enforced by sociopolitical institutions.

REFERENCES

Banuri, T. (1987). *Modernization and its discontents.* World Institute for Development Economics Research.

Boal, A. (2000). *Theater of the oppressed.* Pluto Press.

Dutta, M. (2015). *Theatre for social change* (PhD thesis). Tata Institute of Social Sciences.

Kidd, R. (1985). Popular theatre and nonformal education in the Third World: Five strands of experience. *International Review of Education/Internationale Zeitschrift Für Erziehungswissenschaft / Revue Internationale L'éducation, 30*(3), 265–287.

Melkote, S. R., & Leslie Steeves, H. (2001). *Communication for development in the third world: Theory and practice for empowerment.* SAGE Publications.

Pieterse, J. N. (1998). My paradigm or yours? Alternative development, post-development, reflexive development. *Development and Change, 29*(2), 343–373.

Prasad, K. (2009). *Communication for development.* BR Publishing Corporation.

Schininà, G. (2004). Here we are: Social theatre and some open questions about its developments. *The Drama Review, 48*(3), 17–31.

Thompson, J., & Schechner, R. (2004). Why 'Social theatre'? *The Drama Review, 48*(3), 11–16.

Wang, G., & Dissanayake, W. (1984). *Continuity and change in communication systems: An Asian perspective.* Ablex Publishing Corporation.

Chapter 12

Doing Theatre, Fighting Stigma
Budhan Theatre and the Creative Struggle
of the Chharas

Dakxinkumar Bajrange[1]

'It's important to change the perception of the common man'. These are the words of Dakxinkumar Bajrange, an award-winning film-maker, playwright and director with Budhan Theatre, a community theatre group run by the Chhara denotified tribe (DNT) in Chharanagar in Ahmedabad, Gujarat. At the time of India's independence, 127 communities in India remained classified as 'criminal tribes' under the Criminal Tribes Act, 1871, which was based on the then prevalent theories of criminal tendency being hereditary. These tribes were denotified later under the Criminal Tribes Act, 1952, but with their marking as 'habitual offenders' in subsequent legislations and, more importantly, in the institutional memory of law enforcement agencies, the stigma associated with being part of a DNT persisted. The members of the Chhara community often have to face 'physical, social and psychological struggle' due to 'stigmatization as a criminal', as described on the Budhan Theatre website.

---

[1] Mr Bajrange was interviewed for this essay. Ms Maanvi provided editorial assistance.

Within Gujarat, Chharanagar has a reputation of being a ghetto, with the community historically being part of the illicit liquor trade. This perception is reflected in police attitudes towards the community. In 2018, 29 people residing in Chharanagar were booked under various sections of the Indian Penal Code (IPC) after an alleged skirmish between a policeman on patrol and members of the community (Oza, 2018). Several people, including a photojournalist and three lawyers, were injured in the raids. This led to widespread anger in the wider community, and external support from theatre artists and activists poured in. This gradual change in perception of the Chharas, from 'criminals' to respected theatre artists, is where Budhan Theatre comes in.

Established in 1998, Budhan Theatre aims to address the stigma associated with DNTs in India, through street plays and expressionist theatre, and also involve the Chhara community in art and activism. As a community media project, Budhan Theatre is inextricably woven with the community it represents and mobilizes. Most of the plays include actors and directors from the Chhara community, and their theatre is often a response to brutality against DNTs across India.

Combining local knowledge with theatrical practices, Budhan Theatre has performed nearly 50 plays across India, with some of their popular plays like *Budhan Bolta Hai* also finding an audience online. How did a theatre group so rooted in the identity of a community begin? What are the challenges it faced along the way? And what place does it see for itself in a sociopolitical landscape that is increasingly hostile to political theatre?

'WE ONLY HAVE OUR BODIES TO RAISE OUR VOICES': GENESIS OF BUDHAN THEATRE

Budhan Theatre's beginnings can be traced to a murder. In February 1998, Budhan Sabar was murdered by the police in Purulia in West Bengal (D'Souza, 1999). Sabar belonged to another DNT, Kheria Sabar. According to his wife Shyamoli, he was stopped by the police, arrested and beaten to death without any reason. The police contested this version of events. However, in July of the same year, the Calcutta

High Court ruled in favour of Sabar and his family. The judgement also 'made clear just how arrogantly the police behave with DNTs' (D'Souza, 1999).

This incident was the catalyst for Budhan Theatre's first play, *Budhan Bolta Hai*. The foundations for a theatre group to start had been laid in the community by the noted writers and activists Mahasweta Devi and Ganesh Devy in 1998. When they came, Bajrange says, 'They wanted to do something with the community relating to education. At the time, Chharas were considered to be a criminal tribe. Through that interaction they came to know about the history of the place and wanted to establish a counter-narrative through theatre'. They helped establish a library in the community, which gave impetus to the genesis of Budhan Theatre.

Writing about witnessing the first few performances in Chharanagar, Devy (2000) writes:

> The young men and women surprised us by performing an extremely effective play, in the genre of street play, about police atrocities on denotified communities.... There was hardly anybody in the audience who was not profoundly moved to see the Chhara youth enacting the entire Budhan Sabar case. With what passion, what ease they act, these Chhara boys and girls! Some of them have their fathers, brothers, relatives in police custody and jails. There was very little in the play which was not part of their daily lives. (Devy, 2000, p. 56)

Drawing a historical context of the community, Bajrange underlines the fact that 'the community itself was never criminal, but that is the dominant perception of the people in the state towards us'. 'The Chharas were a persecuted community under the 1871 law (Criminal Tribes Act). In colonial times, the British could not understand why the community was moving from one place to another. After Independence, they were further persecuted under the Criminal Tribes Act, 1952', adds Bajrange, locating the nomadic origins of the community.

The Criminal Tribes Act, 1952, which repealed the earlier act, however did not have provisions for constitutional guarantees for DNTs. This meant negligible access to education and employment opportunities, which forced some of the tribes like Chharas to seek recourse in illegal liquor brewing in the dry state of Gujarat (Khurana & Sharma, 2020) and theft.

But the Chharas have been a community rooted deeply in the arts. The community was 'known to have served the British royalty' through 'theatrical and dance performances' (Khurana & Sharma, 2020). It was this skill that eventually led to the community-led effort of Budhan Theatre. A slogan on the official website of Budhan Theatre loudly proclaims, 'Born actors, NOT born criminals'.

'We were forced into criminality. With strong sanctions put against the community by those in power, one could not do much in the society', reminds Bajrange. He says,

> Chharas were actually very good actors and it is this talent that they used even while engaging in thefts. A senior person would almost stage a theft like a director—they would do reconnaissance of the place in advance and prepare a plan. While one junior would distract the target through various means, another will decamp with the valuables. It involved a lot of skills—costumes, physical demeanour, manners of speaking, etc. So, while the community indulged in thefts it was something that forced upon us—before anything else we have been actors.

With Budhan Theatre, the Chhara community has come full circle to reject the identities thrust upon them and to fashion a new, confident self that has continuities with their traumatic and complex pasts.

'We only have our bodies to raise our voices', says Bajrange. He adds:

> So, using theatrical grammar and movement, we set about doing so. It was important to put across what had happened with our parents' generation. Every time there is a killing of someone who belongs to the denotified tribe, we brainstorm on how to make a play about it.

To protest brutal police assault on Chharanagar (Satheesh, 2018), the community took out a silent rally on 29 July 2018. They also organized a *besana,* a funeral ritual, to mourn the loss of law and order. The community's response was widely covered in the media and led to several senior police functionaries, as well the political leadership, considering their demand for the guilty policemen to be punished.

PLAYMAKING AND ITS CHALLENGES

How does one determine the success of a play—through the message of the play reaching its intended audience or, as happened with one performance of Budhan Theatre, through the message of the play reaching a surprising target? 'We were performing our adaptation of Dario Fo's "Accidental Death of an Anarchist" when we were approached by a man. He said he liked our play and requested us to perform at his office', shares Bajrange. That man was from the Ahmedabad Crime Branch, and he was taken aback to see a particular actor skilfully play the role of a controversial former high-ranking figure who was charged with involvement in extrajudicial killings.

Budhan Theatre's plays are based on street play techniques, with less reliance on elaborate set design or costumes. The reasons for the same are based on necessity and reflect one of the initial challenges that the theatre group faced. 'We use street theatre because there are no costs. We can use our body and voice as medium. Initially, we had very little knowledge of theatre', explains Bajrange. The theatre group also does not have a dedicated rehearsal space, which according to Dakxin Chhara has trained them to adapt and perform in confined spaces. He points out,

> we usually do the rehearsal on my terrace. But there is no contemporary space for Budhan Theatre to do dedicated rehearsals in. The reason is that we are already a congested community. That is the reason we are not confined to conventional spaces. When we perform, we have no idea whether we will have proper space to do so. We adjust according to available time and space.

Funding is also a challenge. Chhara explains,

> We recently established a trust called Vimukta, because I think it is time to start work on a bigger scale. After dealing with the community, after dealing with the government for so many years, I think it is now time to start work on a large scale. Not just from Chharanagar, but for

all DNTs. Through this trust, I want that the artistic nomadic communities among the denotified tribes are given space to enhance their art in a way that they can earn their livelihood. We want to do this at a district level, state level, and then, national level. The thought behind establishing the Vimukta trust is a push for cultural revolution.

A COMMUNITY'S ACHIEVEMENTS

One of Budhan Theatre's main achievements has been the change in people's perception towards the Chharas, says Bajrange. He explains how, through the plays, the theatre group has performed across Gujarat and elsewhere and the stigma of being a 'criminal' associated with the community has been removed to some extent. He says,

> At least a certain section of the society is not looking at the community as criminals, they are only looking at us as film-makers, theatre artists, writers, dancers, singers, but not criminals. This did not happen earlier; they all used to think Chharas are criminals. I can see this difference in people's attitudes.

In 'Our Stage: Pleasures and Perils of Theatre Practice in India', Chhara explains the impact of Budhan Theatre in how differently people treat Chharanagar. He says,

> As young children we were discriminated against in the class and made to sit with other Chharas on the last bench. But now we feel that people have begun talking to us, even moving closer to us; they come to our 'criminal ghetto.' People have started writing about the library that Mahasweta Devi helped set up; they have started writing about our actors. Gradually there has been a social acceptance of our community. (Bajrange, 2009, p. 106)

Another major achievement he counts is how members of the Chhara community who get involved with Budhan Theatre do not go back to doing petty crimes. He says,

> Actors never go back to criminal activity, despite the financial crisis they may be facing. Whichever actors are there, they become a role model for others in the community, and speak about community

234 | Dakxinkumar Bajrange

issues. They are social leaders, speaking for the larger community of the denotified tribes—not just Chhara—and they negotiate with the state for their rights.

Writing elsewhere, Bajrange notes:

> The awareness about their own identity is the central activity of Budhan Theatre. And...all the Budhan Theatre actors, they are regarded as really good people of the community in the eyes of mainstream society. They get huge respect, huge respect in the field of the arts. Wherever they go, across the country, when they speak about Budhan Theatre, they always get respect. This respect makes them confident, for themselves.... When they speak, when Budhan Theatre members speak, they always speak with great confidence.... Our problem is identity. This is the central point of the Budhan Theatre activity. Members of Budhan Theatre are absolutely clear about their identity issues. And they also know how to counter the issue through dialogue, through the arts. They know this. (Johnston & Bajrange, 2014, p. 462)

The Criminal Tribes Act, 1871 was repealed on 31 August 1952. Since 1998, after the first performance of the Budhan play, the day is celebrated by DNTs across the country as 'Vimukti Divas'—their second Independence Day. It serves as an occasion to demand rights for the oppressed community. Budhan Theatre has played an important role in the celebration of this day and has been spreading awareness about the history of the day through its plays. Bajrange counts this as the third achievement of Budhan Theatre: '31 August is celebrated by all denotified tribes across the country, and the day is marked as an occasion to demand our rights, and to remember history. It is also a time to ask what went wrong in history'. He clarifies that DNTs, numbered at around 60 million, are 'still an oppressed community in India, but now they are asking for their rights based on a deep consciousness of their painful history'.

Despite the emphasis on DNTs, Budhan Theatre's plays are not confined to their issues. The theatre group recruits Dalit actors and regularly adapts plays to show the oppression of Dalit and Muslim groups in Gujarat. For instance, Dario Fo's *Accidental Death of an Anarchist* was adapted to highlight the plight of 'POTA families' in Gujarat. These are families whose members have been arrested under the draconian Prevention of Terrorism Act, 2002. The stigma attached to the families is such that they are known by this moniker. Bajrange explains,

> Our play was not just discussing brutal acts on DNTs, but also the stigma attached to Muslims in the state. The play elaborates on how 'POTA families' are affected and we called them to see the play. We perform on issues of denotified tribes, but we also perform on issues of other communities, like untouchability and police corruption.

USING SOCIAL MEDIA AND FUTURE CHALLENGES

While Budhan Theatre has a robust online presence through its YouTube channel and Facebook page, the group is still wary of using social media as a medium for performance. Bajrange believes that 'theatre is a physical art, and the intimacy between an actor and an audience, cannot be felt on the screen'. However, he acknowledges the reach of social media. 'A play can be seen by 200 to 300 people during a live performance, but if the performance is on the Internet, millions of people can watch it. I am not against the Internet, but the society also has to be sensitised'.

Sensitization of society towards the plight of DNTs and oppressed communities is at the heart of Budhan Theatre's objectives. But doing this is increasingly a challenge for any community media initiative in the contemporary political climate. Working in Ahmedabad, or more broadly Gujarat—which has historically been a Bharatiya Janata Party (BJP) state—Budhan Theatre is alert of the challenges of raising awareness about marginalized groups with a right-wing government in power. Bajrange's motto to address these challenges, however, is simple. 'Try and try until you get success'. He adds,

> the current government is against the marginalised and oppressed communities, and I know that. They are reluctant to facilitate mar-ginalised communities, because the ruling party, which is mostly the party of the upper castes, does not like to give people's rights to them.

> I know it is difficult, but we can't stop the efforts. The ultimate goal of Budhan Theatre and the Vimukta trust are constitutional guarantees for the minorities and denotified tribes. Once we have that, then the second step will be to implement these guarantees.

However, the constitutional guarantees desired by Bajrange still seem a way off. The central government has set up two committees to look into the matter: Renke Commission and Idate Commission. The latest report on the issue was submitted by Idate Commission in 2014, but no action has been taken yet on the rehabilitation of DNTs. A board has been set up by the National Institution for Transforming India (NITI Aayog) to submit its recommendations on the issue (Ramachandran, 2019).

OBJECTIVES OF BUDHAN THEATRE

For Bajrange, art cannot be detached from politics, which is why he believes that Budhan Theatre and its plays cannot shy away from showing reality—even if it is criticized as being too violent. He says,

> One criticism we get is that our plays are too loud, and parents often think they are too violent for children. Which I agree with, but this is the reality. If we don't show this reality, people will not think. When small children here are beaten up in custody, then how can I show them a fantasy? I want to show them the reality, and sensitise them to the larger reality.

Without politics, he argues, 'art is not complete'. For him, and by extension Budhan Theatre, cultural and political change go together. As part of this vision, Budhan Theatre also trains other groups, as well as routinely liaising with non-governmental organizations (NGOs) and educational institutions to design and deliver workshops and courses in a more formal setting.

However, political change to Chharanagar is still a distant dream. Despite the changes in perception about Chharas in the state (from criminals to actors), they still experience everyday discrimination, especially at the hands of the police. According to Roxy Gagdekar, a British Broadcasting Corporation (BBC) journalist based in Gujarat, during the COVID-19 outbreak, 18 people had died in Chharanagar since 15 May, with fears of community transmission (@RoxyChhara, 2020). However, the administration was yet to respond.

A performance of *Budhan Bolta Hai*—the play based on the murder of Budhan Sabar in 1998—is available to watch on YouTube. The performance that took place in Jantar Mantar in Delhi ends on a powerful note, which seemingly condenses the anger and objective of Budhan Theatre. The members of the theatre group come together and, looking straight at the audience, chant loudly, 'Are we second-class citizens?' Their next line is a simple demand, which can be seen as the driving sentiment of Budhan Theatre, and also representative of DNTs across India: 'We want self-respect'.

REFERENCES

@RoxyChhara. (2020, May 29). *Dangerous news—Community transmission has begun in #Chharanagar. 18people have died since May15 in this ghetto. Several sick and admitted. Next #Wuhan is here. Can govt help to stop d transmission and deaths here plz.* https://twitter.com/RoxyChhara/status/1266428875707482113

Bajrange, D. (2009). Assertions. In S. Deshpande, K. V. Akshara, & Sameera Iyengar (Eds.), *Our stage: Pleasures and perils of theatre practice in India.* Tulika Books.

Budhan Theatre. (n.d.). Budhan Theatre: Theatre for community development https://www.budhantheatre.org/

Devy, G. (2000). For a nomad called thief. *India International Centre Quarterly, 27*(2), 51–60. https://www.jstor.org/stable/23005487

D'Souza D. (1999, June 10). *Accused of being accursed.* Rediff on the Net. https://www.rediff.com/news/1999/jun/10dilip.htm

Johnston, C., & Bajrange, D. (2014). Street theatre as democratic politics in Ahmedabad. *Antipode, 46*, 455–476. https://doi.org/10.1111/anti.12053

Khurana, N. A., & Sharma, R. (2020). Gender justice and empowerment: A study of Chhara Bootlegger women of Ahmedabad. In M. Kuruvilla & I. George (Ed.), *Handbook of research on new dimensions of gender mainstreaming and women empowerment* (p. 462). IGI Global.

Oza, N. (2018, July 28). Gujarat: Chhara community furious over police crackdown in Chharanagar. *The Week.* https://www.theweek.in/news/india/2018/07/28/Gujarat-Chhara-community-furious-over-police-crackdown-in-Chharanagar.html

Ramachandran, S. K. (2019, June 16). Key appointments to board for denoti-fied tribes pending. *Hindustan Times*. https://www.hindustantimes.com/india-news/key-appointments-to-board-for-denotified-tribes-pending/story-uQwoGDHSVM74tjyFWmaosO.html

Satheesh, S. (2018). *In Ahmedabad's Chharanagar, court summons to 6 policemen brings hope after night of horror*, https://scroll.in/article/892072/in-ahmedabads-chharana-gar-court-summons-to-six-policemen-brings-hope-after-night-of-horror

Section IV

Trajectories of Change: Spaces of Hope

Chapter 13

A Delicate Weave
The Place of Local Wisdoms in Community
Media Initiatives

Anjali Monteiro and K. P. Jayasankar

INTRODUCTION

A learned Brahmin, while crossing a river, asks the Dalit boatman whether he has read the Rigveda, one of the four canonical texts of Hinduism. Upon learning that the boatman had an opportunity to do so, the Brahmin despondently remarks that a quarter of his life is lost. He persists with his query to the boatman with the next—Yajurveda. The answer is still no, and half of the boatman's life goes. Before the Brahmin could reach the next—Samaveda—a violent storm breaks out. As the boat is about to capsize, the Dalit boatman asks the Brahmin whether he knows how to swim. The Brahmin says no. 'Then all your life is lost!' exclaims the boatman. This story, often narrated by a media activist friend, P. V. Satheesh, sums up the hierarchies and the politics of knowledge.

As we enter worlds that are very different from our own, whether as activists, educators, researchers, film-makers or communicators, and interact with communities within a context of institutionalized hierarchies between 'us' and 'them', it becomes important to keep to the fore an awareness of the politics of knowledge; what is regarded as valid knowledge is contextual, tentative and inserted into flows of power and resistance (Jayasankar & Monteiro, 2016).[1] This encounter with other ways of knowing and being was brought into sharp relief for us during our audiovisual documentation work in Kachchh.

Since 2008, we have been involved in documentation of the music of formerly nomadic, pastoral communities, in the region of Kachchh[2] in the state of Gujarat in India. Gujarat witnessed state-abetted ethnic cleansing directed against the Muslim minorities of the state in 2002, in which over 2,000 people are estimated to have been killed (Jaffrelot, 2003).[3] Kachchh, though a part of Gujarat, remained unaffected by this violence of 2002. We were inspired to explore the sociocultural fabric that makes Kachchh an island of peace in a sea of intolerance and embarked on a process of documenting the Sufi traditions of music, storytelling and poetry that are an integral part of the lives of the pastoralists that live there.[4]

While recording for the film *So Heddan So Hoddan* (Monteiro & Jayasankar, 2011),[5] Haji Umar, a grassroots Sufi scholar, with whom we had the privilege to work, remarked to us about how the exigencies of bringing modernity and economic progress to his village seemed to

---

[1] This chapter draws extensively on a section from Chapter 5 of Jayasankar and Monteiro, 2016, which discusses our work in Kachchh and on Monteiro and Jayasankar (2011).

[2] Also spelt sometimes as 'Kutch', it is a district in the north-western part of Gujarat, bordering Pakistan.

[3] Some parts of the state also have a long history of strife between Hindus and Muslims. The discrimination against Muslims continues to the present day, under the aegis of the Bharatiya Janata Party that allegedly abetted the violence in the name of 'Hindutva' (Hindu-ness as an ideological and political project) and has been in power since 1995.

[4] We have extensive documentation with various musicians and storytellers. We have completed three films—the Kachchh trilogy: *Do Din ka Mela* (Monteiro & Jayasankar, 2009), *So Heddan So Hoddan* (Monteiro & Jayasankar, 2011) and *Jhini Bini Chadariya* (Monteiro & Jayasankar, 2017)—which are discussed later in this chapter.

[5] The second film in the Kachchh trilogy.

override all other dimensions of life, impoverishing both the outsiders (who seek to intervene for change) and the local populace:

> You are the only people, other than Shabnam Virmani,[6] who have come and asked us about our poetry and songs, about Sufism. Everyone else wants to know about crops and seeds, what fertilisers we use, how much we earn, as if that were the only part of our lives that are important. No one talks to us about our stories, songs and traditions. (Haji Umar, personal communication, September 2010)

This focus on economic empowerment, which involves outside intervention in changing local communities, through the imparting of skills or provision of services and infrastructure, while no doubt important and necessary, tends to be pursued to the exclusion of all other modes of engagement. The subaltern becomes a 'respondent' and a 'beneficiary', an object of study and welfare, constituted as an entity with limited agency and knowledge. This then becomes a missed opportunity for the external agent and makes for a one-way flow of information; we often miss out on learning from local knowledge and experience, in the process. Nandy (2012) underlines the importance of local wisdom that is often ignored by those who engage with marginalized communities, such as Dalits and adivasis, pointing to the need to move away from the discourse of victimhood and exploitation to a celebration of their rich and diverse cultural, ecological and intellectual traditions.

There is hence a need to critically interrogate and rethink the relationship between communicators and the communities they work with. Can one work towards building relationships based on trust and mutual respect, on sharing of knowledge and ways of seeing, making it possible to participate in a dialogue that has the potential to problematize these relations of power, transforming both 'us' and 'them'? In many ways, community media initiatives could open up these spaces for mutual learning, given their focus on the 'intangible heritage' of local communities.

---

[6] Shabnam Virmani is a film-maker who has initiated and developed The Kabir Project (www.kabirproject.org). She has done pioneering work on the legacy of Kabir and Bhitai in the subcontinent.

In this chapter, we discuss the community media initiatives of the Kutch Mahila Vikas Sangathan (KMVS), with whom we have collaborated since 2008, in our video documentation work mentioned earlier, on the music of pastoral communities in Kachchh. For over 20 years, since 1998, KMVS, a grassroots organization that works with marginalized women on issues of livelihood, rights and culture, has been doing pioneering work in the area of community media and community radio (CR). This is based on the belief that culture, music, language and lived traditions form an important component of empowerment initiatives. KMVS believes that empowerment has to draw upon traditional wisdoms and competencies, giving them a new context and space to grow. KMVS has worked deeply and consistently in the sphere of culture, in collaboration with local communities. The chapter first discusses our entry point into this space, through our film-making work, and the context and significance of these indigenous cultural traditions, focusing on music. It then goes on to look at a specific project of KMVS, entitled Sur Shala (Melody School, literally), which seeks to facilitate the documentation and teaching–learning of these musical forms. It looks at two stories of teaching–learning from this project. Finally, we return to the idea of what these traditions offer us, in terms of communitarian ways of seeing and being, and the implications of this for community media work and for revisiting the politics of knowledge.

THE KACHCHH TRILOGY

Our ongoing work in Kachchh, which forms the basis for this chapter, has thus far resulted in a trilogy of films, *Do Din ka Mela* (*A Two-Day Fair*, Monteiro & Jayasankar, 2009), *So Heddan So Hoddan* (*Like Here Like There*, Monteiro & Jayasankar, 2011) and *Jhini Bini Chadariya* (*A Delicate Weave*, Monteiro & Jayasankar, 2017). We chanced upon a collection of photographs and music from Kachchh at a friend's place and decided to visit the region in 2008. What followed was a 9-year-long engagement with the musical traditions of the pastoralists of Kachchh; much of this work has been done in collaboration with

KMVS. The first focus was to document and 'archive' some of the rare Sufi musical forms and instruments that were on the verge of 'extinction'. The trilogy was born out of this sustained documentation. One of the major motivations for these films was to explore the ways in which the multi-ethnic communities in this region lived together in harmony, in spite of the fact that this was part of the state of Gujarat, which has witnessed large-scale violence directed at the Muslim minorities. Even when Gujarat burned in 2002, Kachchh remained an oasis of peace.

A Two-Day Fair (Monteiro & Jayasankar, 2009), the first film in the trilogy, features the uncle–nephew duo Mura Lala and Kanjir Rana Sanjot. Mura Lala is an accomplished singer, who sings the verses of Kabir and Bhitai; he is accompanied on the *jodiya pawa* (double flute) by his nephew Kanji Rana Sanjot. Kanji taught himself to play and make his own flutes after hearing the music on the CR. Mura and Kanji are Meghwals, a pastoral Dalit community that lives on the edge of the Great Rann of Kutch, in the western Indian state of Gujarat. They are both daily-wage labourers and subsistence farmers in an arid zone. The film is a two-day journey into the music and everyday life of this duo, set against the backdrop of the Rann. The Great Rann of Kutch is a vast salt marsh/desert that separates India and Pakistan. Before the partition, the Meghwals moved freely across the Rann, between Sindh (now in Pakistan) and Kachchh. The music and culture of the region is a rich tapestry of many traditions and faiths, an affirmation of the syncretic wisdom of the marginalized communities that live in this spectacular yet fragile area.

So Heddan So Hoddan (Monteiro & Jayasankar, 2011) explores the lifeworld of three cousins, their families and the Fakirani Jatt community to which they belong. It focuses on their engagement with the work of Shah Abdul Latif Bhitai, a medieval Sufi poet, who is an iconic figure in the cultural history of Sindh. Bhitai's *Shah Ji Risalo* is a remarkable collection of poems that are sung by many communities in Kachchh and across the border in Sindh (now in Pakistan). Many of the poems draw on the eternal love stories of Umar–Marui and Sasui–Punhu, among others. These songs speak of the pain of parting, of the inevitability of loss and of deep grief that takes one to unknown and mysterious terrains.

Umar Haji Suleiman of Aasirawand village, Abdasa taluka, is a self-taught Sufi scholar; once a cattle herder and now a farmer, he lives his life through the poetry of Bhitai. Umar's cousin, Mustafa Jatt, sings the *baiths* (verses) of Bhitai. He is accompanied on the *surando* by his cousin Usman Jatt. Usman is a truck driver who owns and plays one of the last surviving *surandos* in the region. The *surando* is a peacock-shaped, five-stringed instrument from Sindh.

Before the partition the Maldhari (pastoralist) Jatts moved freely across the Rann, between Sindh (now in Pakistan) and Kachchh. As pastoral ways of living have given way to settlement, borders and industrialization, the older generation struggles to keep alive the rich syncretic legacy of Shah Bhitai, which celebrates diversity and non-difference, suffering and transcendence, transience and survival. These marginal visions of negotiating difference in creative ways resist cultural politics based on tight notions of nation state and national culture; they open up the windows of India's national imaginary.

A Delicate Weave (Monteiro & Jayasankar, 2017), set in various locations of Kachchh, traces four different musical journeys, all converging in the ways they affirm religious diversity, syncretism and love of the other. Drawing on the poetic and musical traditions of Sant Kabir and Shah Bhitai, as well as the folk traditions of the region, these remarkable musicians and singers bear testimony to how these oral traditions of compassion are being passed down from one generation to the next.

Whether it is the group of young men in Bhujodi, who meet every night to sing the *bhajans* of Kabir, or the feisty women from Lakhpat, who quietly subvert gender roles through their music performances, or Noor Mohammad Sodha, who plays and teaches exquisite flute music, or Jiant Khan and his disciples, whose love for the Sufi poet Bhitai is expressed through the ethereal form of *waee* singing—all these passionate musicians keep alive this delicate weave, committed to the project of what Naranbhai Vankar, a carpet weaver and community archivist from Bhujodi, calls 'breaking down the walls'—walls that have been built up through the politics of hate and intolerance.

THE CONTEXT AND CULTURAL SPACE OF KACHCHH

Kachchh region has a long tradition of nomadic pastoralism, with many different communities that moved from the region, across the salt desert known as the Great Rann of Kachchh, to Sindh, now in Pakistan, with their flocks of cattle and camels in search of pastures, in a process of rotational migration. This movement resulted in strong kinship and trade ties between Hindu and Muslim pastoral or Maldhari communities in Kachchh with their counterparts in Sindh and Tharparkar across the Rann. In earlier times, their religious identities were somewhat inconsequential; many of these groups comprised indigenous people, with their own beliefs and practices and hence regarded as being of 'indeterminate' religion; there were also strong fraternal relationships between different communities, across religious persuasion, supported by stories about these ties from mythology and folklore. The Partition of India[7] transformed the lives of these communities forever, accentuating distinct and mutually exclusive religious identities; the new border became a fault line for divides that had never existed. The pastoralists were now hemmed into recently imagined nations, which continued to re-enact the tensions brought into play by the partition.

After 1947, the border was somewhat porous until the India–Pakistan conflict of 1965, after which crossing over became increasingly difficult and the Rann became a militarized zone. The emergence of hard borders, which are fenced and fortified, is not the only threat to the semi-nomadic pastoralism of the Maldharis. The past few decades have witnessed a slow and steady destruction of these ways of life, through the state's environmental policies,[8] the promotion of industrialization,[9] the proliferation of ecologically insensitive tourism and the bureaucracy's condescending and cavalier attitude towards these communities.

---

[7] The partition in 1947 divided the Indian subcontinent into the nations of India and Pakistan. It was a violent schism that resulted in the displacement of over 12 million people and nearly a million deaths.

[8] See http://aquaticcommons.org/2077/1/Kutch.pdf

[9] See https://scroll.in/article/909085/indias-swimming-camels-are-endangered-by-destruction-of-mangroves-in-kutch

Sindh and Kachchh share a common heritage, based on Sufism and other syncretic practices, as well as a shared repertoire of poetry, folk-lore, embroidery, architectural practices and visual culture (Ibrahim, 2008). The Bhakti poetry of Kabir, the 15th-century mystic weaver–poet, is sung and recited across communities and religions. Shah Abdul Latif Bhitai (1689–1782), a Sindhi Sufi poet, wrote the *Shah jo Risalo*, a remarkable collection of poems that continue to be sung by communities throughout Kachchh and Sindh. Many of these poems draw on legendary love stories, which speak of the fragility and finitude of life, the inevitability of grief and an ultimate surrender to and union with the infinite. Hakeem Rahman, a Fakirani Jatt pastoralist in his 80s, speaks of how these oral narratives resonate with their everyday lives:

> We are shepherds; we re-live our lives, our joys and sorrows in the stories of Bhitai. The same camels, the same mountains, the same heat, the same hardships—our experiences are reflected in the melodies of Shah Bhitai. Each melody has its own characteristics that reflect our life. (Hakeem Rahman, personal communication, September 2010)

The poetry of Kabir and Bhitai speaks to the transient and precarious lifeworld of the Maldharis, whose social history has involved living with uncertainty, with the ever-present shadow of disasters (floods, drought, earthquakes) and with constant movement across boundaries. Haji Umar, a self-taught Sufi scholar and cattle herder, articulates the philosophical subtext of these Sufi and Bhakti traditions that affirm unity and non-difference, beyond borders and fixed identities:

> When souls were created, they were just souls. Not Hindus or Muslims or Christians or Sikhs. Just souls. That's from where Bhitai starts his journey. Today, the world has forgotten Bhitai's 'Like here, like there', which points to the universality of human existence. If we understand the true meaning of his verses, we will realise that whether we are Americans or Japanese or Indians or Pakistanis, we are all children of Adam. And I am not as good as the other. The other is better than me. (Haji Umar, personal communication, September 2010)

Perhaps the philosophical traditions of Sufism and Bhakti which underlie the poetry, music and storytelling of many of the Maldhari communities, and which emphasize the frailty of the self, harmony with the other and unity with the cosmos, make for relatively peaceful and mutually dependent coexistence. In contemporary times, this intangible heritage is being precariously eroded, with the disregard for local languages and cultural traditions within the education system, with the onslaught of new forms of entertainment and with changing socioeconomic contexts (tourism and industrialization). It is this context that KMVS has responded through its community media work, which has included both a magazine and CR.

KUTCH MAHILA VIKAS SANGATHAN AND COMMUNITY RADIO

KMVS was one of the first organizations to start producing CR serials in Kutchi language which were broadcast through All India Radio (AIR) from 1998 onwards. These programmes galvanized both local audiences and local artistes. They helped discover singers and musicians who had never performed outside their communities before and helped impart training to youth and women who became CR producers. While the focus of the various series was on development and women's empowerment, KMVS chose to make an entry through extensive use of local folk forms, including music, poetry, legends and stories, given the important role that these play in the lives of the communities that live in Kachchh (Asif Rayma, co-ordinator of Soorvani, personal communication, April 2016). This initiative thus gave a huge impetus to the Kutchi language and cultural forms. It also helped communities and groups within them articulate their issues, voice their concerns and mobilize to protect their interests and rights. Radio Ujjas, which had a regular slot on AIR over a period of 13 years since 1998, produced eight radio series of Kutchi-language programmes which were very popular, and these helped them build a sustained relationship with many artistes and performers.[10]

---

[10] The first series, *Kunjal Panje Kutchji* (*The Sarus Crane of Our Kutch*, December 1999–January 2001, 53 weekly episodes), won the Chameli Devi award in 2000. This was followed by *Tu Jiyaro Aiye* (*To Be Alive*, March–June 2001), *Kutch Lok ji Vani* (*Voice of the People of Kutch*, July 2002–August 2003), *Bandhni Ji Gal* (*Voice of Women*, January 2005–March 2006), *Dariya Gher* (*Taming the Ocean*, September 2006–May 2007) and some others, with a total of more than 500 episodes.

Though the official state language and medium of instruction is Gujarati, the people in Kachchh speak Kutchi and Sindhi, which are not taught in schools. This has also led to a situation where these languages, with their rich poetry and folklore, are being marginalized and gradually getting lost to the new generation. The older generation, though unlettered, continues to uphold these precarious literary traditions through oral narratives. Radio gave a fillip to these traditions and to Kutchi-language programming, hitherto absent from the broadcast media. It also created a space for the younger generation to begin to engage with these cultural forms. Radio is an accessible medium that reaches the pastoralists, given that they would often carry an inexpensive transistor radio (these days, a cell phone) along with them as they travelled with their grazing cattle.

In 2008–2009, we worked with two musicians from the Dalit Meghwal community in making a film;[11] one was the singer Mura Lala (who has since then become quite well known) and the other his nephew Kanji Rana, a young cattle herder and *jodiya pawa* (double flute) player in his 20s. Kanji was inspired to play the double flute after he heard Noor Mohammad Sodha, a master flautist, play in the CR slot. He began to make his own flutes out of polyvinyl chloride (PVC) pipes and taught himself to play, listening to cassette tapes and radio transmissions. This story brings out the transformative potential of CR, as well as its ability to promote and foster local musical traditions and local languages.

In 2012, KMVS started its own CR station in Bhimsar village of Nakhatrana taluka of Kachchh which has been entirely managed by the local women's organization, *Saiyere Jo Sangathan*. This channel continues to broadcast a range of programmes focusing on cultural themes, development and women's empowerment.

Following the success of its radio serials on AIR, which helped give visibility and impetus to local artistes, KMVS began mobilizing them in the form of an organization, Soorvani, which has over 350 members. These musicians face several challenges. As the KMVS website notes:

---

[11] *Do Din Ka Mela* (Monteiro & Jayasankar, 2009), discussed earlier in this chapter.

There are few left. They are not organized. They negotiate for performances independently with middlemen, resulting in exploitation and creating unhealthy competition. They have little practice time. They are often unaware of or unable to access government music promotion schemes and opportunities. They live in remote villages and have little access to a listener market. They struggle to acquire professional skills and performance capabilities. Female folk singers are restrained by patriarchal norms and have few opportunities to learn or engage in their craft. Younger music students suffer from an oppressive, hierarchical relationship with their teachers. Given all these challenges, there is little incentive—financial or communal—for a younger generation of musicians to take up the tradition.[12]

It is in response to these challenges that KMVS has been working on several initiatives. These include: conducting training programmes for artistes at various levels, from beginners to middle-level artistes, to prepare them for performances; organizing programmes for the artistes at the local, district and all-India levels; and taking artistes on exposure visits to other states. In this way, KMVS has tried to work towards building up a community of musical performers who could hone their own practice, learn from others and take their art form beyond the confines of their village. However, as Asif Rayma notes, there was a need to go beyond these initiatives:

We thought that we have to do something beyond performance. From the outset, KMVS had a strong focus on cultural forms and understood the importance of preserving these and reaching them to the new generation. However, our archiving work—we had collected a large body of music and other forms—was not systematically organized. So, we decided to systematize and focus on this aspect. Our community-based archiving is not just limited to art and culture. We even look at aspects such as their lifestyles, their histories. All these communities came from elsewhere, whether Sindh or Rajasthan, and the old people have stories about this history, this movement. We did detailed community mapping on various parameters, including festivals and social customs and celebrations. Along with this, we also tried to understand the importance of music in the lives of various communities, to identify the

---

[12] See http://kmvs.org.in/soorvani/

musicians and the occasions on which they perform. For some communities, such as the *Jats*, music is a very important part of their life. It is not performance for someone else, but a way of self-expression. It reflects their relationship with their environment and the world around them; also their relationship with the various gods and goddesses that are a part of their belief systems. (Asif Rayma, KMVS coordinator of Soorvani, personal communication, April 2016)

Thus, KMVS' research and documentation efforts were based on an early realization of the importance of cultural mapping and documentation of traditional wisdom. KMVS also realized through this process of mapping that some traditions were in danger of disappearing altogether, with the older musicians being unable to pass on the skills or earn a livelihood from music. As Preeti Soni recalls:

> The elders kept the music and other traditions alive, but the young people not interested any longer. There were musical forms like the *Waee*, which had only three singers left or musical instruments like the *surando* or *jodiya pawa*– we realised that these were fast disappearing. So we thought of how can we revive them. We put this to the musicians, we discussed it them. We're not interested in mere documentation. How do we share these with society and try to keep these forms alive, to pass them on? That's how the concept of *Sur Shala* (music school) emerged. (Preeti Soni, Director of KMVS, personal communication, April 2016)

SUR SHALA

The Sur Shala programme, started by KMVS in 2015, attempted to create a support structure and framework for younger musicians to learn from more senior ones. Initially, KMVS started out with the idea of a conventional music school, in a central location like Bhuj or Nirona, where students would come in all day to learn various forms. However, when it took this idea to the senior practitioners, they were unresponsive and not interested in taking this forward. KMVS soon realized that a centralized music school was not a viable solution and instead decided to support a process of decentralized mentoring. According to Ahmed, coordinator of Sur Shala:

Finally, they said we can't come to Bhuj, leaving our work behind. They didn't quite understand the concept of a guru. They said, that's not the way we learn these things. We can sit on Friday and Monday nights with our students and sing with them, as we do in our tradition. So we asked them to do it their way. (Ahmed Sameja, coordinator of Sur Shala, person interview, April, 2016)

KMVS thus decided to use the model of more informal music gatherings that take place in these communities, where senior artistes sing or play along with novices. *Sur Shala* involved 19 senior practitioners who would regularly meet their disciples (a group of 2–10 members) on two nights a week to pass on their musical traditions through singing or playing together. The mentors would meet every month, for an all-day dialogue-cum-musical session, sometimes bringing along some of their disciples. These regular meetings helped ensure that the mentors worked in consonance with each other and that they had an occasion to share their experiences and learn from each other.

The practitioners supported by Sur Shala included singers of *aradhya-vani* (devotional music or *bhajans* sung mainly by the Meghwal community, including the songs of Kabir), *waee* (a meditative Sufi form, based on the work of Shah Abdul Latif Bhitai), *kaafi* (a classical Sufi form, also based on the work of Bhitai and other poets) and *lok geet* (folk music of various communities) and musicians who played the *jodiya pawa*, harmonium, *morchang* (Jew's harp) and *dhol* (a percussion instrument). This programme ran for over a year, and the results are interesting and offer a model for the revival of local and folk traditions.

We started with *Waee*, then *jodiya pawa*, *Aradhyavani* and Sufi and folk music. We got unexpected results. Now there are 10 to 11 people who are beginning to perform Waee, which earlier had only 3 practitioners. They are still learning, but now we are confident that the tradition will continue. When we see new people, younger people singing *aradhya-vani*, we feel very happy. Younger people, in the age group 16-25 are now performing and gaining confidence and interest in these forms. (Asif Rayma, personal communication, April 2016)

Sadly, the funding cycle for Sur Shala ended in 2017, and KMVS was unable to find the resources to continue supporting the programme.

However, many of the groups started through the project continue to meet, practise and perform on their own. In the following sections, we look at two out of the 19 mentoring processes set in motion, in order to understand the issues involved and the potential of this process to generate interest and participation in younger people and to help them become sustainable.

ARADHYAVANI COMMUNITY GROUP AT BHUJODI

Naranbhai Vankar belongs to the Dalit Vankar (weaver) community and lives in Bhujodi, a crafts village with high tourist traffic, home to many national award–winning master craftspeople, particularly weavers. We met him first at a Sur Shala gathering, where he was quietly recording the proceedings and contributing to the discussion among the many musicians assembled there. Naranbhai's moment of epiphany came when he saw the Kabir films by Shabnam Virmani, part of The Kabir Project. He realized the emancipatory and empowering potential of these traditions of Bhakti/Sufism to counter the politics of hate and exclusion:

> According to me, what we're doing is to preserve our culture and the main message is that brotherhood must flourish. The walls that have come up between people these days...to remove them as far as possible, to demolish them, to bind different people of the community together.... If we could spread the message of friendship and brotherhood all over the world, it would be good for the entire humankind! (Narayan Vankar, personal communication, April 2016)

To Naranbhai and his fellow weavers, the singing of bhajans has been a way of life for generations. They are sung to the rhythms of the loom:

> Sant Kabir was a weaver, who while weaving would express himself singing his bhajans. Our elders did the same. I remember my father and my uncle singing bhajans all day, while weaving. Naturally, we also inherited that tradition! These traditions of bhajan singing are such that they give you a hotline to the Absolute! (Narayan Vankar, personal communication, April 2016)

He, as a weaver himself, identifies with Sant Kabir, whose work borrows heavily from the metaphors and imagery from weaving, which becomes a motif for life itself:

Sant Kabir used to weave. He called the journey of life, our human form a shawl...a delicately woven shawl. He would sing that our creator has given us a life like a delicate shawl, which we must keep spotless with sacred thoughts, so that the warp and the weft of our lives stay intact and spotless, without bad deeds and without causing hurt to any living being. (Narayan Vankar, personal communication, April 2016)

Naranbhai, after his encounter with the Kabir films, decided to work with a small group of youngsters who were interested in learning *bhajans* from the older members of the community. The young people began to meet regularly in the nights, and slowly, the group grew in size and, more importantly, began to internalize the philosophy of the traditions of *aradhyavani*. In a group discussion with the young men and Naranbhai,[13] they sum up what this space means to them:

Naranbhai: *Bhajanvani* is our old tradition. There was a time I thought that we would only ever hear these hymns on tape recorders in the future, never live. Others were feeling it too; will this *Bhajanvani* tradition survive or not? But Fate also has its ways, and opens doors. These boys began learning, and that was a great thing. The music of your predecessors (to Bhagatbhai, a senior member) will be passed onto the current generation. That is the hope. There is worth in that music and by learning it we can bring some change into our own lives. (...)

Kinjalbhai: At first I thought these people stay up all night playing, and they don't let others sleep either. But now I'm just as invested as everyone else in this matter.

Naranbhai: We will have to put in effort, and enjoy ourselves too, but that's the only way we can enjoy what Fate has to offer.

Kinjalbhai: A lot of studying and concentrated effort will be needed for this. You can't make butter out of milk without any hard work. There is a process of churning that has to take place. So we have to put in a similar effort.

---

[13] In April 2016.

Interestingly, technology played a facilitative role in the transfer of musical skills, both in this case and in the case of many other mentoring groups; the easy access to cheap cell phones, which can be used to share and communicate recorded content, has been a great boon in keeping these traditions alive and attracting the attention of the younger generation, which has access to these gadgets:

> With the introduction of mobile phones, it's become easy to record and listen to songs. With the help of mobile phones, it became possible to get young people interested in singing, listening and understanding this music, listening to their elders sing. And one day, 3–4 of them decided to learn it formally. (Naranbhai Vankar, personal communication, April 2016)

In the meantime, KMVS's Soorvani programme also decided to work on similar lines, towards documenting and preserving local traditions of music, with the objective of conserving such traditions on the verge of extinction. KMVS actually found a resonance in Naranbhai's efforts in developing its Sur Shala programme.

> Here, we already had a process in place, of younger people learning from the elders. They saw this and decided to work together and spread this sur shala idea to other villages.

Between 2016 and 2017, Naranbhai took up the initiative of being a community archivist for KMVS. He would record and transcribe *bhajans* all across Kachchh, working towards the creation of a rich compendium of poetry and songs. He also taught himself to use computers, in order to listen to the digital recordings and to transcribe them.

> Wherever there is any bhajan programme I record it. I sit all night and record with the artistes. Then I transfer it to the computer in the Soorvani office and listen to it and transcribe it, as well as interpret the hidden meanings of these bhajans, what do they teach us, I try to elaborate on these ideas and give the writer in me an opportunity to try out his talents! This is the work that I do with Soorvani. This gives me a lot of satisfaction and pleasure. (Naranbhai Vankar, personal communication, April 2016)

However, one must keep in mind that the relationship between these musical traditions and the world views of communities is complex, layered and at times contradictory. One has also to consider the larger contemporary political and social ecosystems within which these communities live their lives. For instance, many members of the Vankar community in Bhujodi, including Naranbhai and others espousing these traditions, have recently begun to affirm their Hindu identities, at the expense of a more tolerant, open-ended way of relating to the other. Given the overall politics of hate in the country, which has reached new levels of shrillness and polarization, and also the fact that some of these communities have become more prosperous with the opening up of Kachchh to tourism, there is growing support to the Hindu-supremacist Bharatiya Janata Party and to its leader, Narendra Modi, who is regarded as a figure of pride by many citizens of Gujarat, because of his Gujarati lineage and connections. Hence, one cannot hold on to a romantic view of the rendering of these traditions, seeing them as guaranteeing openness and tolerance. This calls for a critical awareness of the relations of power within which communities are located, which divides them into 'majority' and 'minority' communities, with the state promoting a majoritarian politics and assiduously promoting anti-minority narratives. With this 'Hindutva' politics gaining ground in the region, there are also newer and harder versions of 'Islam' which proscribe the more open-ended syncretic Sufi practices such as music and worship of local Sufi saints (*pirs*) and their shrines (*dargahs*). Noor Mohammed speaks about the difficulties in sustaining his musical practice in these changed circumstances:

> Today, the situation is bad. Music and singing are becoming taboos now! We should try to understand Bhitai's words in his *Rissalos* [verses]: 'The body is a necklace. And the heart its beads. The soul a *Damburo*, whose strings play the song. That affirms God is one. That song, becomes worship. Even for the ones who sleep.' The [orthodox] *Al-e-Hadith* say that we've forgotten God, when we visit Sufi shrines. But God belongs to all. Today many women pilgrims walk to *Haji Pir* [Sufi shrine] and other shrines. Some [orthodox] people put thorns on the road to stop them. (laughing sarcastically) Why only thorns, why not burn the road then? Those who want will go anyway!

These oral traditions, while having the potential to be bulwarks against hatred and intolerance, are under attack from various quarters, from hard affirmations of religious identities and from political manifestations of these, as also from an instrumental modernity that has no place for open-ended narratives of compassion. They are in danger of getting washed away by the tidal wave of hate politics that has become the norm and is normalized and justified by the dominant media today.

WOMEN'S FOLK MUSIC GROUP IN LAKHPAT

Lakhpat is an ancient port town that was once on the banks of the Indus in the 18th century. It was an important centre of trade and commerce. It was from here that the founder of Sikhism, Guru Nanak, started his voyage to the holy city of Mecca in the 16th century AD. There is still a gurdwara here that commemorates this event. Lakhpat, which is only 40 km from India's border with Pakistan, had a profusion of temples, Sufi shrines and mosques, until an earthquake in 1819 moved the river westwards and the port town lost its former status as an important centre of commerce and travel. It gradually fell into ruin, and all the prosperous trading families left the town. The current residents are mainly pastoralists and daily-wage earners from the Muslim Sodha community, with a few Hindu families.

The Sur Shala programme in Lakhpat resulted in the formation of the first women's singing group in Kachchh. Initiated by KMVS, the activity has been spearheaded and mentored by the dynamic sarpanch of Lakhpat, Ramzanbahi Sodha, since 2016. As Zareena Hasam Sodha, one of the members of the group, recalls:

> People from Soorvani came here. Ahmedbhai was the first one to bring the radio. It was a series called: 'Kunjal Panje Kutch Ji'.[14] He used to show it to us, as we were unaware of it. He would then ask us to sing. We were scared to sing on the mike, as we'd never done it before. So Ramzanbhai made us practice. He taught us how to sing to the beat,

---

[14] *The Sarus Crane of Our Kutch* was the name of the first series of radio programmes started by Kutch Mahila Vikas Sangathan (KMVS), which ran from December 1999 for a year.

with the percussion. For six months, after dinner, we'd go to his place, to learn. It is our heart's desire to go forward with this with Soorvani.

Women's social presence in Kachchh, as in many other parts of India, continues to be circumscribed by patriarchal norms. It is in this context that a group that is composed primarily of female singers assumes significance. The women have been able to use this platform to push the envelope of social sanctions to perform in public and to travel to other towns in Kachchh and beyond. Zareena speaks of the process involved and how it has given them self-confidence:

> We went to Bhuj to perform for a Kachchhi audience. It was a great experience and we want more performances. Here, at home, we perform at weddings. Sing all night and return next morning, enjoying ourselves, all night. We have not learnt it formally, but from our hearts, no one taught us. No one learns in one's mother's womb; we learnt from our hearts, not from books either. We don't read and sing. We are unlettered.

As film-makers documenting these empowering musical traditions, it was interesting to observe how the women not only sang but also participated enthusiastically in the process of documentation, guiding us to record their everyday lives, sharing with us those aspects that they felt were significant and noteworthy. They also saw the film as a way to enhance their process of self-empowerment:

> Zareena: We are happy that our recording has been done. People outside will see us perform and we'll get known. We'll also come on TV and you'll make a video cassette. When we get known, we can progress. If we perform outside, we'll go ahead. Sitting at home, nothing will happen. Q: *How about the community's response?*
>
> Zareena: The villagers have no role to play. If our husbands and in-laws permit us, nobody stops us, not the villagers, not the family.

The women's group, which also has male members from Muslim and Hindu communities,[15] draws on the multicultural energies of Lakhpat, where Hindus and Muslims have lived in harmony for centuries. It is

---

[15] There are three men who play the instruments and four female singers, in their 30s and 40s.

perhaps the Sufi traditions, which have been part of the town's history, that make it a unique space in a world that is increasingly polarized along religious lines. As Abdullah Sodha, a self-taught Sufi scholar, says when describing the ethos of Lakhpat:

> Here there are 24 mosques, 24 Sufi shrines, 24 Hindu temples, all in one Lakhpat. This is God's gift! From times immemorial, many Sufi mystics lived in Lakhpat. Our forefathers, our parents followed this practice. They followed certain codes. If Hindus and Muslims live in harmony, there'd be no problems. If we live like brothers. there'll be no cases, fights or violence. We feel happy! (Abdullah Sodha, personal communication, April 2016)

Lakhpat's proximity to the international border with Pakistan and the heavy military security arrangements in the area make the work of Ramzanbhai and the music group all the more critical. Ramzanbhai discusses the significance of music and cultural forms in bringing people together and the role that festivals play in creating an atmosphere of mutual respect and enjoyment of each other's traditions:

> The message of Soorvani is one of unity. Ours is a border area. The message is of unity and brotherhood between Hindus and Muslims (…) The history of Lakhpat is that whether Hindu or Muslim, all celebrate festivals together. Hindu or Muslim, the feeling of brotherhood exists from early times. During Navratri, when they sing *Chhand* or do the *Aarti*…. Our girls and women also dance the *Raas*. In Kachchh, people respect me. Earlier I was the Sarpanch (Village Head) for five years. The Hindu community said that the sarpanch though a Muslim participated in all the 9 days of Navaratri. People would ask how I, as a Muslim and a Haji could play the harmonium, during Navratri. This is my passion, my expression!

LEARNING FROM LOCAL WISDOMS

The contemporary period has witnessed renewed interest in Sufi and other *nirgun* traditions,[16] which, as we have seen, pose a critique to notions of intolerant certainty and hard identities based on conflictual

---

[16] *Nirgun* literally means 'devoid of attributes/qualities' and refers to strands of *bhakti* or worship that see 'God' as formless and all-encompassing. The poems of the medieval Indian Sufi saint Kabir are popular within this tradition.

relations with the other. Predominantly, this has taken the form of a middle-class interest in these traditions, manifested in the processes like The Kabir Project,[17] which is involved in documenting, working with performers, organizing events and making these traditions visible in the public sphere. These kinds of processes are important in sustaining these traditions and introducing new segments of society to them. What is equally important is to foster processes at the local level which ensure that these forms and the world views that underlie them continue to flourish among the communities that have nurtured them and passed them down the generations. This is what Soorvani, Sur Shala and other community media initiatives of KMVS seek to do.

Nevertheless, there are many communities and practitioners, particularly those who retain their *maldhari* (pastoral) way of life, for whom Sufi and Bhakti traditions remain a central way of being and seeing. These traditions have space for subversive and reflexive practices, as in the work of Kabir. Kabir, the medieval weaver–saint– poet, an iconoclastic figure who critically interrogated both Hindu and Muslim religious orthodoxy, points to the insignificance of the self in the cosmos and unpacks the subject as 'only clay, a leaky pot, a jug with nine holes' (Mehrotra, 2011, p. 117). Similarly, the work of Shah Bhitai, among others, is a profound reflection of the finitude of human existence and the alienation and sorrow that mark the human condition. Asif Rayma points to the common thread that runs through these traditions:

> Sufi and Bhakti traditions both emphasise humanism (*manavta*). There is no aspect of life that is not touched by this music. (...) In the past, the various communities were connected to each other, they had social relationships, economic relations, and religious ties. For example, there were common shrines, where people of all religions worshipped. Muslim Lanjas have been playing instruments for the Navaratri celebrations, for many generations, and see it as their duty to do so. (Asif Rayma, personal communication, April 2016)

The strength of many of these pre-modern traditions is in their open-endedness and hence their ability to resist intolerant certainty,

---

[17] For more on The Kabir Project, please refer to https://www.kabirproject.org

which has become a hallmark of our times. In the film *So Heddan So Hoddan*, Haji Umar speaks about the text of Bhitai in terms of its openness to a profusion of interpretations, which makes it boundless and ever elusive:

> One of the learned men was given a couplet from Bhitai's work—just a couple of lines. He interpreted it in 360 different ways and made a huge volume. He took it to Bhitai, who told him that even you spend a lifetime, your interpretation will remain incomplete. This is the greatness of Bhitai's work. What more can one say of it! (Haji Umar, personal communication, September 2010)

Invariably, the onus of keeping alive these fluid oral traditions tends to rest with marginalized communities, whose devotion to these narratives is deep and passionate. Haji Umar narrates another story of his teacher and how he came to learn the *risalos* of Shah Bhitai. His mother was pleased with his teacher and asked him what he wanted in return. He could have asked for the world, but instead he asked that he may be granted the privilege to learn the text by heart, without having to read it! This devotion is what tends to get devalued in the long march to development and modernity, where these local wisdoms are seen as irrelevant and unproductive.

KMVS's work, while focusing on economic and social empowerment, has, unlike many other development initiatives, attempted to listen and learn from the experiences and narratives of the communities it works with. This has enabled it to contribute to a crucial process of helping make these traditions robust and sustainable in a larger context that has little place for them.

> In Sufism, the essence is love. If we have love in our hearts, hate is far away. We were worried about how to reach these values to the younger generation. They may choose or not to adopt them or not, but how do we reach it to them? (Asif Rayma, personal communication, April 2016)

This question remains, as youths, particularly those who have had access to formal education, are slowly being pulled into an urban, aspirational space, where the markers of a good life and of success are increasingly at variance with those of the previous generation, as the following conversation between Haji Umar and Hakeem Rahman points out:[18]

> Haji: *Why aren't young people today doing this?*
> Hakeem:Young people have no interest in these things. No one wants to listen to Kafi.They prefer instrumental music
> Haji: *Like the flute?*
> Hakeem: These days they prefer machines. They all want to roam around on their bikes.

With all these challenges, the community media work of KMVS, over the years, has demonstrated that it is possible to learn from communities, to create networks of like-minded practitioners who espouse traditions of peace and tolerance and to work in a sustained way towards generating fresh interest in these traditions.

Many community media projects, including non-governmental organization (NGO)–driven CR initiatives, tend to use traditional forms merely as vehicles to impart predetermined developmental content. Here, the form is artificially separated from the deeper meaning of these traditions in order to make palatable and popular new content related to externally determined ideas of what constitutes 'development' and 'empowerment'. The community media work of KMVS points to the significance of learning from local traditions of harmony and inclusiveness, thus redefining the shape of community media and the role of community media facilitators and activists.

REFERENCES

Ibrahim, F. (2008). *Settlers, saints and sovereigns*. Routledge.
Jaffrelot, C. (2003, July). *Communal riots in Gujarat: The state at risk?* (Working Paper No. 17). Heidelberg Papers in South Asian and Comparative Politics, South Asia Institute, University of Heidelberg. http://archiv.ub.uniheidelberg.de/volltextserver/4127/1/hpsacp17.pdf

---

[18] Conversation from the film *So Heddan So Hoddan* (Monteiro & Jayasankar, 2011).

Jayasankar, K. P., & Monteiro, A. (2016). *A fly in the curry: Independent documentary film in India*. SAGE Publications.

Mehrotra, A. K. (2011). *Songs of Kabir*. Hachette.

Monteiro, A., & Jayasankar, K. P. (2009). *Do Din ka Mela* (A Two-day Fair). Tata Institute of Social Sciences.

Monteiro, A., & Jayasankar, K. P. (2011, October). Like here like there. *Himal South Asian*.

Monteiro, A., & Jayasankar, K. P. (2011). *So Heddan So Hoddan* (Like Here Like There). Public Service Broadcasting Trust.

Monteiro, A., & Jayasankar, K. P. (2017). *Jhini Bini Chadariya* (A Delicate Weave). Tata Institute of Social Sciences.

Nandy, A. (2012, July 28). Theories of oppression and another dialogue of cultures. *Economic and Political Weekly, XLVII*(30), 39–44.

Chapter 14

Notes on the Political Economy of Community Media

The Self-organizing Power of Communities[1]

Faiz Ullah

INTRODUCTION

While the rights guaranteed by the constitution give all of us the freedom to participate in collective political life, for an overwhelmingly large number of people living on the margins of society, such freedom has proved to be rather meaningless. The desire of the people to lead a life of dignity in a just society has largely been confined to their exercise of casting their votes. Rohit Vemula,[2] the late research scholar and

---

[1] This chapter is a revised and translated version of the author's Hindi essay 'Kucch Kahein, Kucch Karein: Samudayik Media aur Samajik Parivartan', published in *Pratiman: Samay, Samaaj, Sanskriti*, 2019, 14(7), pp. 329–344. The author would like to thank Prof Abhay Kumar Dubey and Prof Ravikant at Centre for the Study of Developing Societies, New Delhi, for their feedback on the essay.

[2] Rohith Vemula (30 January 1989 to 17 January 2016) was suspended from the university and expelled from the hostel on account of his political activism. His suicide was widely recognized as institutional murder in various social circles.

political activist at University of Hyderabad, reflected on this experience in his last letter, accurately and poignantly, when he wrote that

> ...the value of a man was reduced to his immediate identity and nearest possibility. To a vote. To a number. To a thing. Never was a man treated as a mind. As a glorious thing made up of stardust. In every field, in studies, in streets, in politics, and in dying and living. (Vemula, 2016)

Sociologist Andre Beteille (2003) notes that though constitutional guarantees have removed barriers to political participation for the citizens of India, the idea of a politically significant citizen remains unrealized. He argues that 'there has been a quantitative enlargement of citizenship without much qualitative advance…(and) if there is a public domain in which decisions relating to the major institutions of society are made, it is inaccessible to very many Indians' (Beteille, 2003, p. 50), thereby highlighting the lack of participatory and deliberative cultures in Indian democracy. In other words, people's votes matter, but their hopes and aspirations do not. It is because of this narrow, skewed and iniquitous system that demands for social justice and equity appear to be suspect and conspiratorial to those in the centres of power. From universities to factories to neighbourhoods, the lack of substantive freedom to express one's ideas reveals the impoverished state of our contemporary political culture where people are required merely to discharge certain formalities and enact the rituals of participatory democracy.

A significant part of this political culture are the media, which not only organize it through enabling social relations but also shape its form to a large extent. Given the spread, complexity and diversity of modern mass democratic societies, the media are a significant means through which people can share their views, engage each other in discussions and possibly arrive at consensus on issues of common concern. Here the term media loosely refers to the institution of the press that brings different people together, constituting the public sphere. Irrespective of the media's role, such processes are central to democratic functioning, and it is through participating in them that citizens can liaison with the institutions of the state and influence the nature and course of collective social life. Participation in such processes is the essence of citizenship, and every citizen should have the opportunity and capacity to do so. The state and its various constituents too derive their legitimacy through being responsive to such processes, as it is incumbent upon them to respect reasoned public opinion. It is necessary to point out here that there are modes and avenues other than the media to participate in such deliberations, such as voluntary associations, workers' unions and informal collectives and mobilizations.

A casual glance would be sufficient to apprise us of the vibrancy of the contemporary mediascapes. One encounters a new television channel, print or online news magazine or a mobile phone app almost every day. There is a lot of discussion and debate too—probably a bit too much, according to some media scholars and analysts. Could it then be inferred that these media and the debate and discussions they facilitate are accessible for people to participate in or address their interests and well-being?

THE CONTEMPORARY PUBLIC SPHERE

To be meaningful, the public sphere needs to be accessible, inclusive and available for dialogue between various people, irrespective of their status. Everyone, without any difficulty or discrimination, should be welcome to participate in the public sphere, and consensus on issues of the common should be arrived at via rational–critical discourse. These parameters make the public sphere *public* in the truest sense of the word (Habermas, 1991). It should be clear that the public sphere, like contemporary media, as indicated earlier, is not centralized but meta-topical, consisting of related, overlapping and even competing sphericules (Calhoun, 1992), reflecting the hurly burly of public life. It is important to point out that the concept of the public sphere is being used here in a normative sense. While using the concept of public sphere, one is keenly aware of the contestations around it, especially those that have put it to scrutiny in the context of deep historical, social and economic inequalities. This assessment uses the concept of public sphere while being alert to its limitations, as indeed Habermas himself was, vis-à-vis extant power relations and the larger political–economic context.

Even the most expansive public sphere cannot possibly accommodate or represent the aspirations of everyone. It inevitably begins to ignore the concerns of the poor and the oppressed, like the Dalit Bahujan communities, religious minorities, women, people belonging to a non-binary gender and sexual minorities, the working class, the urban poor, large sections of the rural population, etc. They are permanently housed in the waiting room of society and asked to sit still until it is their turn to speak and be heard. Of what significance are the discussions that take place under the shadow of historic and fundamental inequality where some voices are louder than others and get more attention (Fraser, 1992)?

In the Indian context, the idea of public sphere has had its own shortcomings. According to Gail Omvedt (2003),

> the issue is not simply formal presence or debate between strangers, but discussion among equals. Here the 'public' required to be created in terms of building up new human groupings, through redefined and widened bonds of social intercourse, which involve the sharing of water and food. These aspects of human interaction were precisely what were regulated, hierarchicised and made exclusive within the traditional caste society. (Omvedt, 2003, p. 141)

The notion of the public sphere was conceived to interrogate not only the influence of state power but also that of market economy on public life. With the strengthening of capitalist and neoliberal tendencies of the state, several aspects of public life have been thoroughly subjected to the logic of markets. This has had substantial bearing on the meaningfulness and vibrancy of the public sphere. According to Habermas, this has led to the re-feudalization of the people's power (Habermas, 1992). Through this process, the issues that are beneficial for the classes in power are presented as public issues—the common citizens merely give their assent to the decisions made by the powerful classes (Habermas, 1992).

Another critique of the idea of a public sphere which we should perhaps be attentive to is its unremitting focus and belief in communicative rationality—that bad ideas could be shown for what they are when contrasted with good ideas. As recent crises the world over have demonstrably shown us, only good ideas or rational–critical discourse is not enough to shore up the flagging struggles of societies against challenges as varied as climate change, ever-widening economic disparities, muscular nationalism and resurgence of demagogic populism, to name a few. Not only in India but also in several parts of the world, watchdog institutions to protect individual rights, guarantee of due process to ensure justice and pluralism—some of the key characteristics of liberal democracies—are under severe duress today. In what ways could we critically think about widespread erosion of civility that forms the bedrock for a healthy and functioning public sphere and, by extension, democracy?

Despite all the challenges, the idea of a robust and responsive public sphere is central to the functioning of a democracy, which allows for people to engage with the state in a productive way. However, its deep subversion in contemporary societies remains a cause of concern. To retrieve and restore it today would require thinking and commitment to facilitating change not only in the issues of media and communication but also in the structures and processes that underpin them.

POLITICAL-ECONOMIC CONTEXT OF COMMUNITY MEDIA

Mainstream media, which include state-funded or -controlled 'public broadcasting' and privately owned corporate media, are quite significant because of their sheer size and reach. They are considered one of the four pillars of democracy, entrusted with the task of working as a counterbalance to the other three pillars of the state and check their overreaching—essentially the same role as that of public sphere. While, on the one hand, the state-funded or -controlled media are a key part of the state machinery, the privately owned media are different from the other three pillars in a fundamental way—they are profit-seeking. Let us consider these facts briefly.

It is widely agreed that to expand and strengthen the public sphere, public media are very important. India though has never really had an independent public broadcasting enterprise; it has always been beholden to the state. While it is projected that public broadcasting institutions are autonomous, they are not immune to the interference or influence of the government in power—from appointments to programme policies. Criticism of state policies cannot be expected from them. In other words, they are unable to reflect the view of the people. Another related but not very apparent aspect of this is their strong ability to shape the subjectivity of the audience or citizens to suit the priorities of the state. The answers to many questions, such as how do we understand the meaning of being a 'good citizen', what does being an 'ideal woman' mean, how are different eras in history remembered differently, how are abstract ideas of progress and development defined, what is our place in the country and society, etc., could be found in the archives of the public media. In contemporary times, social relationships that should rankle us are normalized largely because the public media have been portraying them as the 'normal' for years, lending them currency and legitimacy. The decisions regarding which direction the country or society should take and what model they should adopt have been taken usually by the state and not by the publics. According to Vineet Kumar (2012),

> there has been a strong hierarchy of authority between the medium and the audiences which dictates the kind of programmes that should be seen and heard by the people—ones that would enable their development and social and national development. As a result, the programmes that have been broadcast—whether they are related to art, culture, politics and history or entertainment, sports and discussions—are animated by this objective. The questions of values, ethics and concerns are essentially connected to these (media systems).[3] (p. 50)

The Supreme Court, in its historic 1995 judgement declaring airwaves to be a public resource, had rightly observed on this matter,

> Diversity of opinions, views, ideas and ideologies is essential to enable the citizens to arrive at informed judgement on all issues touching them. This cannot be provided by a medium controlled by a monopoly—whether the monopoly is of the State or any other individual, group or organization. The broadcasting media should be under the control of the public as distinct from government. (Union of India Vs Cricket Association of Bengal, 1995, p. 105)

Privately owned for-profit media[4] are also not very different. In this case, political interference or influence has been replaced by profit motives.

---

[3] Author's translation.
[4] These are profit-making businesses but are an important part of civic life.

This point needs some clarification, because even as the underlying principles are different, the division may be a bit blurred. Privately owned corporate media, to be sure, are also not free from political meddling. There are many instances of political outfits and individuals having substantial connections to the privately owned media and of media entrepreneurs who play significant political roles in public life.[5] It also bears highlighting here that a large chunk of revenues for corporate media comes from government advertising, which the latter provisions according to its priorities without much transparency (Ghoshal, 2019).

Although the commonly held perception is that private corporate media encouraged consumerism in the early 1990s—the time neoliberal order was officially inaugurated in India—it is important to remember that Doordarshan began incorporating consumerism among viewers much earlier than that (Mankekar, 1999). The entry of both private and global media in India in the 1990s furthered this drive towards commercialization, with a focus on the middle classes at the expense of others, through facilitating, among other things, a close reworking of the national imagination through a strategic interplay of economic and cultural capital (Fernandes, 2000).

This confluence of politics and economics raises a couple of key points for us in the context of the present discussion: one, the ability of the elite to produce popular consensus and influence democratic processes—such consensus naturally works to protect their interests; and two, the deeply entrenched role of both the public and private media sectors in maintaining the status quo. Both ignore the voices and aspirations of the people and emerge, in themselves, as a political power. Many media researchers and analysts are of the view that the mainstream media marginalize the political and intermediary institutions and undermine the capacities of democratic systems to encourage popular participation (Meyer, 2002, p. 139). Or, they themselves are a key part of the governing system, tasked with leading social and political spheres (Cook, 2005, p. 15). Instead of facilitating and encouraging an expansion and enrichment of the public sphere, the mainstream media wish to replace it, assimilate

---

[5] See Thakurta (2015) and Saxena and Atul (2017) for the nexus between the corporate media and the political class.

diverse people and centralize power. Encroaching upon political processes and spheres is one of their strong tendencies.

In the liberal thought circles, where media is seen more as a marketplace of ideas rather than as part of the public sphere, media reform is proposed as a solution to the problems outlined above. It is suggested that programme producers be trained and sensitized. From this point of view, the unyielding attitude the mainstream media have towards the poor and the marginalized is due to the personal shortcomings or biases of the media workers, rather than something that is built into their own structures.

Because of the democratization of technology, today, it has become possible, if not easy, to create alternatives to mainstream media. With the proliferation of documentary films, online news portals and social media networks, we exist in a more media-saturated context than ever before. Following the changes in media policies, the idea of community radio has been realized to some extent. However, it remains to be seen how 'alternative' such initiatives are. If one tried today, it might be possible to get news of people from places whose names one only got to hear in the song request shows of All India Radio. Do such changes mean that more and more people today can participate in the public sphere? If we take a general view, then perhaps yes. Many important issues that the mainstream media did not consider important are finding their way into our conversations today. There are lively debates on the issues of social and economic justice, scrutiny of the functioning of the government and criticism of reactionary ideologies. If we see such developments in the context of the idea of the public sphere, then there is definitely some change, but there are also some inconvenient questions that emerge.

One of the key features of the public sphere is its inclusiveness, and most alternative media[6] initiatives do not seem to be fulfilling it. Public sphere and civil society are both constituted outside the state. The difference between the two is that while the former is open for everyone

---

[6] Initiatives largely run by civil society organizations. The difference between such initiatives and community media initiatives is that in the latter, means of production and operational control belong to the people.

and their common issues, the latter is constituted of organized private individuals, where they come together to realize their limited agendas. It is not being suggested here that the two are mutually exclusive but that there is a difference in the way they are formed and in the way in which they function. Civil society does not necessarily function on democratic principles or work in the interest of the public; take, for example, the elite urban resident welfare associations. Many civil society groups do work for the larger society, but only a select few insiders get to take part in it (Warner, 2001).

Today, there is a broad consensus that while civil society organizations carry out welfare and development activities, their imagination and work processes are not democratic. Here, the decisions are taken by a select few—sponsors or specialists—and then implemented among the people. It is, again, not being suggested here that the decisions are not eventually beneficial to the people but only that they do not emanate from the people. To create good and effective media cannot be an end in itself if it is removed from the material contexts of the people they seek to represent. In fact, it is relatively easier to build effective media *without* the people. What is difficult and important is to work with the people in an inclusive manner through which they can understand and be better placed to deal with social and political issues that affect their lives.

Those civil society organizations that place emphasis on participatory approaches also do not seem to fulfil the criteria for public sphere. In initiatives where participation is encouraged—thought and executed by the people—it is done so within the limits set by the sponsors. A lot of times, people work in the way they imagine they are *expected* to by the sponsors (Mosse, 2001). It has also been found in the functioning of such initiatives that they reproduce the unequal power relations within the communities they work with, benefitting the community elite at the expense of the more marginalized members (Cleaver, 2001). In the context of community radio, such a context has been shaped by the inflexible government policies, where roles and responsibilities are defined very strictly. The core of these policies rest on the patronizing development communication paradigm where the role of the media is to educate the 'masses' (Pavarala, 2013). Also, in the context of alternative media, the term inclusivity assumes other dimensions when it comes to technology. Usually, people are included in only programme production and are kept away from developing an understanding of the technologies they work with. The result is that when faced with a breakdown in technology, people are forced into helplessness. Until experts from outside the community come to solve the problem, everything grinds to a halt.

If the mainstream media represent the views of the state and the capitalist class, then the alternative media largely represent the views of civil society. And if such views have not been formed through debate and discussion among the people, then they lose their vitality, as well as validity. In a functioning democracy, the consensus formed in the public sphere must be reflected in the thinking of civil society and thereafter in the policies of the state. According to Habermas (1964), the idea of the public sphere, where political compromises ought to be ideally legitimized, can only be realized in the mass democracies through '...rational reorganization of social and political power under the mutual control of rival organisations committed to the public sphere in their internal structures as well as in their relations with the state and each other' (Habermas, 1964, p. 55). However, amid the challenges of structural transformations discussed earlier, the evidence points to the contrary. Drawing on the ideas of Antonio Gramsci (1971), large sections of the contemporary Indian civil society seem to have been instrumentalized to facilitate the rolling out of the state's hegemonic project into the public sphere. One is thinking here of non-governmental organizations (NGOs) that have aided the retreat of the state in the matters of welfare and social security for the poor and the associations like trade unions which have become labour bureaucracies bereft of any significant radical agenda. There are many other such examples available before us today which attest to the state's palpable influence and control over civil society through regulation, co-opting and coercion.

Emphasizing institutions, sponsors and specialists at the cost of internal democracy and not taking into account the political–economic disparities have put a lot of people outside the purview of alternative media. Today, an overwhelmingly large number of people are extremely mobile because of large-scale migration or serious disruption caused by information technology–driven ways of structuring work. One is thinking here of millions of people engaged in logistics, services and informal trade and manufacturing. Due to lack of stable work opportunities, people move from one sector to another, one place to another, quite frequently and fluidly. How does the currently unchanging imagination of alternative media serve or promote the interests of such people who live in varied contexts of 'illegality'—informal housing settlements—in the absence of dignified options of livelihood? What about large sections of populations who have been wilfully kept way outside the public spheres or towards whom large sections of the public sphere have turned hostile? They usually only have access to the kind of media infrastructures and content that are considered suspect in the eyes of the state, industry and sometimes even civil society (Titus, 2020). One is tempted, in this context, to invoke in a limited sense the concept of 'political society' as outlined by Partha Chatterjee (2013) as one of the ways to think about varieties of exclusion such sections of the society and communities are subjected to and the ingenious and often transgressive ways in which they negotiate with them—in this particular context, most often, through acts that have little regard for the demands of modern politics or legal property regimes. Ravi Sundaram (2013) suggests that 'piracy destabilizes contemporary media property, and works through both markets and bazaars, both disrupts and enables creativity, and evades issues of the classic commons, while simultaneously radicalizing access to subaltern groups in the Third World' (p. 125).

Cheap feature phones and smart phones, memory cards and data plans have increased the reach of the media today. This has had some effect on both the expansion and deepening of contemporary public spheres. Today, we are beginning to hear the voices of the historically oppressed communities and marginalized sections of society. A new public culture is taking shape where people, freed of socially inherited roles and obligations, are creatively engaging in media criticism and creating their own media. The difficulties that prevented a vast majority of people from joining knowledge and political spheres remain—literacy, social restrictions and unreliable infrastructure—but people have started to work around them on their own strengths.

Consider a few examples. In a village just outside Bareilly, Uttar Pradesh, a 12-volt battery is first charged with a diesel generator and then used for running phones and laptops. For prices ranging from ₹18 to ₹200, one could find unlimited data plans as well. Mobile phones are being used not merely to talk or send text messages but also as a screen replacing television and larger computers (Kumar, 2013). In Dhule, Maharashtra, there is a thriving culture of songs, videos and films—many produced locally—exchanged and accessed through mobile phones. 'Download workers', for a small fee, download, curate and transfer media onto the phones of their clients (Thorat, 2016). This hacking or jugaad outlook has enlivened the public spheres. This is not to glorify the workarounds people have to resort to in the absence of basic facilities but to highlight the increasing capacities of people to take part in the world of ideas. One would be amiss, however, not to highlight the tenuous and inevitable connections that are often drawn between identities and statuses of the groups who usually have to seek recourse to such workarounds. Rai et al. (2015) in their work clearly show why people and groups find the word jugaad either inadequate or plain offensive to describe what they do, bringing into relief the particular caste and class locations that are often associated with the uncritical use and celebration of the term, especially among the privileged. With sensitivity to this context, we could perhaps begin to ask what kinds of ways jugaad opens for us to look at politics afresh, where people do not wait for the solutions—also, leaders and experts—but create, on their own, strategies and resources for democratic participation.

Dr Ratan Lal (2018, p. 146) has elaborated on this particular aspect through his personal experience:

> Cases of atrocities against Dalit and Adivasi communities usually do not make it to the headlines in mainstream media. That's why they made social media their alternative tool...on 17 January 2016 Rohit [Vemula] committed 'suicide'—other than a few channels and news-papers, all the mainstream channels and newspapers were mute. Youth for Buddhist India organised a large public meeting at Jantar Mantar on 23 January. I also took part in it as a speaker. Hundreds of people live streamed my and other colleagues' speeches on Facebook. The coming together of smartphones and Internet along with Facebook, Youtube, and WhatsApp made the event and the news international, which the

mainstream media in India did not even find worth mentioning. After this, several small protests were organised across the country. While the Jantar Mantar protest was unprecedented, it was the first time when thousands of people participated in marches to protest the alleged suicide of a Dalit student.[7]

In *Hans* magazine's special issue on social media, published in September 2018, almost every article has critically engaged with these continuously emerging and changing modalities. The issue's editorial has credited this strengthening and enlivening of the public spheres to new equations of 'technology, language, ideas, distribution, and cultural production' (Ravikant & Vineet Kumar, 2018, p. 9). According to the editors, the public groups using digital media and connected through the Internet are:

> ...writing unencumbered, without making any tall claims. For the people, language and technology, production and distribution, textual articulation and audio-visual experiments are not different things. Not only this, if they have complaints with the world around them or even the output of the traditional media, they choose neither to be its apathetic consumers nor helpless victims. They are now active in the roles of prosumer and producing a lot of textual material and accounts of activities, which till now met a sorry end in the offices of maganizes and newspapers or police stations due to whims and fancies of editors and station house officers respectively. Activities of media and institutions are no longer one-sided refrains; instead they are now becoming multifarious and manifold in terms of production and distribution of content.[8] (p. 9)

It is important to reiterate here the significant changes that wide uptake of digital and online media have brought about in contemporary political culture. The oft-quoted dictum 'that all politics is media politics' rings true today more than ever. It is this strong consensus around the import of digital and online media today that makes them an inevitable variable in analyses of social and political transformation. Making videos of particular events go 'viral' or spreading them like 'fire' or organizing 'Twitter storms' around them are key strategies of all kinds of popular

---

[7] Author's translation.
[8] Author's translation.

mobilizations. It is through participating in these mobilizations that people are beginning to ask questions of transparency and accountability from the powerful online platforms, as well as of lack of public provisioning in access to the Internet. It would also be important to consider in this regard that while the state and civil society considers those living at the margins a mere *target* of their well-intentioned media projects and interventions, in the community media paradigm, people create opportunities to express themselves.

Marginalized groups are rarely asked what their expectations from media interventions are; usually, various kinds of projects are imposed on them. For example, those involved in sponsoring and delivering interventionist Information and Communications Technologies for Development (ICT4D) projects still increasingly view the Internet solely as a mitigating tool for poverty reduction (Arora, 2019). Media projects and interventions are designed and implemented around the notion that while the elite can use the Internet in a variety of ways, it 'should be used by the disenfranchised for nonfrivolous purposes' (Arora, 2019, p. 8). It is rarely asked, if at all: why do the needs of the marginalized need to be different from those of the elite? Or, why should only they have to bear the burden of using the Internet for the right reasons? Why are they not extended the opportunity to connect with the Internet on their own terms?

INDEPENDENT SELF-ORGANIZING AND COMMUNITY MEDIA

Community media are media controlled and run by communities. It can be said that media production and propagation are crucial in the emergence of communities, since communities are rarely a priori entities and are often *mobilized*. Communities can be of people living in the same geographical place, or they can be of people who have come together around common interests or concerns. Community media remain cautious of work practices that emphasize the issues of leadership and representation and are formed by horizontal relationships rather than those built on hierarchy. Special consideration is given to community autonomy in every aspect of the engagement. The need for democratization of the media, that is, to create people's media alternatives to private, state-run and civil society media, is the main motivation behind the rise of community media. Their objective is to facilitate building of community capacities to enable communities to participate meaningfully in collective social and political life. Such participation may or may not have explicitly political motivations or ends that work towards obtaining positive identification or demanding redistribution of resources. Some may just concern themselves with recreation. It may be broadly asserted that there are relatively fewer impediments to participation in community media—all the members of a community can express their views, connect with other people and share these views, and learn and teach (Jenkins et al., 2009). Unlike civil society–led alternative media, the objective here is not to create propaganda material—be it to do with 'development' or 'liberation'—but to get people to 'intervene critically in the situation which surrounds them and whose mark they bear...' (Friere, 1993, p. 49). Participating in such actions sharpens people's understanding of their issues. It is not being suggested here that people are unaware of the issues related to their own lives but that these processes allow people to access deeper knowledge and complex information implicit in an issue and make them explicit (Gauntlett, 2007). Media produced in the process of people coming together to analyse their situation contain a particular account of their experiences which is extremely difficult to highlight in media made by anyone else.

Three thousand workers of Honda Motorcycle and Scooter India (HMSI), Alwar, Rajasthan, struggled for months against their company's management. All the workers, rising above their internal differences, made an attempt in 2015 to form a union. The management, in turn, made every attempt to try to suppress this, including firing more than 800 workers. Many of the workers who were deeply involved in the process of forming a union were dismissed. The following year (2016), on 16 February, a contract worker was hit and abused by a supervisor when he refused to do overtime on the fourth day after working overtime 3 days in a row. Two thousand workers came together to oppose this incident and suspended operations. That evening, bouncers hired by the management and the police attacked the workers. Around 60–70 workers were seriously injured in the attack. The repression continued for several days after the incident. Cases were filed by the police against several workers from among those who had been targeted in the violence. Many were arrested and dismissed from their jobs. Later attempts at assembling for protest were also frustrated by the police and the management. Mainstream media gave barely any coverage to this series of incidents, and where it was reported, as often happens in such cases, the management's perspective was put forward.

In this context, as much as the struggle of the workers was to form unions and participate in collective bargaining or to seek better working conditions, it was also a principled, ideological struggle, according to the many workers one spoke to. In such struggles, which today have become more acute, the mainstream media views generally side with those of the managements or broadly the capitalist class. The news focuses on the losses incurred by the company and not on the violation of the rights of the workers. Workers are represented as inherently violent, as if suggesting they have no other recourse to express their discontent. Burdened by these and many more prejudices, the workers continued with their struggle. HMSI workers tried to create their own narrative of these events. Numerous videos and photos of police repression were posted on video social networking sites, pamphlets were distributed in the neighbourhoods, and information regarding all their activities was shared on social networking sites and updated continually, so that other workers in the region, activists and journalists could access them.

The second example is from Ambujwadi neighbourhood in Malvani, Malad, in suburban Mumbai. Since the year 2000, more than 3,000 families have settled here. The residents here do not have landownership titles, so the fear of eviction always looms large. There is electricity supply in the area, but water shortage is acute. Despite the Bombay High Court orders, the municipal corporation does not recognize the 'illegal' settlements such as Ambujwadi. People have to either buy water from tanker operators or transport it in containers on their bicycles from neighbouring areas. The average monthly expenditure of a family on water falls anywhere between ₹1,000 and ₹1,500—three to five times more than what a middle-class family pays in the same city. Apart from the problem of water, there is a general lack of basic civic amenities, especially health and education.

Students of Mumbai-based Tata Institute of Social Sciences' (TISS) Post Graduate Diploma in Community Media (PGDCM)[9] collaborated with Youth for Unity and Voluntary Action (YUVA)—an organization working in Ambujwadi and other areas in Mumbai—on increasing public participation in civic issues. They collaborated on a community media project with a group of young adults called the Malvani Yuva Parishad (MYP) on issues mentioned earlier which the group had already been addressing. The project began with a workshop where young men and women of the area working in MYP oriented PGDCM students to their work. The PGDCM students in turn initiated a brief but lively discussion on the state of the media and why it is important to be able to express what one feels. Thereafter, the issues on which short videos could be made were discussed and identified. Scripts for the videos were developed collectively. The group also took stock of the technology available for the exercise. MVP had three–four rented laptops that were used for simple, no-frills editing. There were some cameras, but they were not found suitable for work. For a while, it was considered whether mobile phone cameras could be used for filming, since all the participants had one of their own. Members of both the groups eventually decided to use camcorders provided by TISS to PGDCM students for shooting. These cameras were small, easy to use and relatively cheap. This decision was taken on the grounds that working on these cameras would contribute to skill development of MVP members. They would be able to apply the principles of shooting learnt during this exercise to use any camera in future. If they liked working with the handicam, they may even try to buy similar cameras with the help of YUVA. For the next 2 days, MVP members selected four issues to make short videos on, for which they used still pictures and footage from their phone cameras in addition to the footage shot using the camcorders. All these videos were screened in Ambujwadi and uploaded to YouTube. YUVA and MVP decided to use these in their mobilization work.[10]

---

[9] Full disclosure: I was one of the teachers involved in the delivery of the programme and organization of the collaborative project reported here.

[10] The videos could be accessed at https://youtube.com/playlist?list=PLzf0eq oh0RiAYVNJqvc-QtasgIqATa7_R

While there are differences between these two situations, which are very important in their own right, there are also some parallels that are important to consider in the context of the current discussion. First, both the communities, largely through their own resources—ideas, skills, technology—brought forth their struggles into the arena of media. In the first case activists, and in the second students, worked with them as facilitators. It is true, however, of any facilitation process that it cannot be completely free and neutral. Regardless of how alert and sensitive the people involved are, power relationships do impact it. The solution to the problems of such a relationship is probably to remain continually reflexive rather than paper over them. Normalizing unequal power relations or institutionalizing these would be to tie these communities in the same stifling bonds which they struggle against and wish to break.

Unlike most alternative media environments, people who work in the field of community media do not make media themselves. They provide solidarity, encouragement and sometimes even a little bit of philosophical provocation[11] to the people they engage with. Identification of issues, research, strategizing, media production and outreach work are all done by people connected to the community. Community media work is fundamentally political. Its potential is not exhausted at the point of creating media or finding space in the media, but it is a way of using media as a tool in a struggle or process of change.

CONCLUSION

On the surface, it may seem that the struggles of both groups in the illustrations are based on immediate, short-term needs or demands, but in reality, the horizon of these struggles is quite vast. The struggle for wages, better working conditions, water, work and housing is also often the struggle for recognition and dignity. The foremost aspect of these struggles is rejection of identities and attributes ascribed to these communities by the state and the government, as well as by the media

---

[11] A term for mode of engagement often used by artists associated with the Delhi-based Raqs Media Collective.

and the larger society—in the first instance, workers as 'work-shirking' and 'violent', and in the second, people living in informal housing as 'squatters' and a 'burden' on the city. Negating these mythical identities is an important political aspect of the struggles of these communities.

Dehumanization of people is an effective strategy to deny them their rights and political existence (Ranciere, 2009). This is effected by addressing their 'hurt' only as noise and violence. In this situation, political work within communities—of which media are a major dimension—is required to combat this strategy of dehumanization. It becomes important to work in a manner such that what is considered invisible becomes apparent and those who are treated as noisy beings are forwarded as speakers (Ranciere, 2009). It is obvious, then, that voice is needed—voice not merely in the sense of sound but also as that capable of meaningful expression. If voice is a political resource, or capacity, it is vital that it develops (Couldry, 2010). How can voice be recreated in such circumstances? The need is to narrate one's accounts in one's own voice—to be free from the limits of those questions or conditions that are imposed by someone else. Both the Honda workers and members of MYP developed ideas for their media activities from the experiences of their own respective lifeworlds and exercised and learnt skills and strategies that will stay with them for long.

In general, such initiatives do not take the form of an institution—the emphasis is on building the capacity of the people who are involved. As has been mentioned earlier, in this paradigm, people are encouraged to connect with others and work together. It has often been observed that struggles for social and economic justice are weakened or dissipate due to lack of institutionalized support or in the absence of or a change in leadership. In such a situation, investing in enhancing people's capacities reduces this risk to some extent. Where people come together, think and discuss problems, the scope of possibilities widens for informal cooperation and organization based on mutuality. Investing time and energies in such efforts may be seen as rehearsal for the times when the struggles would quicken their pace and people would still not hesitate to initiate self-directed action.

This mode of functioning has its risks too. We fully realize today the risks and consequences of the rising tide of disinformation campaigns and propaganda. Capacity cannot be assumed to be progressive per se. Development of capabilities can be based on reactionary or conservative values, as is now increasingly evident around us. Therefore, to keep these processes aligned with progressive axes, mere media training shall not be enough—political orientation shall be a continual need. According to Taberez Neyazi (2019), the more Internet and mobile communication technologies become commonly available among people, the more rigorous the contestation over the control of public opinion and political power would become. To this end, those involved in contemporary media intervention praxes need to reckon with whether value-free objectivity or the instrumental ways in which media tools and processes are introduced in community media contexts are going to be effective in meeting the contemporary challenges. On the other hand, they would also need to be alert to the excesses of intrusive digital and online technologies, specifically to concerns about disregard of privacy and widespread surveillance, and think about democratic alternatives to private corporation–provided products and services, as mentioned earlier.

Closing the gap between media and politics is a challenge. Barring a few exceptions, most campaigns and movements cannot seem to go beyond the first stage. One of the PGDCM students, after their exercise with MYP, remarked on a conversation they had where they discussed the need to learn effective communication from the advertising industry, where the objective is not to make good and creative advertisements but to 'sell' the advertised commodities. Concluding his article titled 'Jantantra Ke Naye Manch' ('Democracy's New Platforms'), Laxman Yadav (2018) has highlighted this distance and difference between the symbolic and the real quite well:

> …For more or less the same reasons we call social media a people-oriented media, they are also a weapon in the hands of the powers that be. Social media can only give a platform to any rage or voice; it cannot be the basis of any fundamental change. These voices and energy, instead of consolidating, are being fragmented and oppressed. The resistance rising from the margins while using social media will also need to be alert to its limits. (p. 113)

However, limitations and failures could be instructive and should be treated as such. After all, these newer forms of media and political praxes have been resorted to after realizing the severe limitations of reliance on the executive wisdom of leaders and specialists. The contours of such praxes are still emerging, and it would be interesting to see whether spontaneity, improvisation and even mistakes are able to deliver wider opportunities for substantive participation in democratic processes and bring about desired changes.

Community media by themselves, unlike other established media, are not a clearly defined system. They may be conceived of as a perspective or even an ideal to aspire for. It has been seen in numerous projects that people continue to engage in programme production in alternative media solely because they do not wish the project to suffer a breakdown. In a situation like this, the media and mechanisms behind it end up using people. Instead of institutions working for people, it is the people who end up working for the sake of institutions. Media analysts and researchers are also partially responsible for such an unfortunate pass. Some alternative media projects attract so much research attention that they are kept alive for years even when it is clear that they have long outlived their utility. In such distorted conditions, institutions assume so much importance that either the people are sidelined or they get tired and part ways. If we see it as an ideal, community media can be thought of as working to increase the capacity of communities. If a community has the ability, or is able to develop it with a degree of facilitation, then, from communication to political work, it can make participation possible without any proxies or leaders. If there is a mantra that differentiates community media from the rest of the media, it is this—here there is not much of a difference between those who produce media and those who are subjects of it.

It would be perhaps important to remember here that it is often people's own initiatives that lead towards creation of institutions than the other way around. Formal institutions most often impede processes of transformation by adhering to prescribed forms of claim making. At the time of working on the present volume, anti-Citizenship (Amendment) Act, 2019 protests are happening across the country. Whatever limited gains the protestors have been able to make so far have been due to their non-institutional and non-hierarchical make-up and their defiant confidence in their own capacities.

Social order has a static tendency. It especially tends to resist any kind of progressive change, because changes of this nature conflict with and hurt the interests of the ruling elite. Division of all kinds of social roles takes place so as to maintain the status quo. In such a situation, the limits of what or who may be seen, speak and be heard are regulated strictly. A resistance to this static order, which Jacques Ranciere (2010) calls 'Police Order', is the basic element of politics. Democratization of communication technology has shaken this police order that has been our society's inheritance. Due to this, many people are today able to transcend their fixed roles, raising their voice and making their presence felt as they struggle for social justice and transformation.

POSTSCRIPT

A brilliant student and political activist, Rohit Vemula passed away in extremely unfortunate circumstances. His life and all his aspirations were mercilessly extinguished. During his brief life, he lived to the fullest Dr B. R. Ambedkar's call to 'Educate, Agitate, Organise'. He has left clear evidence of this in his concerns and writings.[12] Dr Ambedkar's call, especially for us in India, could be a productive way to begin to think about the tasks and possibilities of community media.

REFERENCES

Arora, P. (2019). *The next billion users: Digital life beyond the west*. Harvard University Press.

Beteille, A. (2003). Conceptualising the public and the private: The public as a social category. In Gurpreet Mahajan (Ed.), *The public and the private: Issues of democratic citizenship* (pp. 37–55). SAGE Publications.

Calhoun, C. (1992). Introduction: Habermas and the public sphere. In C. Calhoun (Ed.), *Habermas and the public sphere* (pp. 1–50). MIT Press.

---

[12] Rohith Vemula's Facebook posts written between 2008 and 2016 have been edited by Henry (2017).

Chatterjee, P. (2013). *Lineages of political society*. Orient Blackswan.

Cleaver, F. (2001). Institutions, agency and the limitations of participatory approaches to development. In B. Cooke & U. Kothari (Eds.), *Participation: The new tyranny?* (pp. 36–55). Zed Books.

Cook, T. E. (2005). *Governing with the news: The news media as a political institution*. University of Chicago Press.

Couldry, N. (2010). *Why voice matters: Culture and politics after neoliberalism*. SAGE Publications.

Fernandes, L. (2000). Nationalizing 'the global': Media images, cultural politics and the middle class in India. *Media, Culture & Society, 22*(5), 611–628.

Fraser, N. (1992). Rethinking the public sphere: A contribution to the critique of actually existing democracy. In C. Calhoun (Ed.), *Habermas and the public sphere* (pp. 109–142). MIT Press.

Friere, P. (1993). *Pedagogy of the oppressed*. Penguin Books.

Gauntlett, D. (2007). *Creative explorations: New approaches to identities and audiences*. Routledge.

Ghoshal, D. (2019). Modi government freezes ads placed in Three Indian Newspaper Groups. https://www.reuters.com/article/us-india-media/modi-government-freezes-ads-placed-in-three-indian-newspaper-groups-idUSKCN1TT1RG

Gramsci, A. (1971). *Selections from the prison notebooks of Antonio Gramsci*. International Publishers.

Habermas, J. (1964). The public sphere: An Encyclopedia article (1964). *New German Critique, 3* (Autumn, 1974), 49–55.

Habermas, J. (1991). *The structural transformation of the public sphere: An inquiry into a category of Bourgeois society* (Trans. Thomas Burger with Frederick Lawrence). MIT Press.

Habermas, J. (1992). Further reflections on the public sphere. In C. Calhoun (Ed.), *Habermas and the public sphere* (Trans. Thomas Burger) (pp. 421–461). MIT Press.

Henry, N. (2017). *Caste is not a rumour*. Juggernaut.

Jenkins, H., Ravi, P., Margaret, W., Katie, C., & Robison, A. J. (2009). *Confronting the challenges of participatory culture: Media education for the 21st century*. MIT Press.

Kumar, V. (2012). *Mandi Mein Media*. Vaani Prakashan.

Kumar, R. (2013). *Bijlee Nahin Battery Kranti Hai*. http://naisadak.blogspot.com/2013/12/blog-post.html

Lal, R. (2018). Dalit Sangharsh aur Social Media. *Hans: Janchetna ka Pragatisheel Katha Masik, 383*(2), 144–148.

Mankekar, P. (1999). *Screening culture, viewing politics: An ethnography of television, womanhood, and nation in postcolonial India*. Duke University Press.

Meyer, T. (2002). *Media democracy: How the media colonize politics*. Polity.

Mosse, D. (2001). 'People's knowledge', participation and patronage: Operations and representations in rural development. In C. Bill & K. Uma (Eds.), *Participation: The new tyranny?* (pp. 16–35) Zed Books.

Neyazi, T. (2019). Internet vernacularisation, mobilisation, and journalism. In R. Shakuntala (Ed.), *Indian journalism in a new Era: Change, challenges, and perspectives* (pp. 95–114). Oxford University Press.

Omvedt, G. (2003). Social justice and public sphere. In G. Mahajan & H. Reifeld (Eds.), *The public and the private: Issues of democratic citizenship* (pp. 130–145). SAGE Publications.

Pavarala, V. (2013, April). Ten years of community radio in India: Towards new solidarities. *EduComm Asia, 17*(2), 2–4.

Rai, A. S., Saigal, A., Thorat, S. (2015). *Jugaad and tactics.* https://www.society-andspace.org/articles/jugaad-and-tactics

Ranciere, J. (2009). *Aesthetics and its discontents.* Polity.

Ranciere, J. (2010). *Dissensus: On politics and aesthetics.* Continuum International Publishing Group.

Ravikant & Vineet Kumar. (2018). Pratibimbit Rakhiye Tahaan. *Hans: Janchetna ka Pragatisheel Katha Masik, 383*(2), 7–10.

Saxena, N., & Atul, D. (2017). *No man's land: Rajiv Chendrashekhar's mission to secure power in media and politics.* https://caravanmagazine.in/reportage/rajeev-chandrasekhar-mission-secure-power-media-and-politics

Sundaram, R.(2013). Revisiting the pirate kingdom. In S. Ravi (Ed.), *No limits: Media studies from India* (pp. 121–140). Oxford University Press.

Supreme Court of India. (2016, August 28). Union of India Vs Cricket Association of Bengal. http://judis.nic.in/supremecourt/imgs1.aspx?filename=10896

Thakurta, P. G. (2015). The business of politics. *Economic and Political Weekly, 50*(35), 30–35.

Thorat, S. (2016). *Identity and download culture: Revolution or farce?* http://sarai.net/identity-and-the-transformation-of-a-work-revolution-or-farce/

Titus, N. (2020). The other cinemas: Recycled content, vulnerable bodies, and the gradual dismantling of publicness. In M. Anjali, K. P. Jayasankar, & A. S. Rai (Eds.), *Diginaka: subaltern politics and digital media in post-Capitalist India* (pp. 168–193). Orient Blackswan.

Vemula, R. (2016, January 17). Last words of Rohith Vemula. *Raiot.* http://raiot.in/last-words-of-rohith-vemula/

Warner, M. (2001). *Publics and counterpublics.* Zone Books.

Yadav, L. (2018). Jantantra ke Naye Manch. *Hans: Janchetna ka Pragatisheel Katha Masik, 383*(2), 109–113.

Chapter 15

Doing Feminist Community Media
Collectivizing in Online Spaces

Shilpa Phadke and Nithila Kanagasabai

In Bernadine Evaristo's (2019), in turn tender and searing, engagement with contemporary feminisms, *Girl, Woman, Other,* the character Megan/Morgan discovers the trans world and feminism online. In the 21st century this is not an aberration but a very familiar scenario. Many young people discover feminism in the virtual world and find not just a world of ideas but also politics, friendship and even romance. There is a growing body of work that documents the articulation of feminisms online.

This chapter seeks to reflect on feminist communities and collectives that have engaged with the online space and that might not meet the definitions of traditional community media groups or organizations. Community media, often framed within a development discourse, is conceptualized as addressing the needs of the underserved and marginalized—fostering their participation, defending their interests and functioning as an alternative to media controlled by state and market interests. Community media movements started gaining ground globally in the 1970s to 'empower' those who have little or no access to 'mass media'. In India, there have been intense advocacy efforts since the late 1990s, pushing for community radio dedicated to local groups in far-flung places, and to address crisis situations. These have been suc-cessful to varying degrees (Pavarala & Malik, 2007). Community video programmes have also gained some ground in the South Asian context. Over the years, there has also been a shift in focus, with community media initiatives focusing on the urban poor. We attempt to expand this understanding of what might constitute a 'media community' by focusing here on more middle-class initiatives. We ask if examining online feminist communities and their networked participation might not just open up questions of feminist organizing but also allow for a re-imagination of what could constitute community media.[1]

We engage with the work of four feminist groups, all of which focus their politics in urban spaces—Girls at Dhabas (GaD), Pinjra Tod (PT), Blank Noise (BN) and Parcham Collective—as we navigate these ques-tions. While these groups are diverse in many ways, what they share in common is the use of online media to build a sense of the larger collective/community. All of them are groups that have begun in the 21st century, with BN, having begun its work in 2003, being the oldest among the four, and are working within what might be seen as a digital age. We turn our attention to these organizations even as we recognize that they may not define their own work as 'community media'.

The advent of online media and increasing access to high-speed, low-cost Internet in India have vastly altered possibilities of media engagement over the past decade. Udupa et al. (2020) argue that technological affordances are necessary but not sufficient conditions for public political participation in a digital age. They use the socio-technical framework of 'millennial India' to unpack the ways in which networked political participation is 'increasingly shaped by *self-work of ordinary publics*' (emphasis ours), while also calling attention to the fact that only about a fourth of India's population is connected to the Internet.

---

[1] We would like to thank Anjali Monteiro, K. P. Jayasankar, Faiz Ullah, Shivani Satija and Chinar Mehta for comments on earlier versions of this chapter.

This chapter is based on eight interviews with women who have been part of these four organizations, three each from GaD and Parcham and one each from BN and PT. Parcham is more locally rooted and addresses a specific community. However, some of its recent online engagements have addressed national concerns. BN began in Bangalore, now called Bengaluru, but has a national reach in terms of its online presence. Its campaigns find takers in cities and towns and even in villages, where it have partnered with grassroots organizations, according to its reports. Both Parcham and BN are now registered trusts and in that sense might be seen as non-governmental organizations (NGOs). PT, though being nationally known and having a larger reach, is largely Delhi-centric and is located in colleges and universities. It is in touch with other groups elsewhere, but all its activities are coordinated in and focused on Delhi and the National Capital Region (NCR). GaD began in Karachi and even today appears to be centred in cities. However, it has a much larger reach online, and its conversation is South Asia–centric. It has also received a fair amount of international press. It is perhaps the best known of the four organizations internationally.

We spoke to Sadia Khatri, co-founder of GaD, Noor Rahman, who joined the core group in 2016 and who feels that her engagement with the collective has shaped not just her politics but also her career in gender advocacy, and Shmyla Khan, a lawyer by profession who chose to join GaD in 2017 after coming across the kind of conversations the collective was able to elicit in the online space. From Parcham, we interviewed Sabah Khan and Salma Ansari, both of whom are co-founders of Parcham, and Muskaan Sayed, one of the earliest members to join, now part of the core group of this collective. From BN, we interviewed Jasmeen Patheja, who has in her own words been a constant thread and facilitator in various campaigns. Yashaswini Basu, who has been part of PT since its inception and continues to support the work of the collective despite moving out of New Delhi, spoke to us about the collective.

We have followed the progress of all four groups closely over the years. One or both of us are connected to three of the four groups in some form or the other. Shilpa has collaborated with GaD and BN and been one of the directors of a film made on Parcham's girls' football team.[2] Nithila has mentored some of Parcham's young writers as they brought out *Urooj*, a community newsletter that amplifies the voice of the youth in Mumbra.

In the first section, we reflect on how ideological communities might emerge online in ways that one might argue are organic. In the second section, we engage with the process of mobilization of these four organizations and the ways in which they have structured themselves as non-hierarchical. In the third section, we examine the critiques these groups have faced, as well as their experiences of being trolled online. In our final section, we argue that these communities represent the creation and documentation of contemporary feminist histories in real time.

FINDING FEMINISMS ONLINE

In 2015, a young woman who had just returned from university in the United States was reflecting on the lack of a personal relationship with her own city and the hope that she might be able to build one. Her hope led her to post two photographs on Instagram of herself at a dhaba in the city, with a hashtag. Another young woman, a journalist in the same city, saw her post and shared a photograph of herself reading at a dhaba with the same hashtag in a different city in the same country.

The hashtag was #GirlsAtDhabas, and the young woman was Sadia Khatri from Karachi. The journalist, Sabahat Zakariya from Lahore, then wrote to Sadia suggesting they start a Tumblr blog (Figure 15.1).[3] Sadia found that the idea resonated more than they might have imagined,

People started sending in a lot of submissions. And not just from Pakistan but also from India and Nepal. There was even one from Colombo and submissions from Bangalore and Mumbai creating a beautiful feeling of solidarity, across borders—a transnational cross border feminist solidarity.

---

[2] The film is titled 'Under the Open Sky' (2017).
[3] See https://girlsatdhabas.tumblr.com/

Figure 15.1 *One of the early images posted on the Girls at Dhabas Tumblr*

Source: https://girlsatdhabas.tumblr.com/post/120357463634/karachi-girlsatdhabas

GaD aims to initiate a conversation around women's negotiations of public spaces in Pakistan. #GirlsAtDhabas went on to become a popular hashtag that mobilized hundreds of women in South Asia and across the world to reimagine their relationships with their cities and to contribute to this visual archive. Noor Rahman, for instance, stumbled upon GaD on Facebook[4] in 2016,

> I had no idea who was behind the GaD. It was just something I saw
> on the internet, and when I showed interest in organising a cycle

---

[4] See https://www.facebook.com/girlsatdhabas/

rally—after an incident in Lahore where a woman cyclist was chased by a group of men in a car leading to her getting injured—I was welcomed into the fold. It turned out that I did know some people in the group, and the collective just grew with more friends joining!

This story of a woman discovering feminist spaces online is not an isolated one.

In the same year, across the fraught Indo-Pak border, in the city of Delhi, another group of women were mobilizing. Jamia Millia Islamia University issued a notice to its female students saying they would no longer be able to get permission to stay out of the hostel after 8 p.m. (Jain, 2015). This led to a round of protests from students which also spread to other colleges in Delhi. PT started its Facebook page in August 2015.[5] Earlier in February of the same year, women of College of Engineering (CET), Thiruvananthapuram, Kerala, were protesting against gendered curfews[6] and started a Facebook page called Break the Curfew.[7] As the idea spread and gathered momentum, other colleges and universities across the country which already had women protesting gendered curfews became more vocal. PT calls itself 'an autonomous collective of women students fighting for a just, accessible, non-discriminatory University and affordable accommodation'.

Being and working in online spaces has thus allowed for persons with similar political leanings to come together and support each other irrespective of their geographical location. More than a decade before GaD or PT made their presence felt, another project began forays into the online space for mobilizing. BN[8] began as Jasmeen Patheja's graduation art project at Srishti Institute of Art, Design and Technology, Bangalore, in 2003. It has since designed a variety of campaigns largely centred on street sexual harassment. These include I Never Ask for It, Meet to Sleep and Akeli Awara Azaad. Jasmeen sees BN as a movement and a socially engaged art practice. She says,

---

[5] See https://www.facebook.com/pinjratod/
[6] See https://www.thehindu.com/news/cities/Thiruvananthapuram/cet-students-break-the-curfew/article7009795.ece
[7] See https://www.facebook.com/Break-the-Curfew-1023798974301453/
[8] See http://blog.blanknoise.org/

We see ourselves as a fluid community of people who come together from different places, spaces, geographies. BN is a community of Action Sheroes where people are taking agency against gender based violence. I see myself as an artist mobilising people to take agency. It's grown into a movement, I always envisioned it to be a movement; a place where persons can step in and take collective responsibility for the issue. It's growing through collaborations.

Sadia, on the other hand, is cautious about using the word movement. Talking about GaD, Sadia explains,

> I see it as a collective, an art project, an archive; I see it in multiple ways. I don't like the word movement because of what the scale of a movement implies. I never write the term movement but there are members who use that word. We do not all represent it the same way. This shows you the multitudes within a single entity.

Speaking about BN, Jasmeen also talks of art practice, 'As an artist, I ask what am I coming in with? We propose ideas but they have no shape until they are co-created by members of public and feminist allies, communities of women and girls we work with'.

Jasmeen extends this idea of BN community to others when she says, 'So it is not one Blank Noise community, but the Why Loiter community[9], the GaD community, the CREA community'.[10] In our interview, Sadia echoes this exact sentiment when she says, 'This is about South Asia which includes Blank Noise and Why Loiter'. When we tell her that Jasmeen talked of GaD too, Sadia is delighted:

> Jasmeen is someone I met online. It was important just knowing that BN has been around for so much longer. To think of different people who came and went. I wanted to know how to sustain a collective? I got a lot of wisdom from her over the years. And I began to realise that things change shape.

Sadia talks about reading the book *Why Loiter*, 'I read it, just as we were having to justify ourselves to the larger feminist community. The book

---

[9] See http://whyloiter.blogspot.com/
[10] See https://www.creaworld.org/

became an important part of the early discussion we were having. It really felt like a map'. The book Sadia mentions, *Why Loiter: Women and Risk on Mumbai Streets* (Phadke et al., 2011), engages with questions of access to the city and is a text that speaks to the concerns of these groups.

Even as these cross-border conversations provide a sense of larger South Asian feminist solidarities, there are relevant conversations to be had within cities as well. Parcham Collective is based out of Mumbra, a predominantly Muslim locality in Thane district. A large number of Muslims were pushed here following the violence unleashed on them in 1992–1993 in Mumbai. On its website, Parcham[11] identifies itself as 'a group of adolescents and women who came together in 2012 to address the growing sense of alienation and othering that we experienced'. Muskaan, a member of Parcham, says,

> My mom shared our posts on the football camps for girls on FB,[12] and someone replied saying their aunt who stays in the US also shared it with her friends. I feel that for most people that this is happening in Mumbra is a novel thing. This is helping change Mumbra's image a lot.

Over the past 8 years, Parcham has engaged youth and women in the area in a variety of activities and campaigns—from conducting football training (Figure 15.2) and matches for young girls to publishing a newsletter, *Urooj*,[13] envisioned as the voice of the youth of Mumbra, and initiating a suitcase library—where volunteers bring a suitcase filled with books to different public spaces across Mumbra on a weekly basis. However, it is its online presence that has also allowed for increased visibility and recognition, as Muskaan points out:

> If you search for Parcham on Google you will get a lot of articles. You will get our Instagram handle, our FB handle. So when we want to tell someone who does not know about us all we have to say is look us up on Google, you'll find it. When you search for football coaching our

---

[11] See https://www.parchamcollective.org/
[12] See https://www.facebook.com/Parcham/
[13] See https://parchamzine.home.blog/

Figure 15.2 *Football Training at Parcham*

Source: Mangesh Gudekar.

photos come up. We also have our documentary on YouTube, people watch that and get to know more about us.[14] So sometimes people follow through and contact us.

Online spaces allow for ideological communities to emerge in ways that, one might argue, are organic. Media that these organizations create, and also invite others to create and curate, generate a debate online and on the streets that speak to gendered citizenship claims.

The 21st century has seen a great deal of feminist organizing in and through digital modes and spaces. This has been seen variously as located in neoliberal impulses, as being able to offer a space to hitherto marginal voices, feminist and others (Thakur, 2020; Ullah, 2020), and as transforming the ways in which the feminist conversation can now take place (Baer, 2016; Linabary et al., 2019). There is also a growing

---

[14] See https://www.youtube.com/watch?v=OjGfxXHSp1o

body of work that looks specifically at young women's relationship with feminism via digital spaces (Jackson, 2018; Keller, 2012, 2019; Rogan & Budgeon, 2018). While all these organizations have a street presence, three of them are distinguished by the creation of a substantial online presence and the capacity to draw in followers and members via their online communication.

Sadia says,

> Loitering on the internet, one ends up talking to people whom one would never have spoken to in real life. It surprises you and gives you so much. Even though I don't know what that person looks like, there is a moment of being seen, of mutual recognition. A lot of messages like that would come from women who are loitering in their own way or taking back the agency for pleasure. It is about being seen. Similarly women have never been allowed to be part of offline spaces either for different reasons. In online spaces you can also talk to the offline.

BUILDING COMMUNITIES

How do these groups see themselves? If we begin with the premise that they do not conform to the vision of the 'community' envisaged by mainstream community media narratives, then it is relevant to reflect on how and why we might be able to designate these groups as communities. We begin by asking them.

Yashaswini of PT responds immediately, 'We call it a collective'. Sabah retorts, 'Confused', and we all burst out laughing. She continues musing more seriously,

> We are not sure if we are an NGO or a collective. We have only two people on a salary. The rest of them do it on their own time. The image of Parcham we want to project is that we have an opinion about what is happening in the country and that football is not just about football.

Jasmeen says,

> Our understanding keeps shifting, has shifted over time. Earlier there was Annie, Hemangini, and there is a different way of relating because

we were of a similar age. And now I'm 40 and our newest intern is 16. Some of our Action Sheroes today had heard of Blank Noise when they were in their early teens.

She laughs, 'There are bound to be differences because of that'.

We ask: Did it feel like a community? Since PT began as a movement, Yashaswini says it felt like a community from the beginning.

The reason why we all came together was because it pertained to each of us so dearly. It automatically multiplied our strength to stand up for this. Some of us wanted to work, study in the library, and come back early in the morning. It was so integral to our everyday lives and our student lives.

Sadia has a clear recollection of that moment,

Initially when we posted something, if someone asked a question one of the admins would respond to the query. A few months later, we saw a question and people who were on the page but not part of GaD started answering. That's the moment at which we felt this was something bigger. We had a discussion about how wonderful it is and how it's taking a life of its own—we don't have to be present 24/7 to defend ourselves.

It is interesting that a large part of organizing takes place on social media. In recent years, WhatsApp has become infamous for its capacity to spread communal hatred and misinformation (Banaji & Ram Bhat, 2019) and is pejoratively known as 'WhatsApp university'. However, in this case, the same app is being used in a different way. All four organizations use WhatsApp to communicate with each other and to discuss and debate issues.

GaD has one central WhatsApp group and three city groups in Karachi, Lahore and Islamabad. It also used to communicate through a closed Facebook group separate from the page, used only by its members. PT has only one central WhatsApp group where all members are located. Seventy per cent of the members are geographically located in Delhi, and the remaining have moved elsewhere. BN used email lists, many of which are still active, and now uses a mix of media—WhatsApp, Facebook and emails—to communicate when it has campaigns.

Sadia says,

> A lot of the language and terminology evolved in the early months of the WhatsApp group. We were discussing the politics of public space. We were talking about class. Also, someone would message on the WhatsApp group and say that this happened to me today and I feel harassed or angry. This was a way of getting support from each other both in relation to real experiences of the city but also zooming out and seeing how it related to GaD.

Shmyla concurs, 'These conversations happen mostly on WhatsApp—we take major decisions about signing a statement or putting out our own, or even joining someone else's protest'.

Yashaswini says of PT, 'We function primarily as a WhatsApp group and communication has never been a problem'. She tells us that there is a single WhatsApp group that continues to be the mainstay of their communication. She adds that while new members have joined and old ones have left, the group icon has remained unchanged all these years. About 30 per cent of the people in this central group live outside Delhi.

Jasmeen tells us that BN has seen so many different phases of organizing. In 2005, there were different chapters of BN in Mumbai, Delhi and Kolkata, as also meetings in Pondicherry and Pune, anchored by different people. She adds that they would connect people they knew who could then be added to city groups. These groups still exist on Google Groups. She adds, 'Even now when Blank Noise issues a mailer, that same mailer goes to all the google groups'.

Each of these groups had extensively thought about and negotiated questions of hierarchy, representation and leadership. Three of the four groups (Parcham, GaD, PT) discussed in this chapter have multiple co-founders, and all of them reported having a dynamic/expanding core group.

Aspects of convenience and choice played an important role in responsibilities assumed, as did geographical location and available skill sets. For instance, Sadia from GaD points out that as GaD expanded and newer members were added to the core group, the personal interests of these members contributed significantly to GaD's street activities. She says,

It happened organically, depending on the membership of the core team. Natasha was interested in cricket, so we had matches. Noor was interested in the cycle rally. Amana did the reading group—everyone brought in something. Some stuck and some things didn't, especially in the offline space, but the online archive is available for anyone.

Yashaswini sees PT similarly, 'We are cause-neutral—but also agnostic in the causes we choose. It's not pre-decided. The element of human rights violation has to be there'. She notes that a lot of organizing depends on 'geographical feasibility'. Muskaan points out that at Parcham the responsibility of managing various social media accounts is divided based on interests and skills sets:

All of us in the core group share the password and upload pictures on social media. I, for instance, suggest hashtags so it gets more visibility. I am on Insta a lot, so I know whom to tag and how to increase visibility. Sabah reviews or edits something related to politics. She does a lot of the writing on FB. If we have to edit a video, a picture, then Salma does it.

What is also evident from these conversations is the shape-shifting nature of these collectives. While their primary political impulse remains stable, their modes of engagement, as well as the issues that they engage with, are open to change. For instance, Parcham, which began with the girls' football initiative in Mumbra in 2012, with an idea to encourage girls to lay claims to public space for leisure—spaces that have traditionally been denied to women—has in 2019, with the funding of Samata Fellowship from Committee of Resource Organizations (CORO) For Literacy, started a newsletter/blog called *Urooj*, which provides a space for the Muslim youth of Mumbra to learn about and reflect on issues of governance and identity, among other things. PT, which started out as a campaign to push curfew hours, evolved into a larger movement that challenges the gendered restrictions in the name of safety, and it has now become a larger student-led movement that is at the forefront of protests challenging hostel-fee hikes.

Many of the collectives are open to sharing their ideas with feminist groups elsewhere and to these groups replicating/reworking some of their campaigns. Parcham is open to working with other NGOs in the city to help kickstart local girls' football teams. Sabah echoes the sentiments of many other members of Parcham when she says, 'It needn't be Parcham—as long as the politics is spreading. If they create their own organisation or collective, we are happy to help'. BN has actively designed interventions and approaches in its art practice with the intention of it being replicated by allies offering guidelines and toolkits (Figure 15.3). Jasmeen says,

> An idea has no shape or meaning unless someone makes it their own. Meet to Sleep is built with allies. Our work relies on the power and strength of collaborations, both with members of the public and feminist allies including Why Loiter, GaD and many more.

In fact, Jasmeen says she stumbled upon an account called Blank Noise Bhilai on Orkut. This suggests that these narratives and ideas travelled and were taken on by groups that were not directly connected to BN.

Over time, certain faces have become recognizable, more visible than others, bringing up the question of representation. However, the collectives like GaD and PT have been defined by the fact that they are leaderless. Speaking about PT, Yashaswini says, 'Even the founding members don't want to be seen as founders or something. It's always everybody together'. Sadia too points out, 'My face became associated with GaD and though you need spokespeople, it takes away from the collective. Not everyone is comfortable being in public and speaking, and I ended up doing a lot of the interviews'. While BN started off as Jasmeen's student art project, she feels that her own role in the community has changed in keeping with how the community itself has evolved, 'We see ourselves as a fluid community of people who come together from different places, spaces, and geographies, who step in because we want to do something about this issue'.

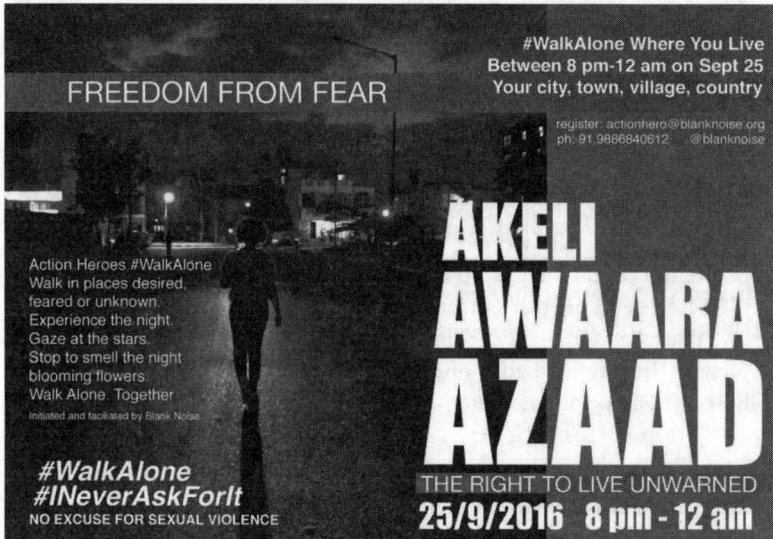

Figure 15.3 *A Poster for the 'Walk Alone' Campaign of Blank Noise, September 2016*

Source: https://www.jasmeenpatheja.com/blank-noise

These communities then appear to approximate the values that community media holds—the desire for democracy, a flat structure, a space where different people find voice, are able to publish, put out ideas, express dissent and engage in debates.

ENGAGING CONTESTATIONS

The attempt to seek a non-hierarchical organizational structure then allows for contestations, a messy history, a shifting space and politics with plenty of disagreement. This section unpacks the ways in which these collectives create and engage in online spaces[15]. All four organizations engage with multiple social media platforms.

---

[15] BN has a Facebook private group with 5,086 members; it also has a page that has 10,257 followers. BN has 2,871 followers on Instagram and 4,848 followers on Twitter, and 12,200 tweets (@BlankNoise) (as of 25 May 2020).

The collectives we engage with viewed the online space and streets as contiguous and co-constitutive spaces. They made meaning of their own activities from the standpoint of those restricted from claiming space—whether online or on the streets. Often the online space was also viewed as a training ground for street activism. Shmyla reflects,

> A lot of us found the space to learn before we moved to offline spaces—how to rally support, how to counter backlash. We started in online spaces and then moved to offline community engagement and GaD has been a big part of that. It also showed that a lot of women are told that why don't you *do* something about it rather than talk on the internet. But we have gone on to have the bike rally. I think we learnt how to translate online rhetoric into offline spaces.

While they were aware of the usual dismissals of activism online— accusations of slacktivism, of being armchair feminists—they were alert to possibilities opened up through working simultaneously in online and street spaces. They particularly welcomed the opportunity for peer learning through connecting to similar groups and collectives. Engaging on online platforms also encouraged those tentative about performing their politics on the streets to learn, question and develop their own political positions over time. Speaking about how GaD in particular and online activism at large have paved the way for much larger street movements, Shmyla says,

> The internet was seen as something trivial. But we discovered a lot of feminist spaces through the internet, where we started to talk about these things. GaD members also met online. The internet has also

---

PT has a very active Facebook page with 43,177 followers, a Twitter account (@PinjraTod) with 8,527 followers and 4,907 tweets (as of 8 May 2020), a blog at https://pinjratod.wordpress.com/ where narratives, songs, slogans and events have been archived and an Instagram page with over 15,700 followers and 592 posts.

GaD has recorded 760 posts and 10,500 followers on Instagram, 3,772 tweets and 6,766 followers on Twitter (@girlsatdhabas) (last tweet on October 2019), 58,799 followers on Facebook (as of 25 May 2020) and a blog at girlsatdhabas. wordpress.com

Parcham has an online presence on Facebook, Instagram and YouTube. It also has a website detailing the work of the collective and another that hosts the newsletter.

helped mobilise for larger events online, for instance the *aurat march*.[16] A lot of women in the organising committee have met online and I cannot imagine the aurat march happening without the internet.

Online communities have facilitated a more long-term involvement with these communities by allowing members who move out of particular geographical locations where the collective is based to continue participating. Yashaswini from PT says,

> Social media has been vital for our existence. A lot of our communication has depended on social media. I moved out of Delhi in 2017; since then my involvement has been more in terms of communication and tertiary support. For me this is important because this is a collective that will remain close to my heart. Many comrades like myself who resonate with the movement find that this is the only way to stay in touch.

While these feminist collectives recognized the enabling effect online media had, they were acutely conscious and constantly grappling with the question of using corporate media platforms and what that meant for their work. Speaking about negotiating the use of corporate media, Sadia invokes Audre Lourde (1984) when she says,

> We had a policy that we will not collaborate with any corporate organisation or be funded by them. This made the question of engaging on platforms like Facebook and Instagram all the more pertinent. After a lot of thought, what we arrived at was that we are never going to be outside of complicity. There is some degree of existing within the master's house. We can admit it and work within it. Subversion is possible within the master's house.

Another concern that was articulated was that of surveillance. Noting how members of the group engage the platform differently from their individual accounts and the social media pages of the collectives, Muskaan points out:

---

[16] An annual multi-city political demonstration in Pakistan to mark International Women's Day on 8 March.

We think a lot about *how* to write, what to post and when, so that it is political, but not attacking. Because we feel monitored all the time. Everyone is. So we are very clear about writing such that it does not offend someone. We check with Sabah since she has a lot of experience. When I post in my personal account I am very direct, but in Parcham's account we have to be careful not to be offensive to anyone or aggressive.

Recounting instances of being trolled on online spaces, especially on Facebook, Shmyla says,

I don't know if the trolling was coordinated because we didn't track it but it seemed coordinated because a lot of people would start commenting at the same time. It became more organised as the years moved on. There was lots of individual harassment but also propaganda about online spaces. Trolls would photoshop the posters we had at rallies and write sexually explicit stuff which ended up being shared.

She went on to point out that most misogynist comments were from accounts featuring nationalistic symbols, like the national flag, thus drawing attention to the relationships between jingoism and increasing misogyny.

Noor avers, 'A lot of people would also make fun or troll pictures from the rallies. They'd say we are funded by the West and peddling some anti-state agenda. They would take pictures from these events, photoshop obscenities onto them and post them'.

When asked about whether Parcham had faced any backlash on online spaces, Sabah admitted that while the collective's page itself has not seen much trolling, individual pages, like hers, have. 'In 2014, when we were working for a secular election—in various groups there was immense hate—when I wrote about demonetisation, people wrote terrible things on my wall'.

Reflecting on the nature of comments that feminist activists are subject to, both in online spaces and the streets, Yashaswini remembers the kind of rhetoric that they faced in the initial days of PT.

Even some people at the university had bitter things to say about us. Accusations about loose morals and talking about the kind of families we came from. So the critique was never about the mode or methodology of our resistance but the easiest way out for them was to demonise women.

Interestingly, though GaD itself did not participate in the Aurat March as a collective, many of its members like Shmyla did, and she looks back at the online harassment they were subjected to as part of GaD as having prepared them in some ways for the backlash that a much larger movement such as the Aurat March went on to elicit.

In an attempt to make visible the kind of labour that goes into tackling online harassment, GaD also decided to curate the hate speech targeted at them in online spaces. Shmyla recalls,

> What we did was collect all the comments as screenshots and put them up as an album. We never had an explicit conversation about this. I believe that what we do online is performative and I believe that there is a value in that. This would sometimes encourage male allies to step up and respond.

Feminists from these collectives were also vigilant about not conflating criticism and trolling. Shmyla points out that their work has often been trivialized,

> Often Left circles are so dismissive of online spaces—they feel we reproduce class structures. There is, no doubt, a lot of disdain for the online element. It was like what do you do apart from putting things online or putting up an event every 3 or 6 months and then putting it online.

Jasmeen points out that similar questions have been levelled against BN,

> When we were organising Meet To Sleep someone on Twitter asked, how are the homeless going to do this? I felt her rage. I painfully, but surely, understood her rage. Painful because the response was not aware of that fact that we were indeed conscious of this question, and because it was challenging to have that conversation directly on Twitter. It was not trolling, it was a critique. But it didn't leave room for a conversation. There is no way I can argue this nor want to, but

I can listen in to this response and allow it to inform how we shape our practice.

Criticisms have also come in from other feminists, as Shmyla points out:

> The criticism we took seriously was from feminists was that we were unable to be intersectional or be part of other movements. There is some valid criticism that we were not able to have working class women or even middle class women coming to our events. For the bike rally—because we had to rent bikes. We could all pitch in but that is an inherent problem with the event because it has an entry fee. Using online spaces for mobilisation limits your reach—most of our posts are in English not Urdu. English, because a lot of us are English medium types—personally I can talk in Urdu a lot but my written Urdu is not as good. For us to do it also feels phony. It would have been different if there were women who were naturally inclined towards Urdu.

PT has also been subject to similar criticisms. Yashaswini says,

> Sometimes we've been criticized by senior activists. We see these as constructive criticisms, ones which make us think. We've been accused of being selective in our solidarities. And also in terms of the solution oriented aspect—many have asked us what is the next step? Maybe we have to think of that too.

In 2019, a group of nine Bahujan, Muslim, and tribal women issued a statement announcing that they were leaving the movement because it was not inclusive or properly representative. They argued that PT was not representative of women from marginalized races, castes and religions (Lama & Maharaj, 2019). PT responded to these in a statement it released (Pinjra Tod, 2019).

These critiques frame the limitations of using online platforms for activism, as well as the mandates of these organizations and their capacity to be representative. Despite the fact that these critiques are relevant and are acknowledged as such by the organizations, nonetheless, they are able to negotiate the digital in ways that allow for a complex and nuanced debate in the building of a feminist community.

DOCUMENTING FEMINIST HISTORIES

Artist Sheba Chhachhi photographically documented the women's movement in the 1980s and 1990s.[17] She has since stopped documenting it, arguing that this work is already being done by many people armed with cameras in a digital time.

Since the 1990s, the digital sphere has been inundated with images from various movements in ways that demonstrate that Chhachhi is indeed right—that there is no dearth of documentation now. In fact, so prolific is this process that even these four groups, three of which are not even a decade old, have a body of work online and on the streets which can be seen as an archive. In our conversations, these feminist collectives expressed concern about the question of archiving.

There is a desire to put all of this work, articles, updates and images and archive them where they might be accessible. Yashaswini says, 'We need to think more about sustainability and also archiving. We need to think of how to immortalise what we have done so far. There is so much beautiful artwork. We want to archive that and take it to different platforms'.

Jasmeen and Sadia also point to the ephemeral nature of digital platforms and the online space more generally. Jasmeen says,

> Earlier we used a mapping platform, but the interface was unstable, with bugs that needed to be fixed often. Our work wasn't always accessible when needed, most often not showing on our website. We really liked the platform but its unstable nature wasn't helpful, and then they shut down too.

Sadia adds to this sense of temporality, 'We want to create an archive outside of Facebook or Instagram so it is an independent website. Because if FB shuts down, we will lose our archive. You can't rely on these things. So this is important in terms of agency also'.

---

[17] For some details, see https://aaa.org.hk/en/collections/search/archive/photo-documentation-of-om-swaha-from-the-sheba-chhachhi-archive

Along with the desire to archive and to preserve for posterity is also an acceptance that this space is ephemeral and that that is not always a problem. Increasingly, platforms have spaces for inputs intended to last only for a specific duration. Sadia suggests that this sense of the fleetingness of the image or text also provides a space of articulation, separate and perhaps just as powerful. She says,

> Social media is a contentious space. It is open and changing and impossible to study or absorb fully. Insta story wasn't a thing earlier. These things that literally disappear in 24 hours. A lot of art and politics gets performed in these spaces that will not be outside of those holding power, what I want to say is that I don't want to take away from the power of that.

While there is acceptance of the temporality of some of the work being shared in the digital realm, there are also connections that live on after the spaces and words have vanished. For instance, BN, which has been around since the early 2000s, used Orkut as a platform to build communities until 2008. The core group has been able to stay in touch with some of the initial supporters and members of the BN community via mailing lists.

This sense of ephemerality is not simply restricted to online spaces but also seeps into their understanding of themselves as collectives too. And so, while GaD recognizes its contribution to the discourse of women's access to public spaces, it is open to the idea that the purpose and form of GaD might have run its course, but the lessons learnt and the connections made would lead to evolving and invigorating political actions and formations. Shmyla observes,

> For many of us, GaD has been a gateway into other forms of politics. Because it was not seen as hardcore protesting like joining the left wing parties, it allowed more people to participate. It gave me the tools to learn to organise, brought us together, and equipped us to deal with backlash. I wish we could have been more active, but one of the problems was we couldn't get a lot of new members, we did not have a set structure for a long time, and after that initial ah-ha moment died out, we are asking ourselves—what more can we do?

One of the reasons Shmyla suggests that GaD might not continue in its present form is because of the sense that its engagements have already produced tangible results in terms of altering the discourse of women's access to public space, or at the very least in bringing concerns of women's safety in the context of leisure into the main-stream narrative.

Shmyla gestures to one particular speech given by no less a person than the current prime minister of Pakistan,

> One of the moments we thought we actually mainstreamed the con-versation about public spaces was that in one of his first speeches Imran Khan talked about safety and women going to parks. For such a right-wing prime minister who came to power at the behest of the army and does not need to appeal to women in any way to say this! We were so excited. He may not know about GaD but at least people around him were familiar with that discourse.

This idea of transforming the discourse is also suggested by Muskaan, who talks about how Mumbra as a predominantly Muslim area was seen from the outside as a result of Parcham's work:

> I simply started by reposting from my mom's account and that's how my mother's friends got to know about Parcham and they were sur-prised by it—that there was an organisation that did this sort of work in *Mumbra! There's football in Mumbra!* My mom came to Mumbra after the 92–93 riots. Earlier she used to stay in Kanjurmarg. She used to live in a non-Muslim area with mixed communities. So her friends were not aware of Mumbra. They had their misconceptions about the place, that it is backward. But when they saw those posts, they changed their mindsets and started appreciating my mom—Wow, you are sending your daughter to play football!

Muskaan's narrative is a reminder that these ideas acquire a life of their own when sent forth into cyberspace. Even as WhatsApp messages fuel fake news and a politics of hate (Banaji & Ram Bhat, 2019), at the same time, there are also other kinds of oppositional discourses circulating online.

At some point in our interviews, every single person talks about the friendships they have found during their engagement in these organizations. Friendships in many cases also facilitated the beginnings of these organizations. Sadia points out that initially, when they started out online, she reached out to women with whom she was having conversations in regard to how to access the city of Karachi and also to friends in Lahore, telling them she was making them administrators of the page. She says, 'I had vetted them and I knew we had similar politics. Not that we did not have disagreements regarding the politics, we did. But just people I had worked with and could trust. An Islamabad chapter started because Mehrbano moved there'.

Shmyla said, 'Women were drawn to GaD when they saw it online'. There was no decision to recruit.

> If someone sent a direct message online, we would invite them to something or add them to a city chapter. Someone would say they had a friend who'd moved cities and is keen on feminist politics. I was friends with someone in Islamabad and they put me in touch with the group in Lahore. We'd meet outside of GaD to just hang out. We'd call them to come over for a cup of tea. A lot of the friendship came instinctively.

She also recognized that GaD tended to attract women who came from a similar class background: 'A lot of us were drawn to GaD because of friendships and personal connections, and consensus building was based in empathy and understanding but it also replicated our class'.

Jasmeen says,

> I feel some of my dearest friends came out of BN—especially the community in 2005–06. Even now, I might call Annie or Hemangini from that time period to talk about something. Blank Noise is built on the collective knowledge, labour and lived herstories of its community.

The idea of friendship is central to Parcham's vision of its work. Salma says, 'Parcham is an organisation that attempts to build friendships. It tries to overcome narrowmindedness and build a society of equity. This society needs to be one where everyone is equal and we can build this through friendship and love'.

Reflecting on what it meant to grow as an organization in terms of building relationships, Sadia says,

> While it started with friends, with the surge of new members we had to find ways to absorb new members into fabrics of trust. If distrust started happening we had to find ways of building from there. This had a role to play in the shifting dynamics of GaD. In 2018, we organised a retreat—as a way to build this community. We applied for funding and got about 19 or 20 people, most of whom had not met each other in person, to come together for a 3-day workshop where we had sessions about our ideas of GaD, of course, but also to speak about who each of us was, where we were from and what mattered to us as individuals.

As many suggest, these organizations fostered a sense of community both on the streets and online. People who had never met became 'friends'. It made conversations, friendship and organizing possible even across the Indo-Pak border. Figure 15.4 shows Sadia Khatri of GaD in a T-shirt designed for one of BN's campaigns.

Figure 15.4 *Blank Noise Meets Girls at Dhabas*

Source: https://www.facebook.com/blanknoise/photos/a.10151129865824534/10156325590609534/?type=3&theater

Women from different organizations also met serendipitously in other spaces and found that their organizations were encountering similar reactions. Yashaswini says,

> When I had gone to the UK to study law, one of my classmates, Amana, was closely involved with the GaD and we had a couple of discussions. We spoke about how PT and GaD were similar in some ways—they were being seen as irreverent in their cultural context and it was a similar case for PT here.

These are conversations that also bring forth a sense of the South Asian subcontinent and the resonances of its peculiar misogynies.

The work these organizations do online and on the streets has contributed significantly to transforming the discourse of how women are seen in relation to the public, whether it is in demanding the end of hostel curfews, campaigning against street sexual harassment, girls playing football in public maidans, or sitting at dhabas claiming the right to do nothing. Their work foregrounds the idea that the document-ing of feminist history can be something that is collectively done, in a sense the writing of feminist historiography in real time. This real-time documentation then becomes an archive, perhaps fleeting, ephemeral and temporary but nonetheless an archive that leaves traces all over the Internet, often creating epiphanies for others.

CONCLUDING COMMENTS

'Individual women would get targeted at bike rallies and talk about it online. When we talked of this backlash, we were told this is not real backlash—real activism is getting picked up by the army', said Shmyla talking about how their activism was seen as not serious.

At the time all of us laughed at how activism was seen in a hierarchy. As we were talking to Shmyla, feminists in Pakistan were engaging in a legal battle to be allowed to have the Aurat March on 8 March.[18] However, even as we were writing this chapter, two activists of PT,

---

[18] See https://www.dawn.com/news/1538075

Devangana Kalita and Natasha Narwal, had been arrested for participating in the protests against the Citizenship (Amendment) Act, and
Shmyla's comment comes back to haunt us.[19]

While these communities have focused on specific issues, they have
also engaged with larger concerns that might be read as belonging to
the realm of citizenship. Much of their work has focused on gendered
claims to citizenship in articulating the right to public space, public
play, and leisure, the right to be treated as adult citizens and the right
to safe and open housing, among others. Their interventions on the
streets have been documented and performed on online media, itself,
a form of activism.

It may also be worthwhile to acknowledge that these collectives
reflect deeply on the question of feminisms themselves. Their functioning holds space for contestations, for challenges, debates and the
articulation of dissent and disagreement. There is little or no assumption
that they will agree all the time, or indeed that being in complete agreement on everything is the basis of their collaboration. There appears
to be an implicit understanding that as long as they have core areas of
agreement, they can work together, and across differences.

Rather than thinking of communities as fixed and stable entities that
aspire to upscale or grow in one direction, we ask if it is possible to
allow for *ephemerality and shape shifting,* without in any way undermining
or undoing the value of their political work, or indeed of the material
artefacts they produce. In fact, one might see the transient nature of
these spaces as their strength, rethinking the idea of the community
itself, implicitly challenging the notion of identities as stable. This allows
for a narrative that focuses on *feminist identities as evolving rather than
fixed,* in rapidly changing social and cultural contexts, and in doing so
offering us a vision of a new kind of politics.

In thinking through the multiple complexities of networked feminist
political participation, we argue for the expansion of the conception
of a community to include those that are *ideologically assembled rather*

<hr>

[19] See https://scroll.in/latest/962769/delhi-violence-police-arrest-two-pinjra-
tod-members-for-anti-caa-protest-in-february

than geographically contained. These scattered feminist communities might challenge the idea that there is a community out there which is always already in existence and to which technological capabilities can be imparted to produce 'community media'. Instead, we argue for the possibility of re-imagining the idea of community as *implicitly partial and in a constant state of becoming.*

Taking this line of argument further, one might envision the possibility that community media may also include spontaneous deployment of media platforms that these scattered communities are already embedded in, even if those platforms are acknowledged to be fraught and compromised spaces. If we allow for this possibility, then we might imagine that these spaces may be used subversively to further progressive, even radical, agendas.

REFERENCES

Baer, H. (2016). Redoing feminism: Digital activism, body politics and neoliberalism. *Feminist Media Studies, 161,* 17–34.

Banaji, S., & Ram Bhat. (2019). *WhatsApp Vigilantes: An exploration of citizen reception and circulation of WhatsApp misinformation linked to mob violence in India.* Department of Media and Communications, LSE. https://www.lse.ac.uk/media-and-communications/assets/documents/research/projects/WhatsApp-Misinformation-Report.pdf

Evaristo, B. (2019). *Girl, Woman, Other.* Hamish Hamilton.

Jackson, S. (2018). Young feminists, feminism and digital media. *Feminism & Psychology, 28*(1), 32–49. https://doi.org/10.1177/0959353517716952

Jain, M. (2015, August 15). *Jamia's 'no late nights' diktat for women is yet another reminder of sexist hostel rules.* Scroll.in. https://scroll.in/article/748528/jamias-no-late-nights-diktat-for-women-is-yet-another-reminder-of-sexist-hostel-rules

Keller, J. M. (2012). Virtual feminisms, information. *Communication & Society, 15*(3), 429–447. https://dx.doi.org/10.1080/1369118X.2011.642890

Keller, J. M. (2019). 'Oh, she's a Tumblr feminist': Exploring the platform vernacular of girls' Social Media Feminisms. *Social Media + Society.* https://doi.org/10.1177/2056305119867442

Lama, S. T. K., & Maharaj, S. (2019). *Statement: Why we decided to leave Pinjra Tod.* Roundtable India. https://roundtableindia.co.in/index.php?option=com_content&view=article&id=9582:statement-why-we-decided-to-leave-pinjra-tod&catid=129:events-and-activism&Itemid=195

Linabary, J. R., Corple, D. J., & Cooky, C. (2019). Feminist activism in digital space: Postfeminist contradictions in #WhyIStayed. *New Media & Society.* https://doi.org/10.1177/1461444819884635

Lorde, A. (2018). *The master's tools will never dismantle the master's house.* Penguin Classics.

Pavarala, V., & Malik, K. (2007). *Other voices: The struggle for community radio in India.* SAGE Publications.

Phadke, S., Khan, S., & Ranade, S. (2011). *Why Loiter? Women and risk on Mumbai streets.* Penguin.

Phadke, S., Ullah, F., & Titus, N. (2017). *Under the open sky.* https://www.youtube.com/watch?v=OjGfxXHSp1o&ab_channel=SMCSchannel

Pinjra Tod. (2019). Women on the edge of time: Reflections from Pinjra Tod. https://pinjratod.wordpress.com/2019/03/20/women-on-the-edge-of-time-reflections-from-pinjra-tod/

Rogan, F., & Budgeon, S. (2018). The personal is political: Assessing feminist fundamentals in the digital age. *Social Sciences, 7*(8), 132. https://doi.org/10.3390/socsci7080132

Thakur, A. K. (2020). New media and the Dalit counter-public sphere. *Television & New Media, 21*(4), 360–375.

Udupa, S., Venkatraman, S., & Khan, A. (2020). Millennial India: Global digital politics in context. *Television and New Media, 21*(4), 343–359. https://doi.org/10.1177/1527476419870516

Ullah, F. (2020). Digital media and the changing nature of labor action. *Television & New Media, 21*(4), 376–391. https://doi.org/10.1177/1527476419869117

Chapter 16

'Divided We Stand, United We Fall'

The Newfound Wisdom of Digital Age Communication Technology

Hemant Babu

The ochre hue of the Hong Kong skyline at dusk was still visible through the dense mesh of streetlights around Legislative Council Complex during the attempted siege by a group of citizens to protest against the Fugitive Offenders Amendment Bill in July 2019.[1] A few

---

[1] At the time of handing over Hong Kong to China, British Hong Kong had passed laws effectively barring extradition of Hong Kong citizens to mainland China for criminal proceedings in order to safeguard the 'one country, two systems' formula. This of course did not go down well with Beijing, which started attempts at rolling these laws back. The push came in 2017 when mainland China had to resort to 'abduction' of Hong Kong billionaire Xiao Jianhua, who was wanted in a graft case. He was stated to be literally abducted from his apartment in Hong Kong by Chinese security forces. Later, in 2018, a Hong Kong resident murdered his pregnant girlfriend in Taiwan and returned to Hong Kong. This incident provided a much-needed rationale for Chinese authorities to push for a law that could enable the Hong Kong chief executive to transfer any fugitive to any jurisdiction for which Hong Kong lacked extradition treaty. The introduction of a bill to this effect resulted in eruption of protests from the pro-democracy forces in Hong Kong which feared that the real motive of the law was to suppress

yards away, sitting side by side on the pavement, a group of young girls were glued to their mobile screens. One of them looked up when a television (TV) journalist asked her if she was getting any network to call or surf. 'Nope, but we use FireChat', the girl said matter-of-factly.

Usually, in protests, where a large number of people gather in a relatively smaller geographical area, it is difficult, if not impossible, to use the mobile phone due to unusual congestion on the nearby cellular towers—that is, if the authorities have not shut them down in the first place.

After the Arab Spring,[2] numerous studies underscored the role that Facebook, Twitter and YouTube played in mobilizing public opinion, coordinating protest and drawing global attention to the protests taking place on the streets of many cities across the Arab world. On Cairo streets, the opinion makers used Facebook to form public opinion, used Twitter to coordinate protest actions and used YouTube to broadcast all over the world.

Ironically, the corporate-run social media that amplified public opinion during the Arab Spring turned into formidable tools of oppression during the Hong Kong uprising, forcing the protesters to resort to unconventional, decentralized and open-source[3] platforms that were not driven by profit-oriented corporations.

---

political dissent in Hong Kong. Millions of Hong Kong residents marched in the streets, forcing the authority to officially withdraw the bill.

[2] In early 2010, there were a series of anti-government protests, uprisings and even armed rebellions across many countries in the Arab world. Egypt, Libya, Yemen, Syria and Bahrain witnessed massive violent protests, while other countries, like Lebanon, Jordan, Morocco, Sudan and Kuwait, saw unprecedented street protests. Social media played the most important role in the mobilization process, forcing governments to shut down the Internet completely or block sites used by the protesters.

[3] The term 'open source' refers to something people can modify and share because its design is publicly accessible. The term originated in the context of software development to designate a specific approach to creating computer programmes. Today, however, 'open source' designates a broader set of values—what we call 'the open source way'. Open-source projects, products or initiatives embrace and celebrate principles of open exchange, collaborative participation, rapid prototyping, transparency, meritocracy and community-oriented development.

That something had been rotting within the traditional media ecology was a fact about which no one needed any convincing. General disillusionment with the mass media, as pre-millennial generations were exposed to, was evident on the streets on many occasions across the globe. The biases and ineptness of print media only worsened with the emergence of TV. It is quite another story that in mainland China or large parts of the Arab world there was no or very few independent print media anyway.[4]

During the Arab Spring uprising, the protesters were aware that the traditional print media and satellite TV had turned hostile to democratic values and plurality, and so they relied on social media for mobilization. In India too, TV viewers have witnessed how those protesting against the Citizenship (Amendment) Act had booed a certain section of TV journalists away from the scene of protest for their non-journalistic and partisan behaviour night after night during the so-called prime-time TV.

Do these phenomena indicate the onset of social media as the most influential form of societal communication? Not really, as the pro-democracy movement in Hong Kong soon realized to its peril. The corporate-controlled giant social media platforms had already started showing their susceptibility to social and political manipulation while emerging as a looming threat to individual privacy.

The two versions of social media—one controlled by the corporate giants and the second controlled by the authoritarian Chinese state—grossly failed as a medium of social communication in Hong Kong and mainland China. Citizens were largely aware that the Chinese media, be it the state-owned or -controlled newspapers or TV, were worthless to an independent mind. The social media platforms that were freely

---

[4] There is a large body of work from various scholars illustrating the state of media freedom in authoritarian China and the politically chaotic Arab world. It is not possible to list them all here, but a few representative works are listed here:
- Eurasia Review as accessed on May 22, 2020: https://www.eurasiareview.com/24122010-freedom-of-the-press-in-the-arab-world/
- Arab Media Report: https://arabmediareport.it/en/la-liberta-di-stampa-nel-mondo-arabo/
- Reporters Without Borders ranking of countries in respect to Press Freedom: https://rsf.org/en/ranking.

available to them were also a well-designed cocoon, since none of the popular social media platforms like Facebook, Twitter, Instagram or WhatsApp were allowed to function in mainland China, where the government has created its own versions of these platforms which are very closely monitored.

But even in Hong Kong, where the popular social media platforms were available freely, the people soon understood that their privacy was not safe in the hands of the corporations, which were either vulnerable to political pressures or willingly yielded to them.

This was the time and circumstances when a paradigm shift in the construct of social media began. A few unassuming tech platforms and networking architectures acquired unprecedented attention not only among the protesters but also among those who closely monitored the developments on the Hong Kong streets. A desperate search and small-scale experiments had already begun for what could be described as community media or alternative media, which are imagined to be the vanguard of plurality, democratic values, participatory equality and freedom from political and corporate interference.

The activists of the resistance movement in Hong Kong, for obvious reasons, preferred only those communication tools that did not compromise on the users' privacy and used decentralized communication protocols. Local Crypto, a global peer-to-peer cryptocurrency exchange, put out a blog titled 'Digital Resistance: security & privacy tips from Hong Kong protesters',[5] which has now acquired a status of being a safety handbook for protesters across the world. The blog not only has some basic tips to safeguard privacy while using one's mobile device, but it also has a list of recommended platforms, apps and other technological and strategic approaches that could be an essential part of the digital toolkit of resistance movements. Some of the tips in the blog are quite intriguing. For example, the lack of centralized control and coordination of the movement is now seen as the most important tool, rather than as a weakness, as it was seen in sociopolitical movements in the pre-digital era.

---

[5] See https://medium.com/crypto-punks/digital-resistance-security-privacy-tips-from-hong-kong-protesters-37ff9ef73129

Two key concepts often used in the discourse over the politics of technology are the guiding principles of the recommendations. These concepts can be described as:

- Rejection of classical corporate-provided communication technology and embrace of open source; and
- Preference to technology that operates on decentralized architecture.

Before going into the theoretical aspects of these two concepts, let us look at the praxis.

One of the most used applications during the Hong Kong resistance has been Telegram, a chat application for mobile phones. On the face of it, there is not much difference between Facebook-owned WhatsApp and Telegram. Both claim to be the fastest messengers with end-to-end encryption and a whole lot of identical features. One major difference between the two is that unlike WhatsApp, Telegram is an open-source platform. One can download the source code from its website and examine if it is doing anything more than what it claims to be doing, that is, if one has the competency to examine software code.

Yet another major difference between the two apps is that Telegram claims it does not need to make money, unlike WhatsApp, which needs to earn profits to keep Facebook's return on investment positive. To support its claim, Telegram says

> Pavel Durov, who shares our vision, supplied Telegram with a generous donation, so we have quite enough money for the time being. If Telegram runs out, we will introduce non-essential paid options to support the infrastructure and finance developer salaries. But making profits will never be an end-goal for Telegram.[6]

WhatsApp, on the other hand, has been a proprietary platform of Facebook with the clearly stated intention of generating profits, even though it is available to its users free of cost.

---

[6] See https://telegram.org/faq#q-how-are-you-going-to-make-money-out-of-this

However, it should be noted here that all the proprietary software or apps that are offered free of cost to the end users are not really 'free' in true sense. It only means that these applications are being monetized in unconventional or non-traditional methods. These alternative methods are not so explicitly mentioned in the privacy policy of these apps, which most users do not bother to read. For example, all users of WhatsApp pay data costs for using the app that is ostensibly free. In addition to this, every user ends up being a minuscule but a significant part of the database that these companies sell in part or in full to virtually make a fortune.

It is important, at this juncture, to acquaint ourselves with the life and work of Pavel Durov, cited earlier in the context of the Telegram app. Durov was born in Russia in 1984. His father, Valery Durov, was a doctor of classical philological sciences, attached as head of the department to Saint Petersburg State University. Pavel was better known as a creator of Vkontakte, or vk, which is a social networking site like Facebook for Russian speakers.

Vkontakte was set up by Durov in 2006 and acquired approximately 88 million users by 2014. It was around this time that his troubles with the Vladimir Putin government began over his repeated refusal to block groups and individuals seen as the political opposition to the regime. The Kremlin's frustration against Vkontakte had started around 2011 in the wake of parliamentary elections that brought Vladimir Putin back at the helm. Putin was stated to take a hands-off approach when it came to the Internet, but the sites like Vkontakte gained tremendous popularity among young Russians. In Saint Petersburg, Vkontakte nourished many anti-Putin rallies, which began to swell from a gathering of a few thousands to a couple of hundred thousands as the elections approached. Overt and covert pressure was put on Vkontakte, but Pavel Durov stood his ground and refused to block profiles of the opposition leaders. He also rejected requests from all quarters to share personal details of Ukrainian protest leaders. The face-off between Durov and the Kremlin finally resulted in the former being thrown out from the helm of Vkontakte through complex corporate manipulation. Soon he, along with his brother, went into exile. As per the *Moscow Times* report dated 28 April 2014, Durov had taken Saint Kitts and Nevis citizenship through the one-time donation route. The same report suggested that the Vkontakte network would now fall under the 'full control' of Kremlin-linked Rosneft Chief Executive Officer (CEO) Igor Sechin and Vkontakte billionaire shareholder Alisher Usmanov.[7]

Telegram has displayed a commitment to open source. Pavel Durov's brother Nikolai developed a custom data protocol that was secure and optimized for work across multiple data centres. But most importantly, it was open. On its website, Telegram says,

> Our API is open, and we welcome developers to create their own Telegram apps. We also have a Bot API, a platform for developers that allows anyone to easily build specialized tools for Telegram, integrate any services, and even accept payments from users around the world.

At the time of writing this chapter, Telegram's development team, mostly comprising highly skilled software developers from Saint Petersburg, is based in Dubai. When the heat started mounting in Russia, the team swiftly migrated to Berlin, London and Singapore before landing up in Dubai. 'We're currently happy with Dubai, although we are ready to relocate again if local regulations change', the Telegram website says.

On several occasions during the protest in Hong Kong, Telegram became extremely sluggish and even stopped working due to massive distributed denial-of-service attacks (DDoS). These attacks are common occurrences around the world. Simply put, somewhere in the world, someone wants to shut down or silence some or the other web service daily. DDoS attacks are attempts to make an online service unavailable for some time through overwhelming servers and bandwidth with a large amount of junk data. Such attacks target a variety of services ranging from banking to news, from information to social communications. Jigsaw LLC, a Google subsidiary in collaboration with Arbor Networks, monitors these attacks on a real-time basis and publishes

---

[7] See https://www.themoscowtimes.com/2014/04/28/vkontakte-founder-pavel-durov-becomes-citizen-of-st-kitts-and-nevis-a34733

them on its website. Explaining the methodology and enormity of the problem, the website says:

> Botnets can generate huge floods of traffic to overwhelm a target. These floods can be generated in multiple ways, such as sending more connection requests than a server can handle, or having computers send the victim huge amounts of random data to use up the target's bandwidth. Some attacks are so big they can max out a country's international cable capacity.... Specialized online marketplaces exist to buy and sell botnets or individual DDoS attacks. Using these underground markets, anyone can pay a nominal fee to silence websites they disagree with or disrupt an organization's online operations. A week-long DDoS attack, capable of taking a small organization offline can cost as little as $150.[8]

Following a series of such attacks on Telegram, its founder Durov indicated the source of these attacks on Telegram. In June 2019, he tweeted that most of the attacking IP addresses were based in China. He said state actor–sized attacks had coincided with protests in Hong Kong.[9]

While open-source code was considered the strength of Telegram, the centralized nature of its technology proved to be vulnerable to the planned attack. This is where hitherto obscured players entered the media ecology. The messaging applications like FireChat and Bridgefy offered decentralized peer-to-peer connectivity between mobile devices, making it possible to communicate without Global System for Mobile Communications (GSM) signals or Internet connectivity. These applications utilized what is known as mesh networking or ad hoc network protocol. Every mobile device is essentially a transceiver, capable of transmitting and receiving electromagnetic signals. Mobile devices communicate with each other through radio devices owned by telecom operators, but they can never communicate directly, even though they are capable of such connectivity. FireChat and Bridgefy

---

[8] See https://www.digitalattackmap.com/#anim=1&color=0&country=ALL &list=0&time=18310&view=map

[9] See https://www.businessinsider.nl/telegram-blames-ddos-attack-on-china-2019-6?international=true&r=US

made use of this capability and allowed mobile devices to communicate with each other even in the absence of GSM networks. Both these applications facilitate communicating one-to-one or even broadcasting a message for all the devices in Wi-Fi or Bluetooth range, or even forming a daisy chain to cover sizeable distances.

The website of FireChat, developed by a United States-based company called Open Garden, boldly announces:

> No Internet Required.... FireChat has been utilised by community organizers, emergency responders and private citizens to communicate when cut off from outside networks, including pro-democracy protests in Taiwan and Hong Kong, natural disasters in Ecuador and Kashmir, and off-the-grid events like Burning Man and Summit at Sea.... Our decentralised protocol offers censorship-resistant security and encryption that takes control back from unscrupulous ISPs, government agencies and hostile regimes. When people build the Internet themselves, no evil empire can control it.[10]

When Pink Floyd sang '...Together we stand, Divided we fall...' in their famous number 'Hey You' in 1979, they probably did not know that the opposite would also be true in the cyber world almost 40 years later. Divided or decentralized infrastructure for social networking platforms has become a preferred choice of many users even as the giants like the micro-blogging site Twitter resort to illiberal and intrusive policies for account verification and suspension. Moreover, the armies of political trolls–led abuses and harassment over social networks have become a serious threat to free speech. Attempts at amplifying certain views or silencing some others have become an essential part of many racist and sectarian political projects across the world. It was against this background that a fresh college graduate from Germany, Eugen Rochko, began working on Mastodon, which emerged, in a very short span, as a potential 'Twitter-killer'.

Mastodon, in a short span of time, has acquired more than 4.4 million users. It is essentially a free and open-source framework that can give anyone a capability to host a Twitter-like platform in less than

---

[10] See https://www.opengarden.com/firechat/

a day's work. This means there are thousands of Mastodon instances (servers) across the world which use a standard set of protocols, making it possible for them to exchange information with each other and allowing their users to interact with each other seamlessly. As there are many servers, there are many user policies. A user can choose which one suits them the most. And if one does not find a suitable policy, one could always start their own server with their own policy and seamlessly connect with other users on other servers.

During the Arab Spring, the resistance movement used the social networking sites like Facebook for mobilizing and organizing protests. However, in the recent past, resistance movements across the world have largely used lesser-known tools for organizational consultation and participation.

The Cantonese-speaking protesters in Hong Kong used a social platform called LIHKG as the main control room for the protests. LIHKG is used for proposing ideas, organizing events, discussing tactics and strategies, crowdfunding ad campaigns, conducting investigations, sharing memes, posters, arts, videos or songs and translating content to reach an international audience. The content is visible to the public, but to engage, a user must have an account. However, it is not easy to have an account in LIHKG, which requires a certain type of email addresses like the one provided by Hong Kong Internet Service Providers or an institution of higher education located in Hong Kong. This particular feature of LIHKG came in handy to ensure that people from mainland China did not participate in the discussions.

However, as the movement grew and international support started pouring in, the resistance movement learnt a trick or two from the open-source and decentralized software development process and started using GitHub, a development portal acquired by Microsoft in 2018, for organizing events. There is a GitHub page for organization of events, crowdfunding and consultation. On the page, one can create issues and submit pull requests with suggestions and recommendations. This means that just about anyone can participate and influence a movement.

GitHub is based on Git, which essentially is a distributed version-control system for tracking changes in source code during the software development process. It was originally developed by Linus Torvalds, the famous creator of Linux operating system (OS). While creating it, Torvalds would not have imagined that his system would be used for organizing protests.

The key here is the interpretative flexibility. There are substantial examples to prove that technology developed in an open process is capable of producing different outcomes—sometimes quite different from the original idea—depending on the social circumstances of development. Such technological innovation, as a result, enjoys longevity and operational relevance.

The idea of technological determinism has been seen, for quite some time now, as a major impediment to equal access and democratic usage of communication technology. Technological determinists believe that technology is an autonomous agent of change. Technological advancement shapes societies in ways the technological artefacts determine. Given that technological innovation, at least in the popular perception, is controlled and directed by capital, it has always led to the generation of surplus capital rather than being a catalyst for human development. Most critiques of communication technology see it as a tool for manipulative consent engineering, leading to curtailment of free speech.

A considerable amount of work has been done by the Council of Europe,[11] a platform promoted and maintained by 14 international non-governmental organizations (NGOs) and journalists' associations, in defence of journalists and freedom of speech. The council has produced many fact sheets on the larger subject of freedom of speech and the state of press freedom. A cursory look at these fact sheets pertaining to freedom of expression, new media and new technologies suggests how the centralized databases generated by modern communication applications enable states and law enforcers to undertake mass surveillance, political persecution and covert attacks on the freedom of speech.

The resultant scholarly turn, away from technological determinism and towards social construction of technology (SCOT), is clearly seen in the communication practices on the ground. SCOT theorists argue

---

[11] See https://coe.int

that technology does not, or should not, shape human action, but it is human action that should shape technology. Many technological innovations in the past have been re-examined and reinterpreted by Wiebe Bijker, Thomas Hughes and Trevor Pinch (1987) in support of this idea.

Some of the events in the recent past have shown us how individuals and groups, without any preconceived notion of technological innovation or entrepreneurship, have begun to emerge on a global platform, to declare that if available technology does not offer what they need, they would create their own.

These events essentially tell us that the meaning of communication technology is not derived or fixed by its design or original intention, but it arises through an active interaction between technology, its users and their dynamic social and political circumstances. That the transformative power of technology is vested in its users and their interpretation, rather than in its design and original intention, is a thought that holds the power to transform the popular notion of technology itself.

The political construction of media technology, which has so far been top-down, hierarchical and non-participatory, seems to be turning now into a socially constructed technology that promises to be decentralized, democratic and plural. The emerging trend towards taking charge of technological developmental processes and resultant outcomes is certainly showing some green shoots in the charred landscape of media technology.

REFERENCE

Bijker, W. E., Hughes, T. P., & Pinch, T. (1987). *The social construction of technological systems: New directions in sociology and history of technology*. MIT Press.

About the Editors and Contributors

EDITORS

Faiz Ullah is an assistant professor at the School of Media and Cultural Studies, TISS, Mumbai, where he teaches courses in media studies, community media and journalism. He has published research-based articles on the political economy of media, work and labour, documentary film and participatory cultures in various journals and edited volumes. In 2016, he co-directed a short documentary, *Under the Open Sky*, featuring a young women's sports initiative in Mumbai, focusing on women's access to public spaces. In 2017, he co-translated noted Urdu writer Intizar Hussain's cultural history of Delhi as *Once There was a City Named Dilli*. Professor Ullah's feature pieces and book reviews have appeared in the *Book Review India*, *Biblio*, *Scroll*, the *Wire*, *Mint*, the *Tribune*, *Kafila*, *Raiot* and *Art India*, among others.

Anjali Monteiro is a retired professor from the School of Media and Cultural Studies, TISS, Mumbai. She is involved in documentary production, media teaching and research. She played a key role in the setting up of the MA programme in Media and Cultural Studies at TISS, the first of its kind in India, and has done pioneering and innovative work in critical media education in India. Along with Professor K. P. Jayasankar, she has co-directed several award-winning documentaries that have been screened in festivals across the world. Professor Monteiro writes in the broad areas of censorship, documentary film and media and cultural studies and has contributed to scholarly journals and edited volumes. Her most recent publications are *A Fly in the Curry: Independent Documentary Film in India*, SAGE Publications, 2016, written jointly with Professor K. P. Jayasankar, which won a special mention for the best book on cinema in the National Film

Awards, 2016, and *DigiNaka: Subaltern Politics and Digital Media in Post-Capitalist India*, co-edited with Anjali Monteiro, K. P. Jayasankar, Amit S. Rai (Eds.), Orient BlackSwan, 2020. Professor Monteiro is a recipient of many fellowships. She has been a Howard Thomas Memorial Fellow in Media Studies, a Fulbright visiting lecturer, an Erasmus Mundus scholar and an Indian Council for Cultural Relations (ICCR) Visiting Professor, all at various international universities. She is active in campaigns for freedom of expression.

K. P. Jayasankar is a retired professor, School of Media and Cultural Studies, TISS, Mumbai. He is involved in media production, teaching and research and has played a key role in setting up the School of Media and Cultural Studies at TISS. Jointly with Professor Anjali Monteiro, he has made over 35 documentaries and won 33 national and international awards at documentary film festivals. Their most recent awards for their Kachchh trilogy are the Basil Wright Prize 2013 for *So Heddan So Hoddan (Like Here Like There)* and Commendation of the Jury, Intangible Culture Category, 2019, for *A Delicate Weave* at the Royal Anthropological Institute Festival, United Kingdom. Along with Professor Monteiro, he was an invited artist at the Kochi-Muziris Biennale 2018, where *Saacha (The Loom)* was showcased as an installation. Professor Jayasankar has served as jury and as festival consultant and director at several film festivals in India. He has mentored many student and fellowship documentary film projects as commissioning editor. His most recent publications co-authored with Professor Monteiro are *A Fly in the Curry: Independent Documentary Film in India*, SAGE Publications, 2016, for which he received a special mention for the best book on cinema in the President's National Film Awards, 2016, and *DigiNaka: Subaltern Politics and Digital Media in Post-Capitalist India*, co-edited with Anjali Monteiro, K. P. Jayasankar, Amit S. Rai (Eds.), 2020. He is a recipient of several scholarships and awards, including the DAAD scholarship at Heidelberg University, the Howard Thomas Memorial Commonwealth fellowship at Goldsmith's College, London, the Erasmus Mundus scholarship at Lund University and the Key Technology Partner scholarship at University of Technology, Sydney.

CONTRIBUTORS

Mahtab Alam is a Delhi-based multilingual journalist, researcher and podcaster. His areas of interest include issues related to politics, law, media, literature, the environment and human rights. Mahtab is former executive editor of *The Wire* Urdu and currently writes for the *Wire* (in English, Urdu and Hindi), apart from BBC Urdu, Independent Urdu, *Down to Earth* and *Samkaleen Janmat*. He is a guest podcaster with SunoIndia.in and the founder of Radio Urdu, an exclusive platform for podcasts in Urdu.

Hemant Babu is a communications and open-source technology enthusiast. He worked as a journalist for a decade and a half. Later, he branched out to create an open-source technology environment that enables free and independent media ecology. He founded Nomad, an organization that helped many community groups in starting local radio stations. Nomad is known for its flagship low-powered frequency modulation (FM) transmitter that was adopted by many community radio stations in India, Africa and Bhutan. Nomad is also known for its contribution in popularizing open-source education technology resources.

Dakxinkumar Bajrange is an award-winning film-maker, playwright and activist from the Chhara denotified tribe of Ahmedabad in the western part of India. He is a recipient of Ford Foundation International Fellowship (2010–2011) to undertake graduate studies at University of Leeds, United Kingdom. His book *Budhan Bolta Hai (Budhan Speaks)* was awarded the first prize for Best Creative Writing on Human Rights by the National Human Rights Commission (NHRC) for 2010–2011. He is a recipient of many awards for his films and fellowships. Currently, he is the Artistic Director at Budhan Theatre (www.budhantheatre.org) and runs his film production house Nomad Movies Pvt. Ltd.

Bidu Bhusan Dash is an assistant professor and Course Coordinator at the School of Mass Communication, Kalinga Institute of Industrial Technology (KIIT) Deemed to be University, Bhubaneswar. He was Charles Wallace India Trust Visiting Fellow at the School of Oriental and African Studies (SOAS) University of London (2015–2016) and

Child Rights and You (CRY) National Child Rights Research Fellow (2013–2014). He obtained his doctoral degree from TISS and taught at Savitribai Phule Pune University. His research and teaching interests are communication for social change and sociology of communication.

Madhura Dutta is a development sector professional working in rural India for about two decades. Starting her career at Contact Base, a national NGO, using culture for sustainable and inclusive development, she has subsequently worked at UNESCO as National Program Officer for Culture, headed All India Artisans and Craftworkers Welfare Association (a national apex membership body of weavers and artisans) as its Executive Director and worked as National Programme Advisor for Corporate Social Responsibility (CSR). Currently, she is an independent consultant and a freelance writer for various journals/blogs/newspapers.

Shweta Ghosh is a national award–winning film-maker and practice-based researcher. She is currently lecturer and PhD researcher at the Department of Film, Theatre & Television, University of Reading, United Kingdom. Her work explores film-making processes, on-screen representation, identity and creative practice in India and the Global South. Shweta's ongoing PhD practice research explores disability and film/video expression, and the sociocultural contexts of accessibility and equity that circumscribe film-making by people with disabilities in contemporary urban India.

Nithila Kanagasabai is an assistant professor at the School of Media and Cultural Studies, TISS, Mumbai, where she teaches courses in research methods and video production. Her areas of interest include feminist media studies, feminist pedagogy, journalism studies, academic mobilities, research cultures and digital media. In the past, she has worked as a news reporter with NDTV and Times Now.

Kanchan K. Malik is a professor in the Department of Communication, University of Hyderabad, India. She is also a Faculty Fellow with the UNESCO Chair on Community Media since 2011 and Editor of the newsletter *CR News*. She has taught postgraduate journalism and mass communication courses for over 20 years. Her research has contributed to policy advocacy efforts for community radio in India. Her scholastic and research interests include women in community communications, community media and the public sphere, journalism studies, media laws and ethics and communication for social change. She is the co-author of the much-cited book *Other Voices: The Struggle for Community Radio in India* (SAGE Publications, 2007). Her recent book, *Community Radio in South Asia: Reclaiming the Airwaves* (2020), is co-edited with Vinod Pavarala.

Madhavi Manchi finished her PhD in Media and Cultural Studies from the TISS, Mumbai. She currently lives in Auckland, New Zealand, and is a researcher at University of Auckland. Her latest research work is interdisciplinary, with a focus on critical food studies, indigenous youth health and indigenous perspectives on sexual violence prevention. When not working, she enjoys a good science fiction or fantasy book.

Raees Mohammed, formerly known as Ravichandran Bathran, is the founder of Dalit Camera. His academic life is reflective of and shaped by his life experiences and the political narrative thereof. His work is fundamentally concerned with human dignity, self-respect and understanding the sociology of humiliation arising out of the caste system in India. Raees has successfully founded a YouTube channel called Dalit Camera. With 35,000 subscribers and an approximate 4.8 million viewership (August 2017), the channel is the first digital multilingual channel ever dedicated to anti-caste issues. He now has founded Nilgiri All India Sanitation Workers Self-Respect Trade Union to address caste in sanitation work.

Vinod Pavarala is a senior professor in the Department of Communication, University of Hyderabad, where he has also held the United Nations Educational, Scientific and Cultural Organization (UNESCO) Chair on Community Media since 2011. Through two decades of research and policy advocacy, he has been at the forefront of the struggle for freeing of the airwaves in India and South Asia. He has addressed several international forums on community media. He serves as the Chair of the Community Communication and Alternative Media (CCAM) section of the International Association for Media and Communication Research (IAMCR) and is on the boards of several international journals. He is the co-author of the much-cited book *Other Voices: The Struggle for Community Radio in India* (SAGE Publications, 2007). His recent book, *Community Radio in South Asia: Reclaiming the Airwaves* (2020), is co-edited with Kanchan K. Malik.

Shilpa Phadke is a professor at the School of Media and Cultural Studies, TISS, Mumbai. She is co-author of *Why Loiter? Women and Risk on Mumbai Streets* (2011) and co-director of the documentary *Under the Open Sky* (2017). She has published widely both academically and in popular media. Her areas of interest include cities and public spaces, middle-class sexuality, practices of consumption, feminist pedagogy, feminist mothering, young women's relationship with feminism and online public spaces.

Shweta Radhakrishnan is a PhD student with the Department of Religion at Columbia University and an award winning film-maker. Her chapter in this volume draws from her experience working with community radio Mandakini ki Aawaz, as part of the organization People's Power Collective. As a Sahapedia-UNESCO fellow, she has also explored the role of community radio in heritage conservation in India. Shweta, an alumna of the School of Media and Cultural Studies, has also been interested in questions of changing urban spaces, gender and education and religion and ritual practices in India.

Nina Sabnani is a professor at the IDC School of Design, Indian Institute of Technology (IIT), Bombay, and an artist and storyteller who uses film, illustration and writing. Graduating from the Faculty of Fine Arts, Vadodara, she received a master's degree in film from Syracuse University, New York, which she pursued as a Fulbright Fellow. Her doctoral thesis on the Kaavad tradition has been published as a book: *Kaavad Tradition of Rajasthan: A Portable Pilgrimage*. She taught animation at the National Institute of Design, Ahmedabad, for two decades and has made several award-winning films. In 2018, she received the Lifetime Achievement Award for Illustration at the Tata Literature Live! festival in Mumbai.

Nikhil Thomas Titus is a PhD scholar at the University of Pittsburgh, United States. He has an MA in Media and Cultural Studies from the TISS, Mumbai. His research focuses on themes of low-cost film exhibition, stardom, urban infrastructure, piracy and migrant narratives. He is a documentary film-maker and a contributor to the community media education space in India.

Index